Thomas R. Köhler

Social-Media-Management

Chancen der Neuen Medien nutzen –
Risiken für Unternehmen vermeiden

*Mit sofort einsetzbaren Beispielen
für Social Media Guidelines*

Verleger: IDG Business Media GmbH, 80807 München

Konzept und Redaktion: Thomas R. Köhler

Lektorat: Dr. Renate Oettinger

Umschlaggestaltung: VoxelAir GmbH, 71229 Leonberg

Grafik und Layout: Vornehm Mediengestaltung GmbH, 81549 München

Druck und Bindearbeit: Strauss GmbH, 69509 Mörlenbach

ISBN 978-3-942922-02-9

Printed in Germany

Bibliografische Information der Deutschen Nationalbibliothek:
Die Deutsche Nationalbibliothek verzeichnet diese Publikation in der Deutschen Nationalbibliografie; detaillierte bibliografische Daten sind im Internet über http://dnb.d-nb.de abrufbar.

Inhalt

Social-Media-Management

Vorwort

Seit Jahren wird über Social-Media-Aktivitäten im Unternehmen diskutiert. Ob Unternehmens-Blog, Facebook-Fanpage oder Twitter-Kanal – im Marketing-Mix vieler Unternehmen sind diese längst feste Bestandteile.

Aber Social Media lässt sich nicht auf die Rolle als Absatzkanal oder Recruitment-Option reduzieren, sondern durchdringt zunehmend alle Lebens- und Arbeitsbereiche. Der eigene Mitarbeiter wird – unter Umständen ganz unfreiwillig – zum „Unternehmenssprecher" – allein durch eine unbedachte Äußerung auf einer Plattform im Web 2.0. Möglicher Imageschaden inklusive.

Eine Regelung der Social-Media-Nutzung („Social-Media-Richtlinie" oder „Policy" oder „Guideline") wird daher von den meisten Unternehmen als notwendig erachtet. Dennoch ist die Unsicherheit über die richtige Ausgestaltung groß.

In diesem Buch werden – ausgehend von mehr als 50 analysierten Guidelines von Unternehmen und Organisationen der verschiedensten Branchen – praxisgerechte Empfehlungen für die Entwicklung einer eigenen Social Media Policy gegeben.

Der Schwerpunkt liegt dabei nicht nur auf der Risikovermeidung, sondern vielmehr auf der Schaffung eines positiven Bezugsrahmens, der es dem Unternehmen erlaubt, seine in Sozialen Netzwerken aktiven Mitarbeiter als positive Fürsprecher, vielleicht sogar als eine neue Art von „Markenbotschafter" zu sehen und zum richtigen Umgang mit Facebook, Twitter und Co. anzuleiten – Zum Wohle des Unternehmens.

München, im Juni 2011
Thomas R. Köhler

Social-Media-Grundlagen

Wenn es einen Begriff gibt, der die Internetentwicklung der vergangenen Jahre nachhaltig geprägt hat, dann ist das Social Media – synonym auch oft mit Web 2.0 bezeichnet. Social Media steht für eine Vielzahl von Diensten und Internetangeboten, deren Kern die persönliche Interaktion ist.

Die wesentlichen Anwendungen sind:
- Soziale Netzwerke mit privatem Fokus (Facebook, Myspace, StudiVZ, Wer-kennt-wen),
- Business-Netzwerke (Xing, LinkedIn, ...),
- Blogs und Mikroblogs (Twitter),
- Wikis,
- Content Sharing,
- Bewertungsplattformen und
- Crowdsourcing.

Gemeinsames Merkmal: Die Inhalte kommen von den Nutzern
Auch wenn man die Anfänge von sozialer Interaktion im World Wide Web – etwa im Rahmen von Foren – bereits auf die 90er-Jahre des zurückliegenden Jahrhunderts verorten kann, kam der Durchbruch erst in den „Nullerjahren" – etwa ab dem Jahr 2004.
Ob Schüler, Student, Arbeitnehmer oder Führungskraft: Sie alle nutzen Soziale Netzwerke, um „im Kontakt zu bleiben", das heißt, Kontakte zu pflegen oder neue Kontakte aufzubauen, vielleicht gar neue Kunden zu gewinnen oder sich für eine Beförderung oder eine neue berufliche Herausforderung zu empfehlen.

Den Motiven für die Nutzung des Social Web hat der Branchenverband Bitkom ein wenig detaillierter (in einer repräsentativen Befragung in Deutschland 2010) nachgespürt. Als Gründe für die Teilnahme wurden von den Befragten genannt:
- Kontaktpflege mit Freunden und Bekannten: 78 Prozent,
- Austausch zu gleichen Interessen: 41 Prozent,
- Finden neuer Freunde und Bekannter: 30 Prozent,
- Kontaktpflege für den Beruf: 7 Prozent,
- Gewinnen neuer Kunden: 4 Prozent,
- Finden eines Lebenspartners: 4 Prozent und
- Suche nach erotischer Abwechslung: 4 Prozent.

Nach den Ergebnissen dieser Studie hat jeder zweite Nutzer (51 Prozent) bereits neue private Kontakte geknüpft. 40 Prozent haben interessante Einladungen zu Treffen oder Veranstaltungen erhalten.
Bei den oben bereits benannten Sozialen Netzwerken mit privatem Fokus sind die hierzulande bekanntesten Vertreter – neben dem Platzhirschen „Facebook" – „Myspace", „SchülerVZ", „StudiVZ", „Wer-kennt-wen" und „Lokalisten". Die Nutzerzahlen sind durch die Bank rückläufig.

Im Sog der Social Networks

All diese Plattformen entwickeln auf den Nutzer eine starke Sogwirkung, der er sich kaum entziehen kann. Dies reicht bis hin zu Entzugserscheinungen, wie eine Studie ergab, bei der Nutzer für einen bestimmten Zeitraum auf den Einsatz des Sozialen Netzwerks verzichten sollten. Bei der Untersuchung der Universität Maryland sollten sich 1.000 Studierende 24 Stunden lang in Verzicht üben. Die Symptome, die die Probanden zeigten, reichten von „Langeweile" bis zu „Verfolgungswahn", so ein Auszug aus dem Ergebnisbericht. Dort heißt es weiter:

„Medien werden als Erweiterung des Ichs empfunden, ohne die man einen Teil von sich verloren zu haben glaubt", so der Autor der Studie. Die Verbindung mit Medien rund um die Uhr ist Studenten wichtig, besonders um Freundschaften aufzubauen und zu verwalten. So könne es sich heute kein Jugendlicher mit Wunsch nach Sozialleben leisten, nicht auf Facebook aktiv zu sein. Für viele ersetzen virtuelle Kontakte teils die realen, und die Beziehung zu den Medien gilt oft als eine der engsten „Freundschaften" (detaillierte Ergebnisse sind unter http://theworldunplugged.wordpress.com/ nachzulesen).

Auch der längst im Geschäftsleben Etablierte tut gut daran, die überwältigende Präsenz der Kollegen in seiner Branche in Xing oder LinkedIn zum Anlass zu nehmen, dort schnellstens selbst beizutreten und aktiv zu werden. Nach verschiedenen Schätzungen sind bereits rund 80 Prozent aller Führungskräfte in Deutschland bei Xing vertreten. Insgesamt betrachtet ist nach Zahlen von Anfang 2011 die große Mehrzahl der Internetnutzer in Deutschland wie in anderen Ländern in Sozialen Netzwerken aktiv.

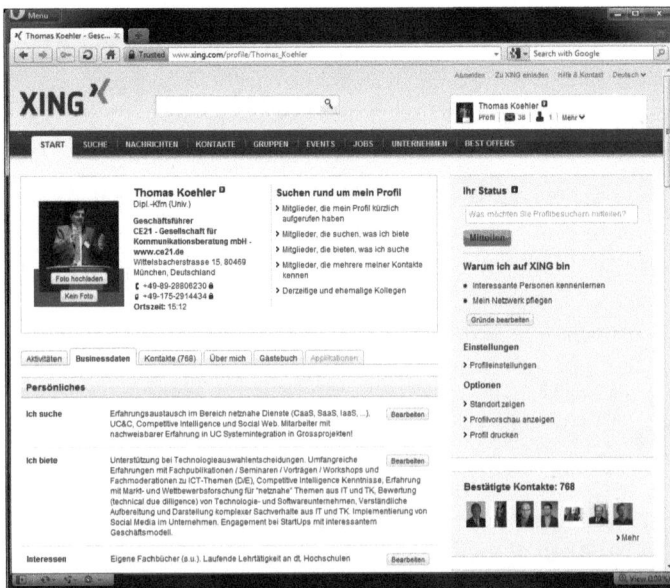

Xing-Beispielprofil
(hier: des Autors)

Kernmerkmal des Social Web ist, dass Nutzer die Möglichkeit haben, sich untereinander auszutauschen. Damit entstehen Beziehungen zwischen den einzelnen Teilnehmern – also nicht mehr wie beim Radio oder Fernsehen zwischen einem Sender und mehreren Empfängern, sondern „unter Gleichen", den sogenannten „Peers". Der Begriff taucht wieder auf, wenn von „Peer-to-peer-Netzen" die Rede ist, von Netzwerken gleichberechtigter Teilnehmer. Im Social-Web-Umfeld kann man nun beobachten, dass innerhalb der Peers Gruppen entstehen, die von besonderem persönlichen Nutzen sind – etwa weil sich dort bestehende Kontakte finden oder andere, bisher fremde Personen, die die gleichen Interessen teilen oder in der gleichen Branche wie der Nutzer tätig sind.

Hat eine solche Struktur einmal eine bestimmte kritische Größe erreicht, dann wird sie quasi unwiderstehlich für andere und zieht weiteres Wachstum nach sich. Das bedeutet auch, dass etwa der zweite Anbieter eines inkompatiblen Netzes gegenüber einem ersten bereits erstarkten Netz kaum noch eine Chance hat, da ein neuer Nutzer – wenn er die Wahl hat – in der Regel immer zu dem erheblich nutzenstärkeren Netz oder Dienst tendieren wird. Damit ist auch erklärt, warum es nur einen E-Mail-Standard gibt oder warum sich neben Facebook und Xing in ihren jeweiligen Segmenten kaum eine Alternative positionieren kann.

Blogs

Bei aller Begeisterung über Soziale Netzwerke als Dreh- und Angelpunkt des Social Web wird gerne übersehen, dass Weblogs (oder kurz Blogs) einen wesentlichen Anteil am Social Web haben. Die Herkunft des Begriffs „Blog" ist leicht zu ermitteln: Web plus Logbuch ergibt kurz Weblog oder noch kürzer Blog. Gemeint ist damit eine Website, auf der wiederkehrend neue Beiträge veröffentlicht werden. Diese werden in umgekehrter chronologischer Reihenfolge angezeigt (der neueste Beitrag erscheint stets ganz oben).

Von regelmäßigen Beiträgen als Merkmal eines Blogs ist zwar oft die Rede, dennoch darf man darunter keine zeitlich fixe Abfolge wie bei einer Tageszeitung (werktäglich neue Ausgabe) oder Zeitschrift (wöchentlich, zweiwöchentlich, monatlich) ausgehen. Die Veröffentlichungshäufigkeit ist typischerweise ereignisgetrieben oder ruht – insbesondere bei privat betriebenen Blogs – auch schon mal mehrere Wochen oder gar Monate.

Blogs sind nicht wirklich ein neues Phänomen. Die ersten Online-Tagebücher tauchten schon in den 90er-Jahren auf. Doch erst um die Jahrtausendwende hat die Zahl der Blogs enorm zugenommen. Betrachtet man die Anzahl der aktiven Blogs, so scheint der Zenit bereits überschritten zu sein. Eine Zählung ist schwierig bis unmöglich, insbesondere da ein Großteil der Blogs als Hobby betrieben wird und häufig bereits nach wenigen Beiträgen nicht mehr fortgeführt wird oder über Monate hinweg ruht.

Blogs lassen sich nach verschiedenen Kriterien eingruppieren:
- nach Anlass: Privat-Blog oder Unternehmens-Blog,
- nach Themenfeld,
- nach zeitlichen Kriterien (z. B. Reise-Blogs),
- nach Art der Veröffentlichung: „traditionell" über Computer oder per Handy („Moblog") und
- nach Medium: Konzentration auf Fotos, Links, Audiobeiträge („Podcasts") oder Videos („Webcasts").

Beispiel für einen
Unternehmens-Blog

Während eine erhebliche Zahl der Weblogs dem Feld der privaten Meinungsäußerung zuzurechnen ist, haben sich in den vergangenen Jahren vielerorts Unternehmens-Weblogs etabliert. Bei einem Unternehmens-Blog äußern sich Mitarbeiter im offiziellen Auftrag ihres Arbeitgebers. Bei Selbstständigen ist eine Unterscheidung zwischen privat und beruflich nicht immer einfach zu treffen. Hier mischen sich häufig private mit geschäftlichen Aktivitäten.

Die erste große Social-Media-Welle, die die Unternehmen erreicht hat, kreiste im Wesentlichen um die Frage, wie ein Unternehmens-Blog sinnvoll zu gestalten sei und wie man mit dort auftauchenden Kommentaren am besten umgehen solle. Nicht wenige der in diesem Buch diskutierten Social-Media-Richtlinien sind in ihrer Urform als Policies für Unternehmens-Blogs entstanden und haben sich mit dem Einsatz weiterer Instrumentarien in ihren Inhalten und ihrer Bedeutung entsprechend erweitert beziehungsweise gewandelt.

Das Erfolgsgeheimnis von Weblogs liegt ganz klar in der einfachen Art der Online-Veröffentlichung. Blogs werden zumeist mithilfe einfacher Content-Management-Systeme

(CMS) betrieben. Von CMS spricht man immer dann, wenn es um die Verwaltung von Website-Inhalten geht. Ein CMS für einen Weblog bietet hier vor allen einen reduzierten Funktionsumfang, der auf die typischen Blog-Funktionen zugeschnitten ist.

Die bekannteste und meistgenutzte Software für Blogs ist Wordpress, für die es eine Vielzahl von Gestaltungsvarianten gibt. Daneben existieren Online-Anbieter, die die Nutzung vorinstallierter Blog-Software ermöglichen.

Typische Bestandteile von Weblog-Systemen sind:
− Kommentarfunktion,
− Permalinks,
− Kategorien (auch „Tags"),
− Trackbacks,
− Blogrolls und
− RSS-Feeds.

Microblogs (Twitter)

Neben Weblogs, die einiges an Aufwand für eine Beitragserstellung − und aus Unternehmenssicht auch für die Moderation eingehender Kommentare − erfordern, hat sich mit „Twitter" ein Social-Web-Angebot entwickelt, das ausschließlich auf kurze Texte setzt. Dieser Dienst ist keine echte Alternative zu einem Weblog, aber durchaus eine interessante Ergänzung. Man spricht hier auch von Mikroblogs.
Bei Twitter lassen sich Kurznachrichten − sogenannte Tweets − mit bis zu 140 Zeichen Länge durch den Nutzer versenden. Empfangen werden diese von den sogenannten „Followern", also einer Art Abonnenten von Twitter-Nachrichten. Gleichzeitig sind die Tweets auch über die Twitter-Suchmaschine abfragbar. Durch die Vielzahl der Nutzer findet sich etwa zu aktuellen Ereignissen eine Vielzahl von Tweets, und man kann auf diese Weise ein „Stimmungsbild" zu einem bestimmten Thema oder Ereignis durch entsprechende Auswertungen erheben.

Betrachtet man die typischen Strukturen bei Twitter, stellt man fest, dass Twitter nur zum Teil die Mechanismen eines sozialen Beziehungsgefüges abbildet und in weiten Teilen einem klassischen Nachrichtenmedium ähnelt.
Anders als in den meisten anderen sozialen Netzwerken gibt es bei Twitter keine „Freundschaft" (zweiseitige Beziehung), sondern nur das einseitige „Follower". Um jemandem „folgen" zu können, ist keine Zustimmung notwendig. Natürlich kann man sich auch gegenseitig folgen, es ist jedoch kein Muss.
Am deutlichsten wird dies, wenn man die Personen oder Organisationen mit den meisten Followern betrachtet. Hier dominieren Schauspieler, Fernsehstars und Politiker (allen voran der US-amerikanische Präsident) und große Unternehmen der Konsumgüterbranche. Die-

sen herausgehobenen Twitter-Nutzern gelingt es, auf direktem Weg ein großes Publikum zu adressieren.
Interessant ist bei Twitter auch die Weiterverbreitung von Inhalten durch „Mundpropaganda" – im Twitter-Jargon Retweets. Auch hieran lässt sich feststellen, dass Twitter eine Sonderrolle einnimmt. Diese Einschätzung belegen auch Studien, beispielsweise einer Forschergruppe aus Korea (http://an.kaist.ac.kr/traces/WWW2010.html), die Twitter-Datenbestände dahingehend analysiert haben.
Tweets lassen sich übrigens nicht nur über das Twitter-Webinterface., sondern über eine Vielzahl von Applikationen, etwa auf dem Mobiltelefon, eingeben oder sogar automatisch generieren – etwa durch automatische Weitersendung von Xing-Statusmeldungen als Tweets oder Maschinen und Geräte, die Systemdaten per Tweet weitergeben („M2M" – Maschine-zu-Maschine-Kommunikation).
Das starke Wachstum der Twitter-Plattform sowie die schnelle und einfach zu realisierende Interaktion mit den „Followern" macht Twitter zu einem attraktiven Social-Media-Dienst für Unternehmen, der jedoch nicht ohne Risiko ist, wie das Fallbeispiel „Onkyo" im Kapitel zu Social-Media-Risiken zeigt. Eine Social Media Policy sollte stets so formuliert sein, dass zumindest implizit Twitter mit abgedeckt wird.

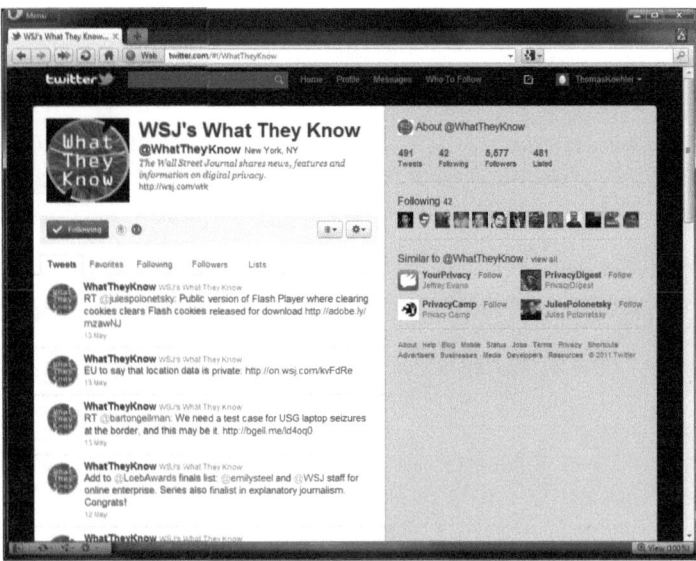

Twitter
(hier Beispiel-Account
mit Nachrichten)

Wikis

Ebenfalls zum Social Web zählt man Wikis. Dem durchschnittlichen Anwender sind Wikis vor allem in Form von Wikipedia, dem anwendergenerierten Universallexikon im Internet, geläufig. Hier kann jeder Anwender nicht nur passiver Nutzer, sondern auch Autor sein – unterschiedliche Meinungen werden von den Anwendern quasi „unter ihresgleichen" ausdiskutiert. Wikis gelten daher immer als Musterbeispiel für die sogenannte „Weisheit der Massen", auch wenn im Detail die Abstimmung der Nutzer untereinander nicht immer zu den bestmöglichen Ergebnissen führt und Fälle bekannt sind, in denen die Diskussion zwischen den Autoren in Rechthaberei, sogenannte „Edit Wars", umschlägt.

Jenseits der Musteranwendung Wikipedia lassen sich diese Mechanismen auch für andere Projekte nutzen, in denen es um das Sammeln von Informationen und um den Wissensaustausch geht. Nicht selten werden daher Wikis auch innerhalb von Unternehmen zu bestimmten Themen eingesetzt. Einige Organisationen entwickeln beispielsweise auch ihre Social-Media-Richtlinien mithilfe des Wiki-Prinzips – ein Fallbeispiel hierzu wird später im Buch noch diskutiert.

Auch Wikipedia selbst wird von Unternehmen zur Öffentlichkeitsarbeit genutzt. Allerdings ist dies wegen der unterschiedlichen Auffassungen anderer Wikipedia-Autoren, die möglicherweise von den Äußerungen der Unternehmen abweichen, nicht ganz ohne Risiko.

Contentsharing

Neben den Wikis – bei denen es im Wesentlichen um Texte geht – gibt es zahlreiche andere Anwendungen für den Austausch von Inhalten, die dem Social Web zugerechnet werden können. Während man rein technische Plattformen für Filesharing, wie etwa load. to oder rapidshare, nicht zu Social Media zählt, existiert eine Vielzahl von Anwendungen, bei denen zwar Inhaltebereitstellung und Diffusion im Mittelpunkt stehen, die aber aufgrund direkter Interaktion sowie Kommentar- und Bewertungsfunktionen eine „soziale Komponente" haben. Dazu zählen unter anderem Flickr (zur Bereitstellung von Fotos), YouTube (zur Bereitstellung von Videos), Dienste für Social Bookmarking und Anbieter wie Slideshare, die Präsentationen in den gängigen Präsentationsformaten wie PowerPoint und Apple Keynote, aber auch PDF- und Word-Dokumente online abruf- und kommentierbar machen.

Zahlreiche dieser Contentsharing-Angebote erfreuen sich nicht nur bei Endnutzern großer Beliebtheit. Ob Firmen-Channel bei YouTube oder Fotos vom jüngsten Firmenfest bei Flickr: Die Bandbreite ist groß. Naturgemäß dominiert aber die geschäftliche Komponente bei Spezialdiensten, insbesondere bei Slideshare.

Nicht wenige Firmen veröffentlichen darauf nicht nur die Handouts zu ihrem Vortrags-Events, sondern nutzen die Plattform auch zur Bereitstellung ihrer Social Media Guidelines, soweit sie diese als veröffentlichungswürdig erachten.

Social Media bietet noch zahlreiche weitere Varianten der Interaktion. Zwei für Unternehmensanwendungen besonders relevante seien hier abschließend erwähnt: Bewertungsplattformen und Crowdsourcing.

Zahlreiche Social-Media-Anwendungen bringen Bewertungs- und Kommentarfunktionen bereits mit. Bekanntestes Beispiel ist der Facebook-„Like"-Button, von dem bereits die Rede war. Doch insbesondere für Unternehmen, die im Business-to-Consumer (B-to-C)-Geschäft mit Produkten und Dienstleistungen online wie offline aktiv sind, lohnt es sich, spezielle Bewertungsplattformen im Auge zu behalten, die es zu allen möglichen Themen gibt – vom Arzt-Ranking bis zur Restaurantbewertung. Wie man hier richtig agiert, wird im weiteren Verlauf anhand von Beispielen diskutiert.

Slideshare
(Beispiel)

Bewertungsplattformen

Ranking und Rating sind im Social Web inzwischen allgegenwärtig. Ob Amazon-Buchbewertung, eBay-Anbieterprofil oder Hotelbewertung bei HRS – bewertet wird heute praktisch überall, auf Anbieter-Websites und auf speziellen Bewertungsportalen wie „Holidaycheck", „meinprof.de", „Anwaltvergleich24". Bewertungsportale sind inzwischen Alltag im Web und Bestandteil der Geschäftskultur, bergen aber für Unternehmen Risiken, etwa hinsichtlich Falschbewertung. Dazu später mehr in den Beispielen.

Crowdsourcing

Faszinierende Möglichkeiten für die Zukunft verspricht auch die Nutzung von Ideen und Arbeitsleistungen von Kunden und Interessenten von der Produktentwicklung bis zum Vertrieb. Unter dem Schlagwort „Crowdsourcing" fasst man hier eine Vielzahl von Initiativen und häufig individuellen Lösungen zusammen, die helfen können, den Austausch zwischen Unternehmen und Endkunden zu beiderseitigem Nutzen zu intensivieren, aber auch ihre eigene Dynamik und ihre ureigenen Risiken haben.

Adaption von Social Media im betrieblichen Umfeld

Betrachtet man nun – unabhängig von den Diensten – die Entwicklung der Adaption von Social Media im Unternehmen, dann lässt sich diese in den meisten Fällen an einem gemeinsamen Beginn festmachen:
Am Anfang steht stets der Einsatz in Werbung und Public Relations. Nicht selten ist der Unternehmens-Blog der Start. Doch häufig verkünden Werbeagenturen die Botschaft, dass es nun ohne eigene Facebook-Fanpage nicht mehr geht, und ehe man sich's versieht, ist man mittendrin im Social-Media-Geschehen – und benötigt eine Policy, wie in diesem Buch beschrieben.
Weitere Schritte können aus den Bereichen Vertriebsunterstützung oder Produktentwicklung kommen oder – und das ist gar nicht so selten – aus dem Kunden-Support, hofft man doch nicht selten auf Kosteneinsparungen, wenn sich die Nutzer untereinander selbst helfen, statt die Support-Hotline zu strapazieren.
Social Media als Kern-Feature eines Produktes oder einer Dienstleistung zu etablieren ist manchmal – aber längst nicht immer – die Konsequenz einer immer weiteren Durchdringung der Unternehmen durch Social Media.

Risiken und Fallstricke von Social Media im Unternehmen

Spricht man über Social Media im betrieblichen Umfeld, so werden nicht selten Anekdoten aus der Kategorie „Pleiten, Pech und Pannen" aufs Tablett gebracht – praktisch jeder kennt eine Firma, in der sich eine Social-Media-Marketing-Aktivität als Bumerang erwiesen hat. Häufiger noch scheint der Fall, in dem sich Mitarbeiter selbst – durch unbedachte Aktionen und Äußerungen – ins Abseits manövriert haben.

Insbesondere Letzteres soll mit Social Media Guidelines vermieden werden, wodurch sich ein möglicherweise entstehender Schaden vom Unternehmen abwenden lässt.

Zeitverschwendung Social Media

„Der einzige Weg, eine Versuchung loszuwerden, ist, ihr nachzugeben."

(Oscar Wilde)

Auch und gerade bei Social Media, von dessen Attraktivität die Rede war, scheint es nicht einfach zu sein, „davon zu lassen" – Diskussion über Verbote hin oder her. Nach einem von der Zeitschrift Computerworld (http://www.computerworld.com/s/article/9135795/Study_Facebook_use_cuts_productivity_at_work) zitierten Forschungsbericht der Firma Nucleus Research büßen Unternehmen, die Facebook erlauben, rund 1,5 % ihrer gesamten Produktivität ein. In der in den USA durchgeführten Befragung kamen Spitzenwerte von bis zu zwei Stunden Facebook-Nutzung am Tag während der Arbeitszeit ans Tageslicht. Die durchschnittliche tägliche Nutzungsdauer von Facebook wurde in dieser Studie mit rund 15 Minuten ermittelt.

Die öffentliche Verwaltung ist von dem Phänomen nicht verschont geblieben: Bekannt wurde der Fall der Schweizer Kantonalverwaltung. Dort hat man festgestellt, dass insgesamt erstaunliche 4 % des Netzwerk-Traffics nur mit Facebook zu tun haben, nach verschiedenen Medienberichten waren es weit über 10 % der Arbeitszeit, die von der Arbeitszeit der Staatsdiener allein in die Nutzung dieses Netzwerks geflossen sind. Die Konsequenz: ein klares Verbot.

Im internationalen Vergleich liegt man jedoch mit den genannten 4 % Netzwerk-Traffic noch deutlich zurück. So berichtet eine Studie des Sicherheitsanbieters Network-Box in den USA, dass rund 6,8 % aller Webzugriffe am Arbeitsplatz auf das Konto von Facebook gehen. Forrester Research spricht in einer Studie sogar von rund 30 % des Netzwerkdatenverkehrs in Unternehmen, die auf das Konto von Social Networks gehen. Selbst an Hochschulen gerät die Produktivität mit Blick auf Facebook unter Druck. Die Ohio State University will herausgefunden haben, dass intensive Facebook-Nutzer weniger lernen und schlechtere Noten bekommen als Nicht- oder Wenignutzer.

Geht man nun davon aus, dass Facebook nur einen – wenn auch signifikanten – Teil der nicht arbeitsplatzrelevanten Internetnutzung ausmacht, drängt sich eine Frage förmlich auf: *Warum verbietet man nicht Social Media und Webnutzung am Arbeitsplatz?* Doch so einfach, wie es scheint, ist es nicht – nicht nur, dass das vorliegende Buch dann an dieser Stelle mit einer klaren „Abschaltempfehlung" enden würde. Es ist schlicht die Wirklichkeit, die eine einfache Schwarz-Weiß-Unterscheidung beim Thema Social Media nicht erlaubt: Widersprüchliche und den oben genannten Studien widersprechende Ergebnisse erhält man bereits, wenn man die Arbeitnehmer selbst fragt. Nach einer Untersuchung aus Großbritannien (http://myjobgroup.co.uk) sind 14 % der befragten Arbeitnehmer der Meinung, dass sie durch Social-Media-Nutzung während der Arbeitszeit unproduktiver werden, während immerhin 10 % vom Gegenteil überzeugt sind.

Es gibt aber durchaus auch Stimmen pro Internet- beziehungsweise Social-Media-Nutzung am Arbeitsplatz: So berichtet die Universität Melbourne (Australien) in einer Studie (http://uninews.unimelb.edu.au/news/5750/) davon, dass Internetnutzung am Arbeitsplatz die Arbeitsproduktivität um 9 % steigern kann, immer vorausgesetzt, dass eine Grenze von 20 % der Arbeitszeit nicht überschritten wird. Man hat auch gleich eine Bezeichnung für diesen Sachverhalt in petto: WILB (Workplace Internet Leisure Browsing). Nach dem Studienautor Dr. Brent Croker (Department of Management and Marketing) liegt der Grund für diese scheinbar widersinnige Ergebniskonstellation in der menschlichen Natur. WILB sieht er als Mittel, nach Tiefpunkten in der Konzentrationsfähigkeit geistig wieder zu Kräften zu kommen.

Ohne mit obiger Aufzählung einen Anspruch auf Vollständigkeit erheben zu wollen, ist offensichtlich, dass eine einheitliche Linie in den Studien zum Thema „Produktivitätseffekte von Social Media am Arbeitsplatz" aufgrund der Vielfalt und Vielschichtigkeit der Ergebnisse nicht auszumachen ist. Bemerkenswert ist auch die hohe Unschärfe, die es – wie in anderen Fällen von Studien und Statistiken auch – nahelegt, sich jeweils die Ergebnisse mit Blick auf den Auftraggeber und dessen mögliche Interessenlage detailliert anzusehen. Zudem empfiehlt sich dem interessierten Leser ein Blick in das Buch „So lügt man mit Statistik" (Walter Krämer, Piper Verlag, inzwischen in der 12. Auflage erschienen).

Wie man es auch dreht und wendet, am Ende wird man bei derartigen Betrachtungen sehr schnell reduziert auf die Frage, wie genau man denn Arbeitsproduktivität in typischen heutigen Schreibtischjobs bewerten kann. In der oben angesprochenen Verwaltung mag das für einzelne Aufgabengebiete durchaus noch möglich sein, etwa indem man die bearbeiteten Bauanträge oder Steuererklärungen pro Arbeitstag aufsummiert und eine Vorher-Nachher-Betrachtung anstellt. Auch die eine oder andere Tätigkeit in einem Unternehmen lässt sich vielleicht noch so – etwa nach Anzahl der bearbeiteten Reisekostenanträge pro Stunde – dokumentieren. Die große Masse der Bürotätigkeiten – die der sogenannten Wissensarbeiter – entzieht sich aber weitgehend harten Messkriterien. Wollte man hier den Einfluss von Social Media ermitteln, müsste man – ceteris paribus, also bei sonst unveränderten beziehungsweise unveränderbaren Rahmenbedingungen – den Umsatz mal mit und mal ohne Social-Media-Nutzung ermitteln. Es liegt auf der Hand, dass dies bestenfalls in einigen realitätsfernen Modellen funktionieren kann.

Auch die Mitarbeiter selbst zu fragen liefert bestenfalls ein verzerrtes oder – je nach Fragesituation und -methodik – schöngefärbtes Abbild der Wirklichkeit.

Zudem wird der kundige Leser jetzt einwenden, dass die private Webnutzung und damit auch die private Social-Media-Nutzung im Unternehmen eine Folge der seit Jahren zu beobachtenden Vermischung von Arbeit und Freizeit ist, die eben nicht nur dazu führt, dass der Mitarbeiter – dank Mobiltelefon, BlackBerry und Co. – auch in der Freizeit erreichbar für Unternehmensbelange ist und ab und zu Arbeit „mit nach Hause" nimmt – er nimmt auch sein Privatleben ein Stück weit mit ins Büro. In vielen dem Autor bekannten Fällen ist das für das Unternehmen „kein schlechtes Geschäft".

Social Media als Sicherheitsrisiko

Lässt man die in Fachkreisen geführte Debatte um den Produktivitätsverlust beiseite, so stehen – insbesondere bei forschungsorientierten Unternehmen – mögliche Sicherheitsrisiken im Vordergrund der Diskussion rund um eine Social Media Policy.

Verbreitung von Schadsoftware

Nicht unterschätzt werden sollte die Gefahr, die spezielle Schadsoftware für Soziale Netzwerke für den Anwender im Unternehmen und das Unternehmen mit sich bringt. Die erste Schadsoftware, die bei Facebook einen größeren Bekanntheitsgrad erlangt hat, war „Koobface". Die Malware verbreitet sich durch (scheinbar) persönliche Nachrichten und versucht den Anwender auf eine Website zu locken, auf der ihm durch einen „Drive-by-Download" ein Trojaner untergeschoben werden soll. Das besondere Problem hier: Durch den scheinbar vertrauten Charakter der Mail (man kennt ja den Absender) ist die Neigung, auf den beigefügten Link zu klicken, ungleich größer, als wenn dieser per anonymem Spam käme. Im Grunde wiederholt Koobface damit nur die Mechanismen, die bereits bei der Ausbreitung des „I love you"-Virus vor Jahren per E-Mail erfolgreich waren.

In Verbindung mit sogenannten Zero-Day-Attacks, bei denen neue Sicherheitslücken ausgenützt werden, die noch niemand kennt, sind auch gut gepatchte Rechnersysteme anfällig für derartige Schädlinge und können damit zum Einfallstor für Hackerangriffe werden.

Risiken für Datenschutz und Privatsphäre

Social-Media-Nutzung kann Risiken für Datenschutz und Privatsphäre beinhalten. Das ist zunächst eine triviale Erkenntnis. Im Rahmen dieses Buches ist es aber dennoch wichtig, genau diesen Punkt zu adressieren, da die Risiken eben nicht nur für die handelnde Person bestehen, sondern auch Dritte durch eigene Handlungen tangiert werden können. Dies ist insbesondere im Unternehmensumfeld kritisch, da die Folgen in der Preisgabe von Unternehmensdaten und Geschäftsgeheimnissen liegen können oder möglicherweise das Verhältnis zu Lieferanten und Kunden oder auch der Mitarbeiter untereinander belasten. Eine ganzheitliche Betrachtung dieser Aspekte aus Unternehmenssicht ist daher stets sinnvoll. Folgende Risiken bestehen konkret:

- Verletzung der eigenen Privatsphäre durch Preisgabe von zu viel Informationen über sich selbst, verbunden mit dem Risiko, das Opfer von Belästigungen oder Stalking zu werden und durch als „unpassendes Benehmen" wahrgenommenes Verhalten gegebenenfalls auch das Unternehmen in Bedrängnis zu bringen. Auch kann man sich damit zum potenziellen Opfer von Spear-Phishing-Attacken machen. Damit ist gemeint, dass man durch die Datenpreisgabe eine Grundlage legt, die später durch Social Engineering von Unternehmensexternen zu böswilligen Zwecken genutzt wird.
- Verletzung der Privatsphäre von anderen, durch die Preisgabe von zu viel (im Sinne von mehr als notwendig) Informationen über Kunden, Kollegen, Geschäftspartner, Lieferanten und Dritte.
- Preisgabe von vertraulichen firmeninternen Informationen oder Betriebsgeheimnissen des eigenen Unternehmens oder von Lieferanten und Geschäftspartnern.
- Bei andauernden Online-Aktivitäten entsteht eine Sammlung von – unter Umständen bei späterer Betrachtung als unpassend wahrgenommenen – Äußerungen, die aufgrund des Charakters des Internets permanent gespeichert und permanent auffindbar ist.

Hier kommt hinzu, dass Suchmaschinen immer bessere Ergebnisse liefern und zudem spezielle Social-Media-Suchdienste das Auffinden derartiger Zusammenhänge weiter erleichtern.

Es fällt schwer, derartige Risiken in einem weiteren Schritt nach „intern" oder „extern" zu differenzieren, so eng verwoben sind die Bereiche bereits miteinander.

Sollte man als Anbieter im Bereich Social Media aktiv sein oder Online-Aktivitäten weitreichend überwachen – im Branchenjargon wird dies „Social Media Monitoring" genannt –, besteht noch ein besonderes Risiko: Durch eigenes Sammeln von Daten gerät man als Unternehmen schnell in eine rechtliche Grauzone.

Weitere unerwünschte Nebenwirkungen

Soziale Netzwerke machen es dem Nutzer leicht, mehr von sich und von seinen Beziehungen preiszugeben, als er eigentlich möchte. Ein Beispiel: Sowohl Facebook als auch LinkedIn bieten die Möglichkeit, bestehende Kontakte online zu suchen – bei Facebook als sogenannter „Friend Finder", indem man sein eigenes Telefon- oder Outlook-Adressbuch hochlädt. Damit gibt man Firmendaten in die Hand eines Dritten, der als Social-Network-Betreiber häufig ein ausländisches Unternehmen ist, das in der Praxis weder deutschen Gesetzen unterliegt noch vom Anwender in irgendeiner Weise kontrolliert werden kann.

Auch installierte Third-Party-Applikationen können – genauso wie Smartphone-Apps – Risiken beinhalten, etwa im Bereich des Abflusses von Nutzerdaten.

In der Praxis können in Social Networks frei zugängliche Nutzerdaten auch zur Vorbereitung von Social-Engineering-Attacken auf Unternehmen genutzt werden: Durch die detaillierte Kenntnis von Lebensumständen und Vorlieben einer Person kann sich ein Angreifer unter Umständen erfolgreich als diese Person ausgeben und so über persönliche Kontakte (Anrufe, E-Mails) an Passwörter oder Firmeninterna gelangen.

Selbst wenn dies nicht gelingt, kann in bestimmten Branchen allein die Kenntnis der Kontakte zwischen einzelnen Personen Rückschlüsse auf Unternehmensstrategien zulassen, die Geheimschutzanforderungen berühren.

Dies wird an einem fiktiven Beispiel deutlich: Hält ein Entwicklungsingenieur in einem Automobilunternehmen auf einer Online-Plattform Kontakt zu einem Verantwortlichen bei einer Zulieferfirma, die auf Leistungselektronik für Elektromobilität spezialisiert ist, kann ein möglicher Wettbewerber Schlüsse dahingehend ziehen, welche Innovationen bei besagtem Autohersteller in Kürze zu erwarten sind.

Wem dieses Beispiel zu weit hergeholt erscheint, es gibt auch andere: Die Vernetzung zwischen Vertriebsmitarbeiter und Kundenansprechpartner taugt für die Vertriebsabteilung des Wettbewerbers auf der Suche nach neuen Kunden häufig als Indikator, wo sich ein „Cold Call" lohnen könnte.

Social Media Disaster

Die Nutzung von Social Media im Marketing ist – zumindest im B-to-C-Geschäft – längst gängige Praxis. Man hofft hier vor allem auf virale Effekte, also darauf, dass sich „rumspricht", wenn ein Produkt oder eine Dienstleistung besonders gut ist. Gerne ist so mancher Marketier – wenn er nur mittelmäßige Produkte oder solche von geringem Interesse hat – versucht, hier ein wenig nachzuhelfen, etwa indem er sich als zufriedener Anwender ausgibt und das eigene Produkt auf E-Commerce-Seiten und Bewertungsplattformen in den Himmel lobt.

Aber auch sonst kann man sich durch unbedachte Internetaktionen schnell zum Gespött der Online-Community machen oder sich gar deren „geballten Hass" zuziehen.

Die nachfolgenden Abschnitte skizzieren typische (reale) Fälle, deren Implikationen im Kapitel „Social-Media-Management" diskutiert werden.

Gefälschte Produktbewertungen

Beispiel WeTab

Wer erinnert sich noch an Helmut Hoffer von Ankershofen? Als Gründer eines Start-ups war er angetreten, Apple mit einem eigenen Tablet-Rechner mit dem Namen WeTab Konkurrenz zu machen. Als nach missglückter Erstpräsentation – bei der nach Presseberichten statt eines funktionsfähigen Betriebssystems nur ein Video gezeigt wurde – die ersten Besprechungen in der Fachpresse durchweg einen negativen Tenor hatten, griff er zur Selbsthilfe: Sowohl er als auch seine Frau gaben – so wurde später bekannt – bei Amazon unter einem Pseudonym überragend positive Bewertungen für das eigene Produkt ab, ohne dabei zu bedenken, dass eine falsch gesetzte Privacy-Einstellung sie verraten würde.

Eine detaillierte Beschreibung des Vorgangs findet sich übrigens unter dem vielsagenden Titel „W wie WeDepp" hier: http://gutjahr.biz/blog/2010/10/wedepp/.
Die Folge der Aktion: Der Geschäftsführer war für sein Unternehmen untragbar geworden und hat inzwischen sein Amt aufgegeben.

Gefälschte Bewertungen bei Amazon
Amazon-Rezensionen sind wegen ihrer großen Bedeutung für Einkaufsentscheidungen bei Büchern, aber auch bei anderen Produkten wie etwa Unterhaltungselektronik, für Produktanbieter wie Buchautoren wesentlich. Die eigenen Bücher oder Produkte mittels lancierter positiver Rezensionen „raufzuschreiben" und etwa auch – besonders perfide – die tatsächliche oder vermeintliche Konkurrenz „runterzuschreiben", scheint nicht selten als verlockende Option für den einen oder anderen charakterlich nicht gefestigten Anbieter.
Nehmen Sie nur das Buch „Die Facebookfalle" (Sascha Adamek bei HEYNE 2/2011), das sich nicht nur in Titel und Klappentext sehr an Thomas R. Köhler: „Die Internetfalle" (Frankfurter Allgemeine Buch 2010) anlehnt (und dadurch „auffällig" wurde), sondern binnen weniger Tage gleich vier „5-Sterne-Rezensionen" sammelte. Schaut man genauer hin, so stellt man fest, dass die ersten positiven Rezensionen von „Die Facebookfalle" auf Amazon bereits vor der Verfügbarkeit des Buchs im Handel auftauchten. Es drängt sich förmlich der Verdacht auf, dass hier nicht alles mit rechten Dingen zugegangen ist. Aber nicht immer sind die Ansätze derart plump.
Mehr zum Problem gefälschter Produktbewertungen, das in bestimmten Branchen wie der Hotellerie schon epidemische Ausmaße angenommen hat, und Hinweise zu ihrer Enttarnung finden Sie auch im oben genannten Buch „Die Internetfalle" des Autors dieses Ratgebers.
Insgesamt bleibt festzuhalten: Professionell gefälschte „Kundenmeinungen" sind nicht einfach zu erkennen. Dienstleister wie die Hamburger Firma Ethority werben offen mit den besonderen Fähigkeiten ihrer Mitarbeiter, die als „ausgebildete Germanisten" in der Lage sein sollen, auch die richtige Tonalität einer Produktbewertung zu treffen. Ob Bauarbeiter oder Hochschulprofessor – man hat dort nicht nur die „passenden" Meinungen, sondern auch den geeigneten Wortlaut im Angebot.

Beispiel Belkin: Produktbewertungen selbst gekauft
Wie man – eher plump – massenhaft Kundenmeinungen manipuliert, hat der Anbieter von PC-Zubehör Belkin ganz nebenbei offenbart (http://www.crunchgear.com/2009/01/17/belkin-paying-65-cents-for-good-reviews-on-newegg-and-amazon/).

Belkin hatte über die Amazon-Crowdsourcing-Plattform „Mechanical Turk" Endverbraucher gesucht, die für 65 Cent pro Beitrag positive Rezensionen für Belkin-Produkte schreiben sollten. Die Anleitung dazu las sich wie folgt (Übersetzung durch den Autor):
- Schreiben Sie grammatikalisch richtig und nur in US-Englisch.
- Geben Sie stets eine 100 %-Bewertung ab (so hoch wie möglich).
- Ihr Eintrag sollte zwischen 25 und 50 Worte umfassen.

- Schreiben Sie so, als ob Sie das Produkt selbst besitzen und es benutzen.
- Schreiben Sie (das heißt „erfinden Sie") eine Geschichte, warum Sie das Produkt gekauft haben und wie Sie es benutzen.
- Bedanken Sie sich bei der Website für einen derartig guten Deal.
- Markieren Sie andere Kommentare, die negativ ausfallen, als „nicht hilfreich", wenn Sie Ihren Kommentar posten.
- [...]

Beispiel Deutsche Bahn
Übrigens schützt auch „Old-Economy"-Charme nicht vor Torheiten mit Online-Produktbewertungen.
Wie der SPIEGEL (30.05.2009) berichtet, hatte die Deutsche Bahn zwecks positiver PR nicht nur Promis dafür bezahlt, sich in den Medien positiv über die Bahn zu äußern: In einem Rechenschaftsbericht [der damit betrauten Agentur Allendorf Media] vom 26. Juni 2007 heißt es: „Auf der Homepage der Frauenzeitschrift ‚Brigitte' sind wir seit heute registriert und werden dort den vorhandenen Bahnblog mit Kommentaren versehen."
[...] Neben anderen Internetmedien wie tagesschau.de war auch SPIEGEL ONLINE davon betroffen: In insgesamt drei Foren zum Thema Bahn machten sich bezahlte Meinungsmacher breit – jedenfalls rühmte sich Allendorf, dass von den damals 1.400 Beiträgen im Forum „Höhere Fahrpreise" insgesamt 350 vom Konzern bezahlt waren. Auch in den SPIEGEL-ONLINE-Foren „Die Bahn – Ständig neben der Spur?" und „Die Bahn: nicht fit für die Börse?" lag die Quote der platzierten Postings angeblich etwa bei einem Viertel. Tatsächlich fallen Einzelne der Diskussionsteilnehmer nicht nur durch eine fast perfekte Marketing-Sprache auf, sondern auch durch ihre überaus wohlwollende Kommentierung der Bahn."

Was sonst noch schiefgehen kann
Manchmal reicht ein unbedachtes Wort in der Öffentlichkeit, um wütende Proteststürme auszulösen, aber auch eine falsche Anbiederung oder Reaktion auf eine öffentliche Anschuldigung kann im Social Web unerwünschte Reaktionen auslösen.

Beispiel Trigema
Nicht wirklich zu den Früheinsteigern in Sachen Internet zählt Deutschlands bekanntester Textilunternehmer: Wolfgang Grupp mit seiner Firma Trigema. Auch wenn inzwischen Facebook-Fanpage und Online-Shop vorhanden sind – so richtig warm wurde man bei Trigema mit dem Internet nie. Bekannt für seine manchmal spitzen bis aneckenden Kommentare nutzt Wolfgang Grupp jede sich bietende Talkshow, um seine Weltsicht zu verbreiten. In einem Interview mit einem Business-Blog (http://www.innovativ-in.de/blog/2010/05/04/auf-den-punkt-trigema-chef-wolfgang-grupp-zum-web/) verstieg er sich unter anderem zu folgender Äußerung über Twitter:
„Ich beschäftige mich damit nicht. Twitter ist für mich einfach nur dumm, und die Menschen, die das nutzen, sind für mich Idioten. Haben die Menschen eigentlich nichts Besseres zu tun, als über belanglosen Kram zu schreiben? Wen interessiert das?"

Trigema-Facebook-
Seite (Auszug)

Diese Äußerung löste das aus, was man in Social-Media-Kreisen gemeinhin als Shitstorm bezeichnet: eine Welle negativer Äußerungen. In diesem Fall mit der Folge, dass sich Grupp genötigt sah, mit einem offenen Brief auf der eigenen Facebook-Seite die Aussagen zu relativieren, um die Wogen zu glätten.

Beispiel Vodafone

Eine der meistdiskutierten Social-Media-Aktivitäten 2009 war die Vodafone-Kampagne, die mit einer ins Netz übertragenen Pressekonferenz startete. Eigentlich hatte man – auch dank der Hilfe einer renommierten Werbeagentur – alles „richtig" gemacht. Man hat sich geöffnet und Interaktion zugelassen, einen bekannten „Blogger" als „Testimonial" engagiert.

Doch als Reaktion erntete man überwiegend Hohn und Spott.

Den Zusehern war sehr schnell aufgefallen, dass erhebliche Differenzen zwischen Form (Interaktion, Dialog) und Inhalt (klassische Pressekonferenz, in der von „Zielgruppe" und „Testimonials" gesprochen wurde) bestanden. Keine große Sache eigentlich, aber ein klares Indiz dafür, wie sensibel die Online-Nutzer in Sachen Kundenansprache oder -dialog tatsächlich sind.

Beispiel Onkyo

Der Hi-Fi-Hersteller Onkyo, in Fachkreisen besonders anerkannt für seine Surround-Receiver – die zentralen Elemente jeder Surround-Anlage im Wohnzimmer –, operiert in Deutschland mit kleinem Team von nach eigenen Angaben rund zwölf Personen und kleinem Budget. Besonders stolz ist man auf technische Besonderheiten wie den Erweiterungsanschluss, an dem man Zusatzkomponenten wie DAB-Tuner oder iPod-Docks anschließen kann.

Bei dieser Ausgangslage liegt es besonders nahe, Social-Media-Kanäle für den Kontakt zum Kunden zu nutzen. So gibt es seit geraumer Zeit einen Onkyo Twitter Channel mit zunächst eher mäßiger Akzeptanz.

Wie steigert man hier die Nutzerzahl bei gleichzeitiger Qualifizierung der Kontakte? Die Antwort schien schnell gefunden: Man fordert die Nutzer auf, Endgeräte zu registrieren und die Registrierungsdaten per Tweet zu übersenden. Als Incentive bot man ein iPhone-Dock an, das an den oben erwähnten Erweiterungsanschluss, den alle neueren Receiver mitbringen, angeschlossen werden kann (der aber in anderen Nutzungsszenarien nicht verwendbar ist). Da man mit einem gewissen Zuspruch gerechnet hatte, reservierte man immerhin 100 Exemplare der Dockingstationen dafür. Geplant war die Aktion für eine Laufzeit vom 19. Januar bis Ende Januar 2011. Doch schon kurze Zeit nach dem Start geriet die Aktion außer Kontrolle: Die Zahl der eingegangen Registrierungen explodierte förmlich, sodass man sich bereits nach knapp zwei Stunden genötigt sah, „die Reißleine zu ziehen". Was war passiert? Die Aktion hatte eine gefährliche Eigendynamik entwickelt. Kurz gesagt: Es hatte sich herumgesprochen, dass es etwas umsonst gibt. Der Autor selbst – als Besitzer eines Onkyo-Surround-Receivers der größten Baureihe durchaus in der Zielgruppe der Aktion – erhielt eine Mail von einem Bekannten, der explizit darauf hinwies. Neben persönlichen Empfehlungen haben aber – so viel lässt sich in der Rückschau sagen – andere Faktoren die Aktion de facto ruiniert. So breitete sich die Kunde von der Gratis-iPod-Dock-Aktion vor allem über sogenannte Schnäppchen-Websites wie „MyDealz" (www.mydealz.de) aus. Auf derartigen Webangeboten werden die neuesten Schnäppchen und Gratisaktionen diskutiert, samt nicht immer einwandfreien Tipps, wie man sich die angepriesenen Vorteile verschaffen kann.

Im Falle der Onkyo-Twitter-Aktion wurde etwa empfohlen, man könne ja in einen Elektroladen gehen und die Seriennummer vom Karton eines entsprechenden Gerätes abschreiben beziehungsweise abfotografieren, um einen entsprechend für die Aktion notwendigen Registrierungscode zu bekommen.

In der Tat konnte Onkyo nach Aussage von Firmenvertretern genau dies beobachten: Ein nicht unerheblicher Teil der Registrierungen bezog sich auf Geräte, die gerade an den Handel ausgeliefert worden waren und teilweise auch nach Auktionsende noch im Elektromarkt im Regal standen.

Es ist anzunehmen, dass etliche Internetnutzer in Folge das auf diese Weise gratis erlangte iPhone-Dock auf eBay verkauft haben – für etwas „Taschengeld".

Aber diese „Freerider" von den regulären Nutzern zu unterscheiden war im Verlauf der Aktion fast unmöglich geworden. Man entschied sich dazu – weit über die angepeilten 100 Exemplare hinaus –, Geräte auszugeben um keine schlechte Presse zu diskutieren. Dennoch waren entsprechende Foren im Nachgang voll von negativen Kommentaren, etwa in der Art:

„makaber" (Nickname) schreibt am Aktionstag um 19.52 Uhr in einem einschlägigen Forum:
„was ist denn dass für eine sch ...? wieviel Dinger hatten die? 2?
Schön, dass man sich jetzt umsonst die Mühe gemacht hat"

Wenn man davon ausgeht, dass in derartigen Foren die Zahl der aktiv Beitragenden im Regelfall unter 1 % der Forenbesucher liegt (eigene Recherchen des Autors), kann man sich ausrechnen, welch ungewollt negatives Echo die ganze Aktion gebracht hat – gut gemeint ist eben nicht immer gut gemacht, vor allen Dingen, wenn man sich der Dynamik des Internets nicht bewusst ist. In diesem Fall wurde die Aktion mit kleinem Budget im Unternehmen selbst – im Agenturdeutsch „Inhouse" – gemacht und wird nach Aussagen von Unternehmensvertretern so sicher nicht wiederholt. Eine in Social-Media-Marketing erfahrene Agentur hätte derartige Fehler vermutlich vermieden.

Aber was sind nun die wesentlichen Erkenntnisse aus dem Fallbeispiel?
– Planen Sie ein ausreichendes Budget ein.
– Begrenzen Sie Online-Aktionen immer nach der zur Verfügung stehenden Stückzahl, etwa „die ersten hundert".
– Denken Sie immer daran, dass kostenlose Aktionen unter Umständen „Freerider" anlocken, und suchen Sie bereits im Vorfeld nach Möglichkeiten, diese auszuschließen.
– Halten Sie auf jeden Fall einen „Plan B" vor für den Fall, dass Ihre Aktion außer Kontrolle gerät.

Beispiel Nestlé
Die pure Reaktion auf eine öffentliche Anschuldigung kann ebenfalls bereits problematisch sein. So erlebte Nestlé in der Konfrontation mit Greenpeace eine besondere Form von PR-Desaster. Laut verschiedenen Medienberichten verwendet der Nahrungsmittel-Multi Palmöl eines indonesischen Lieferanten, der dafür große Urwaldflächen rodet. Man hatte sich zwar von dem Lieferanten distanziert, aber – so wird verschiedentlich berichtet – über Zwischenhändler weiter bei dem Unternehmen eingekauft. Dies hatte Greenpeace mit einem viralen Video angeprangert, worauf sich verschiedentlich Internetnutzer verbal Luft machten, unter anderem auf der offiziellen Facebook-Seite von Nestlé. Das Unternehmen reagierte unter anderem damit, dass es kritische Äußerungen löschen ließ, was dazu führte, dass sich ein Proteststurm erhob, der um ein Vielfaches stärker war als vor der Löschungsaktion. Inzwischen hat sich Nestlé offiziell entschuldigt.

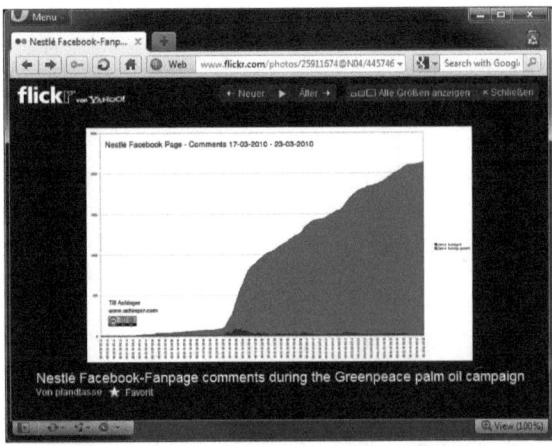

Viraler Effekt bei Nestlé (nach: http://achinger.com/nestles-facebook-fanpage-entwicklung-einer-krise/)

Einen Rat zu geben fällt hier nicht leicht. Klar ist, dass sich ein Unternehmen, das im Web 2.0 aktiv ist, der Kritik aussetzt, zumal mit einer eigenen Facebook-Page, und man gut daran tut, mit Zensur vorsichtig zu sein, da sich das Löschen von kritischen Meinungen in kürzester Zeit zum Proteststurm auswachsen kann.

Beispiel Jack Wolfskin
Der Outdoor-Ausrüster Jack Wolfskin ist bekannt – auch durch sein markenrechtlich geschütztes Logo, das eine Tierpfote zeigt. Nachdem in der Vergangenheit Jack Wolfskin bereits gegen die „taz" – die ebenfalls ein solches Logo besitzt – juristisch vorgegangen ist, da diese Handtücher mit Tierpfoten in ihrem Merchandising-Programm angeboten hat, suchte man sich nun neue Ziele aus.
So wurden mehrere Kleinstunternehmen, die über das Internetportal DaWanda Handarbeiten verkaufen, kostenpflichtig abgemahnt, weil sie mit Tierpfoten bestickte Kopfkissen und ähnliche Gegenstände dort angeboten hatten. Dieses harte und vielfach als unangemessen empfundene Vorgehen von Jack Wolfskin rief vielfache Nutzerproteste und sogar vereinzelt Boykottaufrufe hervor. Erst als der Proteststurm längst die Online-Welt erreicht hatte, lenkte Jack Wolfskin schließlich ein und reagierte mit einer Stellungnahme per Pressemitteilung (zitiert nach: http://www.jack-wolfskin.com/Portaldata/1/Resources/company/Jack_Wolfskin_reagiert_auf_Kritik_beim_Vorgehen_zum_Markenschutz.pdf):

„Jack Wolfskin reagiert auf Kritik beim Vorgehen zum Markenschutz
Die zum Teil heftigen Reaktionen im Internet auf unser Vorgehen in Fällen von Markenrechtsverletzungen führen zu einem Einlenken. Gegen die zehn Anbieter, die Produkte mit Tatzen-Design auf der Plattform DaWanda.de verkauft hatten und daraufhin abgemahnt wurden, werden wir keine weiteren rechtlichen Schritte mehr verfolgen.
Der Schutz unserer Marke hat für uns oberste Priorität. Wir sind immer bemüht, mit Augenmaß und nur dort vorzugehen, wo wir unsere Schutzrechte wirklich gefährdet sehen. Die zum Teil heftige Kritik unserer Kunden in den aktuellen Fällen der DaWanda-Anbieter nehmen wir ernst und zum Anlass, unser Vorgehen kritisch zu hinterfragen. Dies bedeutet, dass wir mit dem Entfernen der betroffenen Produkte von der Internetplattform die Fälle als erledigt ansehen, keine weiteren rechtlichen Schritte verfolgen und den Anbietern die vor allem kritisierten Kosten erlassen.
Darüber hinaus werden wir unser Vorgehen in Fällen von kleingewerblichen Angeboten verändern. Hier werden wir in Zukunft zunächst auf anwaltliche Schritte verzichten und selbst Kontakt aufnehmen. Kommt es zu einer Einigung, sollen Kosten möglichst ganz vermieden werden. Anwaltliche Hilfe soll in Zukunft erst ein letzter Schritt sein.
An der großen Emotionalität, mit der die Debatte geführt wurde, sehen wir, wie hoch die Erwartungshaltung an uns ist. Dem wollen wir gerecht werden. Wir haben uns der Kritik gestellt, unser Vorgehen kritisch durchleuchtet und werden in Zukunft sensibler agieren."

Auch in anderen Fällen hatten und haben Unternehmen, die das Instrument der Abmahnung aus Sicht der Netzgemeinschaft missbräuchlich oder unverhältnismäßig einsetzen, mit ähnlichen Reaktionen zu rechnen.

„Wir basteln uns ein Social-Media-Desaster"

In die Mühlen des Social Web kann man – wie die Beispiele stellvertretend für viele andere zeigen – als Unternehmen auf ganz verschiedene Weise geraten. Einen nicht ganz ernst gemeinten Ratgeber „Zum perfekten Imageschaden im Web 2.0" hat das lesenswerte Magazin t3n im August 2010 unter dem Titel „Wir basteln uns ein Social Media Desaster" veröffentlicht (online unter: http://t3n.de/magazin/10-schritten-perfekten-imageschaden-dank-web-20-basteln-224806/) – der hier abschließend wiedergegeben werden soll. Auf humorvolle Weise beschreibt der Autor „Jan Tißler", was tatsächlich schiefgehen kann und wie falsche Reaktionen die Probleme erst außer Kontrolle geraten lassen:

„Das Social Web bietet jedem viel Potenzial. Das kann man auch sehr gekonnt dazu nutzen, um unangenehm aufzufallen oder seinem Image einen gut sichtbaren Schaden hinzuzufügen. Wie leicht das geht, zeigen wir hier: eine Praxisanleitung in zehn einfachen, gut nachvollziehbaren Schritten.

1. Betrachten Sie das Internet als Ihren Feind

Wie bei vielen Dingen im Leben, ist auch beim Social-Media-Desaster die Grundeinstellung entscheidend. Es ist unumgänglich, dass Sie das Internet als Ihren Feind betrachten. Stellen Sie sich die Horden mürrischer Netzbewohner möglichst plastisch vor, wie sie hämisch auf Sie zeigen und Ihre Angebote und Produkte in den Dreck ziehen. Denken Sie daran: Internetuser sind alle in Kellern wohnende Nerds, die vom wahren Leben keine Ahnung haben. Man muss ihnen nicht mit Respekt begegnen. Gegenüber Ihren Kunden zeigen Sie doch auch gern, wer am längeren Hebel sitzt, nicht wahr? Eben. So ist das auch mit diesem Pack aus dem WWW. Eigentlich noch schlimmer. Steigern Sie sich ruhig rein.

2. Starten Sie trotzdem irgendetwas im Netz

Allein schon fürs Image ist es heutzutage ja nun einmal (leider, leider) notwendig, irgendetwas in diesem Internet auf die Beine zu stellen. Finden Sie heraus, was Ihre Konkurrenten noch nicht tun, und tun Sie genau das – egal, warum. Das nennt man dann einen „Vorsprung". Sie sind schneller als die anderen. Das ist gut. Kennt man ja vom Autofahren.

3. Dieses „Web 2.0" ist wichtig. Seien Sie dabei!

Wie Sie sicher überall lesen, ist dieses „Web 2.0" total wichtig. „Social Media" sagen manche. „Mitmachweb" haben Sie sicher auch schon gehört. Im Grunde kann hier jeder tun, was er will. Immer. Überall. Grauenhaft, oder? Andererseits sieht man, dass manches Unternehmen damit erfolgreich ist. Logisch, dass Sie auch dabei sein wollen. Und das geht super leicht: Einfach bei Twitter einen Account eröffnen und schon sind Sie mittendrin.

4. Berater engagieren, am besten einen „Guru"

Noch besser ist es, sich einen Experten einzukaufen. Dafür gibt es „Social-Media-Berater" oder noch besser: „Social-Media-Gurus". Je protziger die Bezeichnung, desto glaubwürdiger der Geschäftspartner – das kennen Sie ja schon aus Ihrem Alltag. Es gibt noch mehr Erkennungszeichen für einen guten Experten: So hat er eine möglichst bunte Seite bei Twitter, das Wort „Geld verdienen" taucht mehrmals auf und er hat mindestens ein E-Book veröffentlicht. Trifft das alles zu, können Sie blind einen Auftrag erteilen.

5. Menschen sind käuflich. Das gilt auch im Web.
Wie Sie wissen, kann man mit Geld alles erreichen. Warum sollte das im Web nicht auch gelten? Setzen Sie alles in Bewegung, um Aufmerksamkeit zu erlangen. Bezahlen Sie auch gern Leute dafür, dass sie über Sie berichten.

6. Seien Sie laut und aufdringlich
Gehen Sie in die Offensive. Preisen Sie Ihre Produkte möglichst auffällig und konsequent an. Wer am lautesten schreit, bekommt die meisten Kunden. Ist auf dem Hamburger Fischmarkt ja auch so. Schreiben Sie immer wieder Leute an. Wozu sonst gibt es Direct Messages bei Twitter oder das Mailsystem bei Facebook? Sie bekommen wenige Reaktionen? Dann heißt es: Aufwand verdoppeln – so lange, bis es klappt. Viel hilft viel.

7. Wichtig: Einfach laufen lassen
Der Vorteil des Web ist, dass Ihr Social-Media-Guru nur die richtigen Hebel bedienen muss, und der Rest läuft von alleine. Deshalb müssen Sie nichts kontrollieren und auch keine Zeit damit verschwenden, auf Anfragen oder andere Reaktionen einzugehen. In der Zeit können Sie schon wieder zwei neue Aktionen starten! Schließlich geht es hier um Umsatz, Geld, Cash, Kohle! Da sollte man sich nicht mit zwischenmenschlichem Gedöns aufhalten.

8. Wenn etwas schiefläuft: Klappe halten
Ist doch etwas schiefgelaufen? Jemand beschwert sich über Ihre angeblichen „Spam"-Nachrichten? Ihre eingekauften Meinungen sind aufgeflogen? Ihre Produkte oder Dienstleistungen sind vielleicht doch nicht so gut und irgendein Internet-Trottel posaunt es heraus? Sehr gut, das Desaster nimmt seinen Lauf. Einfach aussitzen. Nicht reagieren. So kann sich die Aufregung richtig hochschaukeln und alles Weitere läuft fast wie von selbst. Herrlich.

9. Im Zweifel angreifen
Der Pöbel im Netz krakeelt immer lauter? Sehr gut. Dann sollten Sie jetzt zum Angriff übergehen. Zeigen Sie per Kommentar unter flegelhaften Blogpostings, was Sie vom Autor des Beitrags halten und wie dämlich er sich anstellt. Seien Sie hier sehr klar und eindeutig, sonst verstehen die das nicht. Auch ein gutes Mittel, um die Stimmung weiter anzuheizen: Verschicken Sie Abmahnungen! Ihr Anwalt setzt Ihnen mit Sicherheit gern ein entsprechendes Schreiben auf. Tipp: Abmahnungen gleichlautend an möglichst viele schicken, das potenziert den Effekt enorm!

10. Alles abstreiten. Schuldigen finden.
Okay. Der Wagen ist im Dreck oder an die Wand gefahren? Dann ist jetzt die Zeit für das Finale: Alles abstreiten, als Missverständnis deklarieren und die Schuld möglichst schnell auf jemand anderen abschieben. Herzlichen Glückwunsch: Ihr Social-Media-Desaster ist perfekt."

Social Media im Spannungsfeld von Individuum und Unternehmen

Was wäre, wenn?
- Ein Mitarbeiter einer Restaurantkette postet auf Twitter, die neue Firmenuniform ist „Mist".
- Ein angestellter Lehrer an einer Privatschule hat Fotos auf der eigenen Facebook-Seite hochgeladen, auf denen er bei exzessivem Alkoholkonsum zu beobachten ist.
- Der Chefredakteur einer angesehenen Zeitung postet nach dem Ableben eines Sekten-Gurus seine persönliche Betroffenheit auf Twitter.
- Ein Mitarbeiter eines großen Nahrungsmittelherstellers preist in seinem Blog die gesundheitsfördernde Wirkung von unbehandelter Milch und empfiehlt, diese täglich frisch ab Bauernhof zu kaufen – anstelle von Supermarktware.
- Ein Arzt im Krankenhaus wird Mitglied einer Facebook-Gruppe, die sich für aktive Sterbehilfe einsetzt.
- [...]

All diese Fälle haben sich so oder so ähnlich zugetragen. Wie soll man als Unternehmen damit umgehen? Ist der betrunkene Lehrer nur „Privatsache". Was ist, wenn er bei Facebook mit Schülern „befreundet" ist? Taugt er dann noch als Vorbild? Erwartet man von seinem Chefredakteur nicht eine weltanschaulich neutrale Position, keinesfalls aber die Nähe zu einer Sekte? Ist das Verhalten des Mitarbeiters, der rohe Milch empfiehlt, als geschäftsschädigend zu sanktionieren oder einfach nur Privatsache? Muss ich beim „Facebook-Sterbehilfe-Fan" befürchten, dass er seine ärztlichen Pflichten vergisst, und Patienten vor ihm schützen? Fragen, auf die es keine eindeutige Antwort gibt, die aber vielfach durch eine geeignete Social Media Policy im Vorfeld hätten vermieden werden können.

Dass diese Überlegungen keine bloße Theorie sind, zeigen folgende reale Fälle und deren Folgen für die Betroffenen – Einzelpersonen wie Unternehmen.

Ketchum
Am Morgen vor seiner Präsentation bei FedEx, einem wichtigen Kunden des Unternehmens, postete der Vizepräsident von Ketchum, einer renommierten internationalen Werbeagentur, folgende Nachricht auf Twitter (Übersetzung durch den Autor):
„Ich bin in einer dieser Städte, wo ich mich am Kopf kratze und sage: Ich würde sterben, wenn ich hier leben müsste."
Werbeagentur-Ketchum-VP James Andrews beim Besuch in Memphis. Der Kunde FedEx war „not amused" über das Statement aus dem Management eines Lieferanten. Die Antwort von FedEx (Übersetzung durch den Autor):
„Wir wissen nicht genau, wie viele Millionen Dollar FedEx an Ketchum für Ihre wertvolle und wichtige Arbeit weltweit bezahlt. Wir sind jedoch zuversichtlich, dass es ausreicht,

um einen höheren Grad an Respekt von jemandem in Ihrer Position als Vizepräsident eines Global Players in Ihrer Branche erwarten zu können."

Virgin Atlantic
Nach einem Bericht von „The Independent" vom 01.11.2008 hat Virgin Atlantic (hierzulande bekannt als die Fluggesellschaft des Unternehmers Richard Branson) 13 Crewmitglieder entlassen. Grund waren Facebook-Einträge, bei denen Passagiere beleidigt wurden (unter anderem mit dem Slangausdruck „Chav", für den der Autor keinen deutschen Begriff kennt – und dict.leo.org auch nicht –, der aber vermutlich so etwas wie „Proll" im Deutschen bedeutet → Hinweise zur Aufklärung bitte an den Autor per E-Mail, Twitter, Xing etc).
Neben den despektierlichen Worten für die Passagiere hatten Crewmitglieder im gleichen Zusammenhang auch von Kakerlaken an Bord berichtet.

Facebook bei Krankheit = Kündigung
Wie verschiedene Schweizer Medien und u. a. der Südkurier berichten (http://www.suedkurier. de/region/hochrhein/kanton-basel/Job-verloren-nach-Facebook-Besuch;art372605,3740067), hat die Angestellte einer Firma in Basel durch die Nutzung von Facebook während ihrer Zeit im Krankenstand den Job verloren.
Der Hintergrund: Die 31-Jährige hatte sich wegen Migräne krankgemeldet und angegeben, sie müsse im Dunkeln liegen und könne nicht am Bildschirm arbeiten. Der Arbeitgeber konnte aber feststellen, dass sie zeitgleich auf ihrem Facebook-Profil aktiv war.
Ungeachtet der unterschiedlichen arbeitsrechtlichen Wertung derartiger Vorgänge in der Schweiz ist natürlich auch in Deutschland oder Österreich Ähnliches denkbar.

Israelisches Militär
Wie unter anderem die BBC am 04.03.2010 berichtete, musste ein geplanter Einsatz abgesagt werden. Der Grund war: Ein Soldat hatte auf Facebook im Rahmen seines Status-Updates folgende Andeutungen gemacht: „On wednesay we clean up Quatanah, and on Thursday, God willing, we come home", die konkret auf einen bevorstehenden Einsatz hingewiesen haben.
Neben zehn Tagen Arrest wurde er strafversetzt.

Nonne muss Kloster wegen Facebook verlassen
Neben Unternehmen, Behörden und Militär erwachsen auch im kirchlichen Umfeld Risiken aus der Nutzung von Social Media (http://www.telegraph.co.uk/technology/facebook/8333810/ Spanish-nun-expelled-from-order-over-Facebook-usage.html). Dem Bericht und anderen Medienmeldungen zufolge musste eine Klosterschwester nach über 35 Jahren Klosterzugehörigkeit in Spanien ihr Kloster verlassen. Grund hierfür waren nicht etwa einzelne Äußerungen, sondern allgemein die zu intensive Nutzung von Facebook.
Nachtrag: Mittlerweile hat die ehemalige Nonne eine eigene Facebook-Seite mit mehr als 600 Facebook-Freunden, und ihre offizielle Fan-Seite „gefällt" adressiert mehr als 9.000 Personen (http://www.facebook.com/sorinternet).

BND-Mitarbeiter auf Stellensuche

Wie unter anderem BILD (http://www.bild.de/politik/2010/verlust/ex-bnd-mitarbeitern-droht-haft-und-pensions-verlust-13542640.bild.html) berichtet, waren gleich mehrere Ex-BND-Mitarbeiter mit detaillierten Angaben zu ihrer vorherigen Tätigkeit auf Xing tätig. Da es diesem Personenkreis aber verboten ist, auch nach Beschäftigungsende Angaben zu ihrer Tätigkeit zu machen, die über die Nennung des Arbeitgebers hinausgehen, droht den Stellensuchenden nun ein Strafverfahren – unter Umständen sogar wegen Landesverrats.

Robin Sage

Auch und gerade eine eher passive Nutzung von Social Media kann zu erheblichen Problemen führen, wie das Beispiel „Robin Sage" zeigt.

Inzwischen mit eigenem Wikipedia-Eintrag, die fiktive Person „Robin Sage"

Ein attraktives Bild auf Facebook. Absolventin des renommierten Massachusetts Institute of Technology. Breitet gerne ihr Innerstes bei Twitter aus. Wer möchte nicht mit Robin Sage befreundet sein?

Zahlreiche – vor allem männliche – Internetnutzer reagierten begeistert und überschütteten die attraktive Dame mit Freundschaftsanfragen. Leider vergeblich. Robin Sage ist nicht real. Sie ist nur ein Hirngespinst. Eine Erfindung eines IT-Security-Beraters, dem insbesondere zahlreiche Personen im Umfeld des US-Verteidigungsministeriums auf den Leim gingen.

Erstellt und gepflegt mit einigen markanten Merkmalen, die einen sofort hätten hellhörig werden lassen müssen. So weist allein der Nachname „Sage" auf einen internen Ausdruck für „Spezialkräfte" hin. Die verwendete E-Mail-Adresse nutzte zudem die Domain einer US-Söldnerfirma. Dennoch ließen sich die überwiegend männlichen Kontaktsuchenden davon scheinbar nicht im Geringsten beirren, bis der Schwindel – in diesem Fall durch den Initiator selbst – enttarnt wurde. Vorher gelang es noch, über die gebastelte Identität Kontakt zu rund 300 Mitarbeitern von US-Geheimdiensten, Verteidigungsministerium und Rüstungskonzernen zu bekommen, und in mindestens einem Fall gelang es auch, das Gegenüber zur Weitergabe geheimer Militäreinsatzpläne zu „überreden".

Wie viele Robin Sage es gibt, ist schwer zu sagen. Der Autor geht jedenfalls davon aus, dass dieser Fall alles andere als ein Einzelfall ist. Im Gegenteil: Gerade wenn es darum geht, Unternehmensinformationen auszuspionieren, dürften – wie in diesem Fall – vollständig gefälschte Profile oder entsprechend auf die Interessen der zu adressierenden Zielgruppe hin manipulierte Einträge an der Tagesordnung sein.

Aus Sicht eines Sicherheitsbeauftragten wäre das ein fortgeschrittener Fall von Social Engineering. Die wesentliche Herausforderung für Unternehmen ist hier, die Mitarbeiter entsprechend zu sensibilisieren und auf derartige mögliche Sicherheitsrisiken hinzuweisen und ... nein, das betrifft nicht nur die männlichen Mitarbeiter.

Fazit aus Unternehmenssicht

Übereifrige Mitarbeiter aus Marketing- und Werbeagenturen können durch unbedachte Aktionen ebenso wie „Durchschnittsangestellte" mit unüberlegten Äußerungen die Reputation des eigenen Unternehmens oder der eigenen Organisation ankratzen und damit erheblichen wirtschaftlichen Schaden anrichten. Im Extremfall kann dies zu existenzgefährdenden Krisen führen. Um diese Risiken zu begrenzen, aber die im nächsten Kapitel dargestellten Chancen nicht zu verpassen, sind klare Regeln für den Umgang mit Social Media notwendig.

Erfolgsfaktor Social Media: Wie Unternehmen heute schon erfolgreich Social Media nutzen

Es geht nicht (mehr) ohne Social Media

Gefühlt geht es nicht mehr ohne Social Media – über die addiktive Wirkung von Facebook und Co. wurde bereits gesprochen. Fokussiert man nun rein auf das Business, so steht natürlich „Freunde treffen" nicht im Fokus des Netzwerkens. Daher ist eine globale Studie des Office-Center-Betreibers Regus aus dem Juli 2010 besonders interessant, da hierfür rund 15.000 Business-Anwender befragt wurden.

Demnach nutzen (Mehrfachantworten waren möglich)
- 58 % der Befragten Social Media, um „in Kontakt zu bleiben"
- 54 %, um sich mit speziellen Interessengruppen zu vernetzen,
- 51 %, um mit Kunden oder Kundengruppen zu kommunizieren, und
- 22 %, um einen Job zu finden.

Geht man weg vom einzelnen Mitarbeiter und fragt man nach den Unternehmen, so kommen die Ersteller der Studie zu dem Schluss, dass das Social Web bereits vielfach erfolgreich eingesetzt wird. Während mehr als die Hälfte der Unternehmen aus der Befragung Social Media bereits in irgendeiner Form einsetzen, erklärten stolze 40 Prozent der weltweit befragten Firmen, über Social Networks schon erfolgreich Kunden gewonnen zu haben. Kleine Unternehmen sind dabei nach Datenlage erfolgreicher: Von ihnen akquiriert auf Social-Media-Portalen weltweit mittlerweile fast die Hälfte (44 %) erfolgreich Kunden. Bei den mittelgroßen Firmen ist das nur bei etwas mehr als einem Drittel (36 %) aktuell der Fall. Von den großen Unternehmen gab dies sogar nur ein gutes Viertel der Befragten (28 %) an. Erhebliche Unterschiede gibt es bei den Branchen. IT und Telekommunikation liegen erwartungsgemäß klar in Führung, Marketing, Medien und Beratungsbranche folgen. Finanzwirtschaft, Industrie und Gesundheitswesen sind demgegenüber eher unterentwickelt.

Ein guter Indikator für die Bedeutung von Social Media im Unternehmen sind auch dedizierte Budgets. Hier ist die Quote geringer – über alle Branchen hinweg haben 27 % der befragten Unternehmen ein Budget für Social Media. Bei Medien und Marketing lautet die Vergleichszahl 38 % und in der Finanzbranche 19 %.

Allen Erfolgen zum Trotz: Rund ein Drittel der Unternehmen hält Social Media für grundlegend nicht geeignet für die Kundengewinnung – so das Fazit von Regus.

Auch andere Studien berichten von insgesamt positiven Effekten: McKinsey dokumentiert in einer Studie aus 2009, dass Web 2.0 von erstaunlichen rund 66 % der befragten internationalen Unternehmen als wesentlich angesehen wird, um die Marktposition des Unternehmens zu halten oder auszubauen.

Social Media im Unternehmen

Fast immer geht die Initiative zu Social Media vom Marketing aus, aber es lassen sich auch zahlreiche weitere Ansatzpunkte finden, die – je nach Ausgangslage und Firmenstruktur – eine erhebliche Bedeutung für den Unternehmenserfolg erlangen können.

Marketing

Betrachtet man den Status quo eines Unternehmens heute, so stellt man fest, dass die meisten Aktivitäten sich bisher dort abspielen. Teils geschieht dies aus mehr oder weniger privaten Initiativen heraus. Ähnlich wie es zu Beginn des Online-Zeitalters in so manchem Unternehmen eine „nicht-autorisierte" Firmen-Homepage gab, entstehen nun vielerorts Facebook-Pages, Twitter-Kanäle und andere Social-Web-Aktivitäten, die von Mitarbeitern mal eben in ihrer Freizeit eingerichtet oder – bei starken oder emotionalen Marken nicht selten – von begeisterten Kunden und „Fans" der Marke am Unternehmen vorbei in Eigenregie errichtet wurden.

Spätestens dann, wenn Verwechslungsgefahr einer Fanpage mit einer möglicherweise noch gar nicht installierten offiziellen Aktivität besteht, sollten Unternehmen eingreifen.

Nicht selten sind es aber auch die Marketingverantwortlichen selbst, die – getrieben von Agenturkonzepten und Branchen-News – beschließen, man müsse „dabei sein" im Social-Media-Hype.

Nüchtern betrachtet unterliegt Social Media im Marketing dabei einem regelrechten Hype-Cycle. Während zu Beginn die Unternehmens-Blogs das zentrale Element der Debatte waren und Twitter vor ein bis zwei Jahren seinen „Marketinghöhepunkt" erlebte, scheint heute die „Facebook-Unternehmensseite" die Debatte zu bestimmen – so sehr, dass einige Unternehmen bereits auf die klassische Homepage verzichten und sämtliche Online-Aktivitäten auf das (derzeit) dominierende Netzwerk konzentrieren.

Derartige Fokussierungen mögen im Einzelfall richtig sein, eine generelle Empfehlung lässt sich daraus aber nicht ableiten.

Grundlegend muss jedes Unternehmen – ausgehend von Erfahrungen mit vergleichbaren Unternehmensstrukturen und Branchenverhältnissen – überlegen, welche Maßnahme oder besser welcher Maßnahmen-Mix am besten zum eigenen Profil und zu den eigenen Marketingzielen passt. Eine gute Möglichkeit, sich dem zu nähern, ist der Social-Media-Workshop, von dem in einem separaten Abschnitt die Rede sein wird.

Über Marketingziele sind unzählige Publikationen verfasst worden; welche – jenseits der praktisch immer dominierenden finanziellen – Performance (Umsatz-, Erlössteigerung) im Vordergrund stehen sollte, lässt sich zumindest bei den zu definierenden Teilzielen eingrenzen.

Derartige Teilziele können sein

– die Steigerung der Markenbekanntheit,
– die Steigerung der Bekanntheit des Unternehmens,
– die Steigerung der Abrufzahlen des Online-Auftritts,
– die Steigerung der Verkaufszahlen des eigenen Webshops,

- die Verbesserung des Unternehmens- oder Marken-Images,
- die Verbesserung der Suchmaschinenergebnisse (eigene Auffindbarkeit),
- die Gewinnung von Neukunden,
- die Verminderung der Churn-Rate (besseres „Halten" von Bestandskunden),
- [...]

Was oft vergessen wird: Wesentlich ist dabei die Messbarkeit der Zielerreichung – entweder direkt oder über definierte Parameter, im Branchenjargon auch KPI – Key Performance Indicator – genannt. Bei aller Begeisterung für Social Media im Marketing heute: In jedem Unternehmen kommen derartige Aktivitäten früher oder später auf den Prüfstand, und spätestens dann ist Erfolgsmessung ein wesentliches Thema.

Marktforschung

Marktforschung ist aufwendig, teuer und ungenau – so ein gängiges Vorurteil, mit dem Verantwortliche aus Unternehmen und Marktforschungsdienstleistungsfirmen häufig zu kämpfen haben. Social Media kann dabei helfen, zumindest den online aktiven Teil der eigenen Zielgruppe sehr genau kennenzulernen, was seine Wünsche und Vorstellungen betrifft.

Das geht nicht allein mit herkömmlichen Online-Umfragen, sondern mit dem Einsatz geeigneter Werkzeuge für Social-Media-Monitoring, mit denen sich Erhebungen zu Kundenmeinungen sammeln und auswerten lassen.

Obwohl sich die Anfänge der Entwicklung gut zehn Jahre zurückverfolgen lassen, stehen die Tools dafür technologisch noch relativ am Anfang ihrer Entwicklung. Das Gewinnen eines Meinungsbildes in der Community ist damit – was das Datensammeln angeht – leicht und überschaubar, was die Auswertung angeht, aber durchaus mit Fehlern behaftet, da insbesondere das Verstehen von ironischen oder sarkastischen Äußerungen – wie diese häufig in Kundenforen anzutreffen sind – zumeist noch nicht zuverlässig gelingt beziehungsweise zu Fehldeutungen führt. Die Konsequenz: Ohne Mensch geht es – zumindest bisher – nicht im Social-Media-Monitoring.

Public Relations

Auch die Öffentlichkeitsarbeit (Public Relations – PR) kann von Social Media profitieren – in ihren ureigensten Aufgaben:

- Aufbau und Pflege von Beziehungen zu „Meinungsführern",
- Bereitstellung von relevanten Inhalten mit Mehrwert,
- Verbreitung der eigenen Botschaften und
- Beobachtung der Medienlandschaft.

Während die „Beobachtung" wieder auf das Thema „Social-Media-Monitoring" verweist, unterliegen sowohl Verbreitungswege für Inhalte und Stories als auch die „Meinungsführerschaft" signifikanten Verschiebungen durch Social Media.

Die klassischen Medien (Radio/TV/Print) stecken mitten in einem tief greifenden Wandel. Die viel zitierte „Deutungshoheit" journalistischer Medien steht unter Druck, da sich Nutzer im Internetzeitalter zunehmend direkt – also quellennah – informieren und untereinander über aktuelle Themen austauschen.

Die vielfach geschmähten „Blogger" – ein bekannter Hamburger Werbeagenturchef sprach noch vor wenigen Jahren öffentlich von den „Klowänden des Internets" und meinte damit Blogs – haben in manchen journalistischen Segmenten bereits hohe Relevanz – etwa im Bereich der Mode, da Blogs die oft sehr kurzlebigen neuen Trends erheblich schneller aufgreifen und verbreiten können als die typischerweise im Monatszyklus erscheinenden großen Magazine. Ähnliche Entwicklungen lassen sich etwa auch im Bereich der Autozeitschriften beobachten. Bei der Berichterstattung zu den „Erlkönigen" etwa – jenen neuen, noch geheimen Automodellen, die weithin Interesse bei den Lesern generieren – hat sich die Verbreitungskette weithin geändert. Während früher Profifotografen in auskömmlicher Symbiose mit den großen Zeitungen und Automagazinen die Schlagzeilen machten, sind es heute immer häufiger Zufallsfunde von Privatleuten, die sich – mit Fotohandy und Videokamera aufgezeichnet – zuerst über einschlägige Weblogs, Autoforen und Videoplattformen verbreiten – unter Umständen Wochen, bevor die Mainstream-Autopresse davon berichtet.

Was man hieran bereits deutlich merkt, ist das Entstehen einer Wechselwirkung zwischen Social Media und herkömmlichen Medien, die sich immer häufiger im Internet bedienen, um ihre Formate zu füllen.

Die Unternehmens-PR muss sich auf dieses neue Verhältnis einstellen und tut daher gut daran, die Möglichkeiten und Chancen aktiv zu adressieren, um etwa Twitter, Blogs und Soziale Netzwerke zu nutzen, um Botschaften direkt zu verbreiten und auf eine weitere virale Verbreitung zu hoffen. Diese neue, direkte (statt bisher indirekte) Ansprache erfordert ein Umdenken – sowohl bei der Aufbereitung als auch beim Einsatz der Inhalte. Viele Unternehmen scheitern bereits daran (siehe das „Vodafone"-Beispiel oben).

Nicht vergessen werden sollte zudem, dass man einen „Dialog" anfängt, von dem das Gegenüber erwartet, dass seine Äußerungen und Fragen ernst genommen und beantwortet werden. Um diesem Anspruch gerecht zu werden, werden Ressourcen benötigt, die in der klassischen PR üblicherweise nicht vorhanden sind und eine entsprechend langfristige Planung und Budgetierung brauchen.

Organisatorisch stellt sich die Frage, wie und in welcher Form in einem derartigen auf Social Media fokussierten Szenario noch eine Abgrenzung zum Marketing erfolgen kann oder soll. Wer sollte etwa für den Unternehmens-Blog verantwortlich zeichnen? Die Einrichtung einer gesonderten Verantwortlichkeit für Social Media, die die Bereiche koordiniert, kann eine Lösung sein.

Vertrieb

Ebenfalls nahe am Marketing sind Social-Media-Aktivitäten, die den Vertrieb unterstützen sollen. Während YouTube-Videos, Weblogs und Facebook-Unternehmensseiten bereits weitverbreitet, aber zumeist zum Marketing (oder zur Unternehmens-PR) zu rechnen sind, stehen Social-Media-Vertriebsmaßnahmen noch am Anfang.

Zumeist fokussieren sich die Aktivitäten auf Sonderangebote oder Sonderaktionen für Community-Mitglieder (siehe auch das Onkyo-Beispiel oben) oder auf Coupon-Aktionen. Mit Blick auf die hohe Glaubwürdigkeit persönlicher Empfehlungen ist aber auch die Incentivierung von erfolgreichen Kaufempfehlungen im eigenen Freundeskreis möglich und wird vereinzelt angewandt. In der Autobranche und anderen Bereichen, in denen die Kaufentscheidungen komplex sind, könnte man etwa auch die Produktkonfiguratoren für die Community-Kontakte des Kaufinteressenten öffnen und einen persönlichen Dialog zulassen. Ohne hierzu bereits Marktforschung betrieben zu haben, geht der Autor davon aus, dass bei statusorientierten Käufern die Zahl der verkauften Sonderausstattungen tendenziell steigen wird, wenn der Orderprozess unter den Augen der eigenen Community geschieht.

Denkt man über den unmittelbaren Abverkauf hinaus, so kommt man schnell auf potenzielle neue Erlösmodelle, die mit Social Media erschlossen werden können. Man denke insbesondere an virtuelle Güter oder an zusätzliche Funktionen für existierende Produkte. Derartige neue Konzepte reichen jedoch erheblich weiter als der Vertrieb im Unternehmen selbst; sie sind bereits bei Produktdesign und -entwicklung zu berücksichtigen. Und sie haben massive Rückwirkungen auf das Geschäftsmodell selbst – etwa wenn eine Grundleistung kostenlos oder kostengünstig angeboten wird, während die eigentlichen Erlöse mit bestimmten kostenpflichtigen Funktionen und Leistungen verbunden werden.

Kundenservice und -support

Der beste Kundenservice ist kein Kundenservice – schlicht weil man keinen benötigt. Das sollte das hohe Ziel eines jeden Anbieters sein. In der Praxis hat bereits die erste Internetwelle dazu geführt, dass immer mehr Serviceaufgaben automatisiert wurden beziehungsweise im Kunden-Selbstservice wahrgenommen werden. Dennoch gibt es viele Segmente, in denen Kundenservice im Wesentlichen in Form von den bei Endverbrauchern so unbeliebten Callcentern stattfindet.

Social Media bietet hier zahlreiche Ansätze, nicht nur die Servicekosten zu senken, sondern auch die Kundenzufriedenheit zu erhöhen – einfache Möglichkeiten, die aber bereits einen nicht unerheblichen Teil der Service-Calls ersetzen können und von der Bereitstellung von Anleitungen zum Download oder Video-Tutorien bis hin zur Institutionalisierung von Kundenforen reichen, bei denen Support-Mitarbeiter im Namen des Unternehmens Fragen beantworten oder Kunden – aus Kostensicht wäre das der Idealfall – sich gegenseitig helfen.

Eine Sichtbarkeit der Interaktion bedient dabei unter Umständen viele gleichartige Fälle ohne zusätzlichen Aufwand und erhöht die wahrgenommene Support-Qualität.

Produktentwicklung

Die Produktentwicklung im Unternehmen kann auf vielfache Weise von Social Media profitieren. Zum einen erhält man ungefiltertes Feedback vom Anwender, wenn man systematisch Äußerungen auf den relevanten Plattformen nachverfolgt. Zum anderen kann man jenseits des Monitorings auch selbst aktiv werden und über das Social Web Produkttester und geeignete Kandidaten für Produkt-Workshops finden und vielfach auch steuern – bis hin zur Online-Erfassung der Ergebnisse durch die Teilnehmer selbst.

Damit sind die Vorteile und Chancen des Social Web für die Produktentwicklung aber noch nicht annähernd ausreichend umrissen. Die wesentlichen Vorteile liegen in der Gewinnung von neuen Ideen durch bestehende und potenzielle Kunden. „Open Innovation" –

die Nutzung von Ideen aus dem Web – hat sich für viele Unternehmen als Erfolgsmodell erwiesen. Diese Ideen können sowohl das Produkt selbst als auch das „Drumherum" wie Einkaufserlebnis oder Bestellabläufe betreffen.

Open Innovation ist ein verlässliches Mittel gegen „Betriebsblindheit", benötigt aber diverse Filtermechanismen, wenn durch starke Partizipation besonders viele Ideen auf das Unternehmen einprasseln. Man sollte auch davon ausgehen, dass bei manchen Produkten ein Großteil der eingereichten Ideen eine negative Konnotation hat.

Typischerweise nutzen Unternehmen eigens entwickelte Plattformen, um in Sachen Produkt in Austausch mit den Kunden zu treten. Die Kaffeehauskette Starbucks etwa, die durch zu starke Expansion in eine Schieflage geriet, suchte ihr Heil in der Neuorientierung auch durch die Einführung einer derartigen Webanwendung unter dem Titel „My Starbucks Idea".

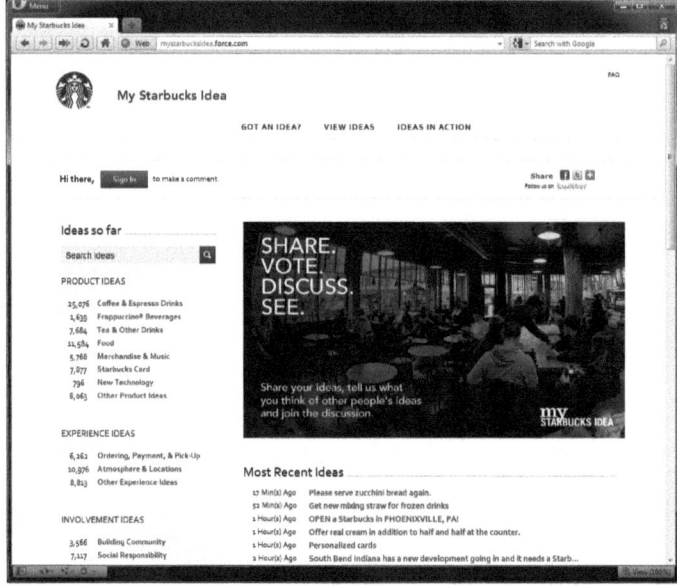

My Starbucks Idea
Crowdsourcing Website

Richtigerweise geht man dort – wie auf anderen Plattformen – davon aus, dass nicht jeder Kunde auch eigene Ideen einbringt, sondern sieht Mechanismen vor, die eine Bewertung eben dieser erlauben, sodass das Unternehmen Rückschlüsse ziehen kann, inwieweit die eingebrachten Ideen Potenzial für eine weitere Verbreitung haben.

Ein weitgehend unentdecktes Anwendungsfeld derartiger Innovationsplattformen sind große Unternehmen innerhalb der eigenen Organisation. Was auf dem Weg zum Endverbraucher funktioniert, kann auch innerhalb der Organisation Nutzen stiften, um etwa Ideen aus anderen Abteilungen „einzufangen". In herkömmlichen Unternehmensstrukturen gehen diese oft unter. „Wenn wir wüssten, was unsere Mitarbeiter wissen" ist demzufolge auch eine häufig gehörte Klage in großen Organisationen.

Produktion

Der flüchtige Leser wird hier vielleicht irritiert sein: Social Media in der Produktion? Erinnerungen werden geweckt, an so unbeliebte Themen wie Heimarbeit. In der Tat ist Social Media in der Produktion so etwas wie „Heimarbeit 2.0". Der international dafür gebräuchliche Ausdruck wurde oben bereits eingeführt: „Crowdsourcing".

Crowdsourcing ist ein von Autoren des Wired-Magazins (http://www.wired.com) in Anlehnung an den Begriff Outsourcing geprägter Ausdruck für die Nutzung von Arbeitskraft, Wissen und Intelligenz von Internetnutzern gegen geringe oder ganz ohne Bezahlung. Als erste größere Implementierung dieser Idee gilt der „Amazon Mechanical Turk", ein innovatives Webprojekt, bei dem menschliche Arbeit über das Internet bereitgestellt wird – fokussiert auf Tätigkeiten, die nicht direkt oder nur unvollständig von Computern geleistet werden können, wie etwa Bildbewertungen.

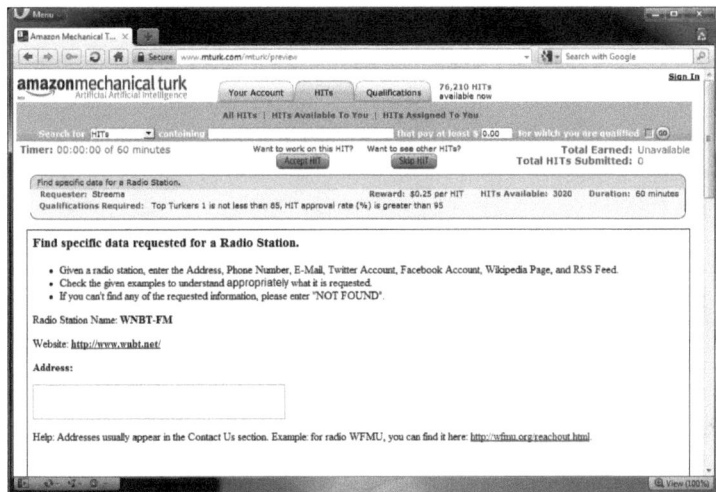

Beispiel für eine Aufgabe bei Amazon Mechanical Turk

Mechanical Turk war ursprünglich die Bezeichnung für einen vermeintlichen Schachautomaten aus dem 18. Jahrhundert. Die Sensation der damaligen Zeit stellte sich als Fälschung heraus – tatsächlich saß ein kleinwüchsiger Mann in dem Gerät und steuerte das Schachspiel über eine ausgeklügelte Mechanik.

Allen derartigen Diensten gemein ist die Grundidee der automatisierten Zerlegung großer Aufgaben in kleine und kleinste Schritte, die an eine Vielzahl von Einzelpersonen über das Netz verteilt werden. Die Zugangshürden sind niedrig – ein Rechner mit Internetzugang und Webbrowser genügt. Jeder Einzelne wird nur nach der Zahl der durchgeführten Arbeitsschritte bezahlt. Die Preisfindung für diese kleinsten Arbeitseinheiten erfolgt in einer Art Auktion.

Während Amazon der Vorreiter war, sind inzwischen zahlreiche andere Anbieter mit ähnlichen Konzepten am Markt. Besonders bemerkenswert ist darunter „Gigwalk" (www.gigwalk.com), bei dem der Anwender mithilfe einer Smartphone-Applikation besondere Aufgaben bekommt, wie etwa die Dokumentation der Beschilderung einer Straßenkreuzung. Auftraggeber sind hier Anbieter von Straßenkarten, Navigationssystemen, Branchenbüchern etc., für die die kleinteilige Erfassung bei Durchführung mit eigenen Kräften ein erheblicher Kostenfaktor wäre, aber die Erfassung durch Personen, die ohnehin in der Gegend sind und sich in einer ruhigen Minute etwas dazuverdienen wollen oder ihre Langeweile bekämpfen möchten, extrem kostengünstig ist.

Dass Crowdsourcing ganze Geschäftsmodelle trägt, sieht man unter anderem an dem Blog-Anbieter „Huffington Post", der für einen dreistelligen Millionenbetrag an AOL verkauft wurde. Das Geschäftsmodell hier: aggregierte Blog-Beiträge von freiwilligen – und zum großen Teil wohl unbezahlten – Kräften.

Personal-Recruiting und -Entwicklung

Die Besetzung frei werdender Stellen und die Rekrutierung geeigneter Nachwuchskräfte ist insbesondere in Zeiten wirtschaftlicher Prosperität problematisch. Dies betrifft insbesondere Unternehmen, die eine nur geringe Bekanntheit haben und beispielsweise nicht auf den von diversen Zeitschriften vorgelegten „Listen der Top-Arbeitgeber" auftauchen. Je nach zu besetzender Stelle suchen Unternehmen daher mit Stellenanzeigen, auf Hochschulkontaktmessen oder mit Headhuntern nach geeigneten Bewerbern.

Social Media kann hier den Zugriff auf die besten beziehungsweise bestgeeigneten Kandidaten verbessern und insbesondere die Kosten der Stellenbesetzung verringern, etwa indem man frühzeitig geeignete Kandidaten identifiziert und an das Unternehmen bindet. Auch für innerbetriebliche Auswahlprozesse eignen sich Social Media, etwa durch Foren im Intranet.

Der Recruiting-Prozess selbst profitiert in der Praxis schon länger von Social Media, da der Großteil der Personaler Kandidaten zumindest stichprobenartig hinsichtlich deren Präsenz auf den gängigsten Plattformen scannt. Inwieweit dies zulässig ist, ist allerdings unter Juristen umstritten. Zumindest öffentlich zugängliche Profile auf Business-orientierten Plattformen wie Xing oder LinkedIn dürften aber diesbezüglich unkritisch zu sein.

Interne Kommunikation

Ebenfalls von Social Media profitieren kann die interne Kommunikation im Unternehmen. Dabei gilt die Regel: Je größer, desto wirksamer. Dabei können sowohl Mitarbeiter – über Abteilungsgrenzen hinweg – Wissen und Ideen austauschen als auch die Geschäftsleitung einen tiefer gehenden Dialog mit einzelnen Mitarbeitern führen.

Interessant ist auch die Möglichkeit, Social-Media-Funktionalitäten im Kontext mit Unternehmenstelefonie zu nutzen. Man spricht dann auch von „Unified Communications".

Beispiele für erfolgreichen Social-Media-Einsatz im Unternehmen

Die nachfolgend aufgeführten Beispiele liefern einen ersten Eindruck über die vielfältigen Einsatzmöglichkeiten und -chancen von Social Media in der Praxis.

Audi

Wie andere Autohersteller nutzt auch Audi Social Media im Wesentlichen als Marketing-werkzeug und schafft es damit, Millionen Menschen dazu zu bringen, „Fans" zu werden.

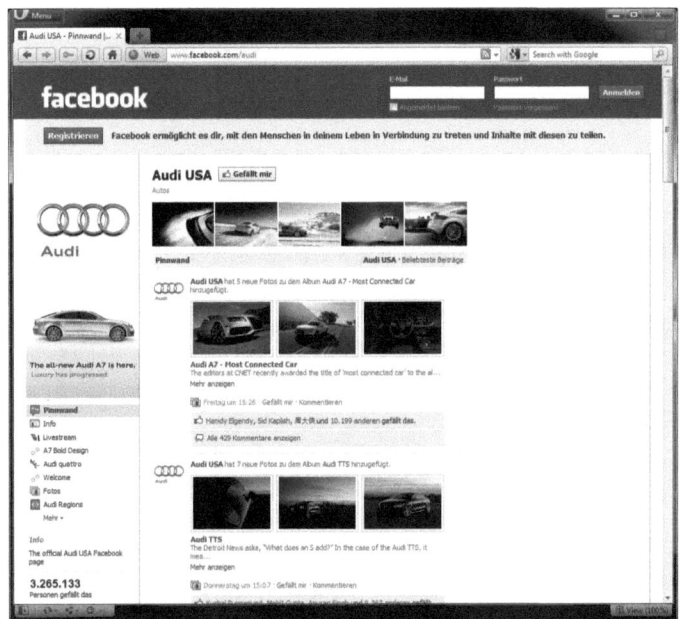

Audi-Facebook-Seite

Verschiedene Medien (http://mashable.com/2011/04/22/audis-facebook-bieber) berichten davon, dass Audi nicht nur besonders viele, sondern auch die engagiertesten Facebook-Fans hat – noch vor dem Teenie-Schwarm Nummer eins Justin Bieber oder Popsängerin Lady Gaga. Dieses Engagement zeigt sich daran, dass Audi nicht nur eine Vielzahl von Fans hat, sondern diese überdurchschnittlich oft bei Status-Updates von Audi den Facebook-„Like"-Button betätigen, also aktiv und affirmativ sind. Dies ist besonders deshalb erstaunlich, weil sich in einer großen Facebook-Studie der Online-Agentur Visibli (http://visibli.com/reports/fbstudy), bei der die Aktivitäten von über 200 Millionen Facebook-Fans ausgewertet wurden, klar ergeben hat, dass Unterhaltungskünstler wie Musiker oder Filmstars im Schnitt erheblich mehr zustimmende Aktivitäten („Like"-Button- Betätigungen, „positive Kommentare") bekommen.

Nach Visibli (http://visibli.com/reports/fbstudy) generiert eine Marke mit einem durchschnittlichen Facebook-Post 54 „Likes" und 9 „Kommentare" (je 100.000 Fans), während ein Unterhaltungskünstler im Schnitt 92 „Likes" und „17" Kommentare (ebenfalls je 100.000 Fans) generiert. Im Falle von Audi und Justin Bieber sind die Vergleichszahlen bei den „Likes" 228 beziehungsweise 181 (Lady Gaga 136).

Während dies ein bisschen wie Zahlenreiterei aussieht, zeigt das Studienergebnis einen wesentlichen Zusammenhang auf: Inhalt zählt, es kommt nicht nur auf die Anzahl der auf Facebook generierten „Gefolgschaft" an. So kann dann auch ein Anbieter wie Audi an die Spitze rücken.

BGLT – Berchtesgadener Land Tourismus

Ein Musterbeispiel für Tourismusmarketing ist die BGLT. Man setzt stark auf Social Media und kann damit bereits deutliche Erfolge erzielen – mit 90.000 Visits pro Monat ist die Website die meistbesuchte „Destinationswebsite". Diese versteht sich als Regionsportal und enthält unter anderem einen Regions-Blog mit zehn externen Autoren. Ausgehend davon werden Plattformen wie Facebook (7830 „Fans", Stand 5/2011), Twitter, Holidaycheck und YouTube angebunden.

BGLT Blog

Seit Herbst 2010 regelt man den Umgang der Mitarbeiter mit Sozialen Medien über eine eigene Richtlinie (siehe Kapitel „Beispielhafte Social Media Guidelines"), die u. a. einen eindeutigen Freiraum auch für die private Nutzung von Facebook vorsieht.

Ferchau Engineering

Der deutsche Ingenieurdienstleister Ferchau Engineering setzt vor allem im Bereich Recruiting auf Social Media. Dabei zeigt Ferchau nicht nur Präsenz auf den gängigen Plattformen (Facebook, Twitter, YouTube und Xing) sondern entwickelt u. a. einen Ideenwettbewerb im Web 2.0

So werden im Rahmen der Ferchau Challenge 2011 Studenten gesucht, die Ideen im Bereich „IT im Alltag" in Form von „Apps" entwickeln und umsetzen.

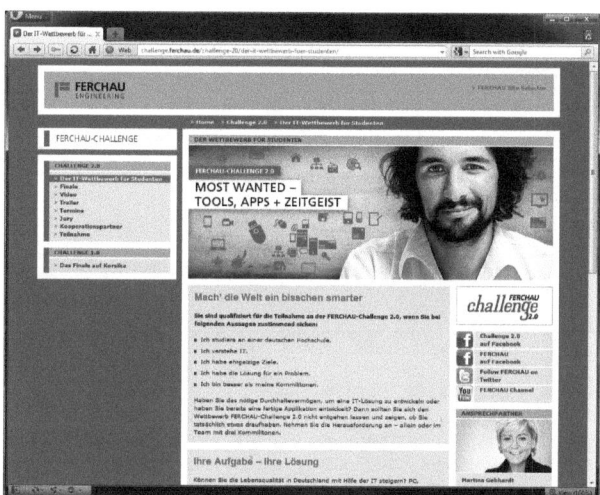

Ferchau-Challenge-Studentenwettbewerb

Telekom

Telekommunikation und IT für private Endanwender ist ein serviceaufwendiges Business, da teilweise komplexe Produkte auf unterschiedlich vorgebildete Anwender – „von ahnungslos bis Freak" – treffen. Jenseits der klassischen Telefon-Hotlines, die beim Anbieter häufig nur begrenzte Akzeptanz finden, kann Social Media dabei helfen, den Kunden-Support zu optimieren:

Seit Frühjahr 2010 ist „Telekom_hilft" auf Twitter als zusätzlicher Kanal für den Kundenservice etabliert worden. Die im Rahmen der Twitter-Initiative eingesetzten Service-Agents haben dabei die Aufgaben,
– Twitter nach potenziellen Servicefällen zu monitoren und Kontakt mit Kunden per Twitter zur Bearbeitung der Fälle aufzunehmen,
– eingehende Anfragen an @Telekom_hilft anzunehmen und
– diese zu bearbeiten.

Zusätzlich wurde nach Unternehmensangaben September 2010 das Pilotprojekt „Telekom_hilft" auf Facebook gestartet. Das Grundprinzip des Twitter-Kundenservices wird hier mit den erweiterten Mitteln der Plattform Facebook weitergeführt und -entwickelt. Zusätzlich gibt es seit Oktober 2010 den Blog „Service-Notizen". Häufig nachgefragte oder aktuell relevante Vertriebs- und Serviceinformationen werden auf www.telekom-hilft. de publiziert.

Das Echo in den Fachmedien wie insbesondere in der Zielgruppe ist außerordentlich positiv und kann – jenseits der direkt Betroffenen und der für diese gelösten Servicefälle – auch positiv auf das Unternehmensimage abstrahlen.

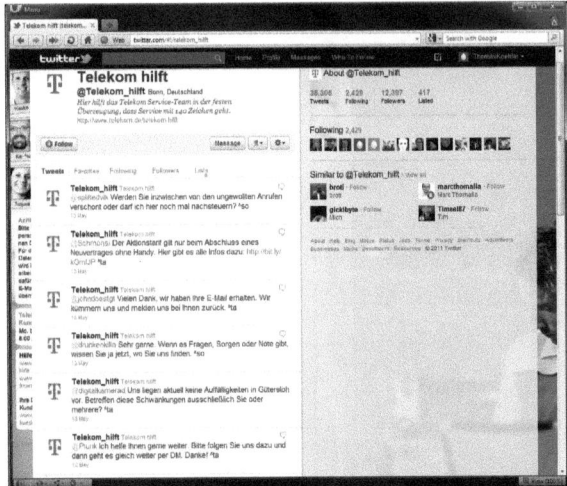

Twitter-Service
der Telekom Deutschland GmbH

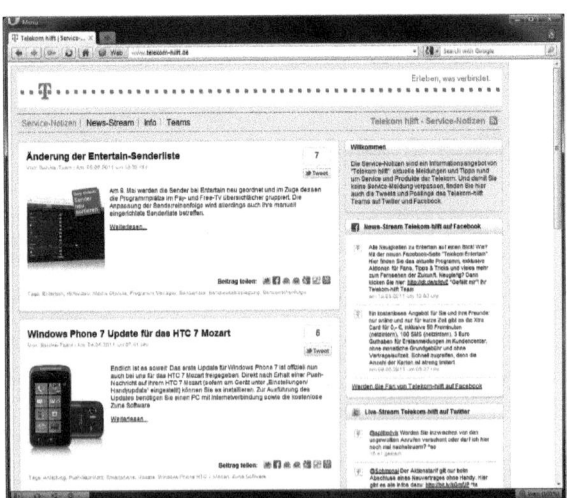

Telekom_hilft-Website & Weblog

Social-Media-Management

Verbote sind keine Lösung

Wird man mit den Auswirkungen von Social Media im Unternehmen zunächst im negativen Kontext konfrontiert, fällt es schwer, nicht sofort nach Verboten zu rufen. Viele Firmen gehen mit der Herausforderung Social Media auf eben diese Weise um. Nach einer weltweiten Studie des Netwerkausrüsters Cisco Systems (2010) ist die Verbotstendenz von Land zu Land unterschiedlich ausgeprägt, wie folgende Übersicht zeigt:

Social Media – Explizite Verbote (Studie von Cisco Systems)
- England 64 %
- Italien 61 %
- Frankreich 51 %
- USA 46 %
- Deutschland 44 %
- Spanien 34 %
- China 21 %

Zu bedenken ist stets, dass – selbst wenn man die Mitarbeiter von der Teilhabe im Social Web weitgehend ausschließt – jedes Telefonat, jedes Kundengespräch oder jede andere Äußerung eines Mitarbeiters mit Kundenkontakt oder eine Mitarbeiterhandlung auch durch den Kunden im Social Web landen kann. Ein unglückliches Verhalten im Einzelfall kann also weite Kreise ziehen. Fälle wie „United breaks guitars" sind inzwischen Legende und selbst in Wikipedia dokumentiert (http://de.wikipedia.org/wiki/United_Breaks_Guitars).
Zum Hintergrund: Ein Musiker, dessen Gitarre beim Lufttransport beschädigt wurde, hatte ein selbst gedrehtes Handyvideo, bei dem er Mitarbeiter der US-Fluggesellschaft bei der Gepäckabfertigung filmte, mit einem eigenen Song unterlegt und auf YouTube hochgeladen.
Spätestens in einem solchen PR-Katastrophenfall muss man mit adäquaten Mitteln reagieren können. Jedes Schweigen von Unternehmensseite würde einem von der „Netzgemeinschaft" als Arroganz ausgelegt und die Verbreitung der negativen Meldung eher noch weiter befeuern.
Zumindest die Option, im richtigen Medium reagieren zu können, sollte man sich als Unternehmen offenhalten.

Social Media intern „verkaufen"

Wie alle neuen Themen muss auch Social Media intern „verkauft" werden. Das Ziel dabei sollte sein, Innovation und Kreativität nicht auszubremsen, sondern zu kanalisieren. Dabei ist es wichtig, die Risiken, die damit einhergehen, zu verstehen und zu adressieren, sodass sie minimiert werden, und das Restrisiko zu akzeptieren. Unkontrollierte Ausbreitung – praktisch ein Social-Media-Blindflug – ist zu vermeiden.

Der Mitarbeiter als Marken-/Unternehmensbotschafter

Die Idee des Mitarbeiters als Marken- oder Unternehmensbotschafter ist kein neuer Gedanke. Sie wird in Fachkreisen seit Jahren diskutiert (siehe z. B. Kapferer, J.: „Strategic Brand Management", Kogan Page 1999).

Darin und in anderen Publikationen wurde schon lange vor dem Eintreffen der Social-Media-Welle darauf hingewiesen, dass der Mitarbeiter einen wesentlichen Beitrag zur wahrgenommenen Unternehmensidentität liefert – im Guten wie unter Umständen auch im Schlechten. Dabei darf das Thema Motivation nicht vergessen werden. Nicht nur Bezahlung und Arbeitsplatzausstattung oder die direkt gelebte Führung für den Mitarbeiter spielen hier eine Rolle, auch Handlungsspielräume sind wichtig. Eben diese Handlungsspielräume erweitern sich nun mit Social Media – zumindest potenziell.

Die Kernfrage, der sich jedes Unternehmen hier stellen muss, lautet: Ermuntere ich alle Mitarbeiter, eine aktive Rolle im Social-Media-Umfeld zu übernehmen, oder selektiere ich gezielt und setze auf eine Gruppe von vom Unternehmen angeleiteten Markenbotschaftern, die die Aufgabe Social-Media-Kommunikation zusätzlich zu dem in ihrem Arbeitsvertrag definierten Stellenprofil wahrnehmen? Dies impliziert kein Überflüssigwerden herkömmlicher Marktkommunikation, aber eine neue Perspektive – weg vom Broadcast, der einseitigen Kommunikation von einem Sender an viele Empfänger, hin zum Dialog.

Die auf Soziale Medien fokussierte Kommunikationsagentur Eck-Kommunikation sieht für die Markenverantwortlichen einen dreifachen Wandel (zitiert nach: www.pr-blogger.de):
- „Sie müssen erstens selbst über die Dialogfähigkeiten verfügen, die Social Media und personalisierte Kommunikation verlangen. Nur so können Sie Mitarbeiter glaubhaft intern beraten und kulturelle Irritationen mit neuen Medien, wie z. B. den Umgang mit Kritik oder die Einbindung von Feedback, vermeiden. Eigene Social-Media-Kompetenz ist allerdings der leichteste, selbstverständliche Schritt in diesem Wandelungsprozess.
- Zweitens müssen Kommunikationsabteilungen die eigenen Mitarbeiter für die neuen Formen der Kommunikation mobilisieren und vor allem motivieren. Dafür muss mitunter das bestehende Arsenal an internen Kommunikationsmaßnahmen angepasst oder um Social-Web-Formate ergänzt werden.
- Drittens müssen die Kommunikationsabteilungen 2.0 über die Kommunikationsmittel der Markensteuerung 2.0 verfügen: Coaching, Training, beratende Begleitung für die

Markenbotschafter und ein hohes Verständnis für die unübersichtliche, manchmal zufallsgetriebene Meinungsbildung im Social Web."

Je nach Unternehmensstruktur, Branche und Umfeld fällt die Antwort auf die Frage nach der Institutionalisierung von Markenbotschaftern unterschiedlich aus. Eine einheitliche Empfehlung kann hierzu nicht ausgesprochen werden.

Die Bedeutung von Social-Media-Richtlinien

Warum eine Social Media Policy

Wird die Einführung einer Social Media Policy im Unternehmen erstmals diskutiert, werden vielfach Stimmen laut, die ein Verbot fordern (s. o.). Unter Umständen werden die Initiatoren auch den Hinweis erhalten, im Arbeitsvertrag werde alles Relevante (Umgang mit Betriebs- und Geschäftsgeheimnissen) ja längst behandelt, eine Policy sei demnach nicht notwendig oder gar überflüssig.

Dem stehen verschiedene Studien entgegen, in denen bis zu zehn Prozent der Befragten berichten, dass ihre Organisation durch unbedachte Social-Media-Nutzung von Mitarbeitern bereits Reputationsschäden erlitten hat.

Fakt ist: Mitarbeiter nutzen Social Media und sind dabei nicht aufzuhalten. Fakt ist auch, dass Nutzer von Sozialen Netzwerken bereits im reinen Privatgebrauch dazu neigen, zu viel von sich preiszugeben oder auch unbedacht Inhalte einstellen, für die sie sich später unter Umständen schämen und von denen sie wünschten, sie hätten diese nie hochgeladen.

Ähnlich wenig Reflektion über das eigene Online-Verhalten darf man auch annehmen, wenn der Mitarbeiter im Unternehmenskontext Soziale Medien nutzt. Eine Social Media Policy kann helfen, das Bewusstsein für die Risiken und Nebenwirkungen der Social-Media-Nutzung im Unternehmenskontext zu entwickeln, und ist auch dann empfehlenswert, wenn Social Media gar nicht aktiv genutzt wird oder werden soll.

Kurz gesagt: Ohne Social Media Policy ist die eigene Organisation verwundbar.

Motivation für Social Media Policies

Während die grundlegende Motivation für eine Social Media Policy zumeist in der Risikovermeidung besteht, erkennt man insbesondere an aktuell erstellten Policies zunehmend anhand der Ausgestaltung, dass nicht nur Risiken vermieden, sondern auch Chancen, die die neuen Kommunikationswege bieten, besser genutzt werden sollen.

Von reaktiver Ausgestaltung der Richtlinien kann man sprechen, wenn der Schwerpunkt auf der Risikovermeidung liegt, etwa durch

– Vermeidung von Informationsabflüssen oder

– Reaktion auf regulatorische Anforderungen (etwa in der Finanzbranche oder in der Finanzkommunikation börsennotierter Unternehmen).

Von proaktiver Ausgestaltung kann man dann sprechen, wenn die Policy den Mitarbeiter zu aktiver Nutzung ermuntert, ihm etwa Beispiele für positives Verhalten vorgibt oder gar den „Mitarbeiter als Markenbotschafter" (s. o.) in den Mittelpunkt stellt. Von einer eher neutralen Ausrichtung kann man sprechen, wenn die Policy detailliert die bekannten Dienste und Sachverhalte regelt, ohne dabei zu innovativ zu werden. Eine Studie von socialmediagovernance.com, die Social Media Policies nach diesen Kriterien gruppiert hat, kommt (mit einer US-dominierten Grundgesamtheit) zu dem Ergebnis, dass sich die untersuchten Richtlinien wie folgt verteilen:
- 15 % Fokussierung auf Risiko
- 48 % Fokussierung auf das Bekannte
- 37 % Fokussierung auf mögliche Vorteile

Die Zahlen für Deutschland und Mitteleuropa dürften dem erheblich hinterherhinken, also bisher stärker auf Risikovermeidung fokussiert sein. Dies legt zumindest eine stichprobenmäßige Befragung von Unternehmen in Deutschland durch den Autor nahe, die aufgrund der geringen Grundgesamtheit aber keine detaillierten Aussagen zulässt.

Social-Media-Strategie versus Social Media Policy
Im Kontext einer aktiven Nutzung von Social Media wird gerne über Social-Media-Strategien diskutiert. Auch wenn es klare Interdependenzen gibt, sollte eine Policy, die im Regelfall für alle Mitarbeiter gilt, zunächst unabhängig davon entwickelt und dann mit der Social-Media-Strategie abgestimmt werden.
Die Entwicklung einer Social-Media-Strategie umfasst im Regelfall:
- Ziel definieren
- Zielpublikum identifizieren
- Delivery-Mechanismen auswählen
- Management-Commitment einholen

Die Ziele können dabei – wie oben dokumentiert – im Bereich Kundengewinnung, Kundenbindung, Steigerung der Markenbekanntheit oder auch Research und Produktentwicklung liegen.
Bei einer Policy hingegen werden – ausgehend von Risiken (und evtl. Chancen) – Rahmenbedingungen definiert, ggf. Konsequenzen, die bei Nichteinhaltung der Policy entstehen, dokumentiert, und zumeist wird definiert, wer im Zweifelsfall als übergeordnete Stelle Entscheidungen zu treffen hat. Eine Social Media Policy als wie auch immer geartete Nebenleistung einer Strategieentwicklung zu sehen führt in die Irre, solange es um alle Mitarbeiter geht. Werden jedoch – was durchaus üblich ist – unterschiedliche Policies entwickelt für
- eine Social Media Policy für sämtliche Mitarbeiter, die alle relevanten Rahmenbedingungen für Social Media beschreibt, oder
- eine Art Betriebsleitfaden für alle, die in Social Media als Teil ihrer Aufgabe arbeiten,
sollte Letzterer als Teil der Entwicklung der Social-Media-Strategie realisiert werden.

Wesentliche Inhalte einer Social Media Policy
Grundgedanken der eigenen Richtlinien sollten mit Blick auf Risiken und Chancen stets sein:
- Sensibilisierung der Mitarbeiter für das Thema
- Erzeugung von Transparenz insbesondere über inoffizielle Aktivitäten
- Schaffung einer Steuerungsmöglichkeit für alle Social-Media-Aktivitäten

Folgende Bestandteile sind dabei wesentlich:
- Regelung der Nutzung (Erlaubnis/Verbot) von Social-Media-Diensten während der Arbeitszeit
- Regelung für den Umgang mit vertraulichen Informationen (Firmeninternas, Betriebs- und Geschäftsgeheimnissen)
- Regelung für die Einhaltung von Urheber- und Wettbewerbsrecht
- Regelung für den Umgang mit Warenzeichen, Logos etc.
- Regelung für allgemeines Kommunikationsverhalten (Höflichkeit, Vermeidung von Ironie und Sarkasmus, um Missverständnisse möglichst auszuschließen, Fokussierung auf Fakten statt auf Meinungen)

Die Rolle des Betriebsrats
Mit Blick auf das Betriebsverfassungsgesetz ist nach gängiger Rechtsmeinung auch der Betriebsrat bei der Einführung einer Social Media Policy zu befragen, da dieser bei Fragen der Ordnung des Betriebes und des Verhaltens der Arbeitnehmer im Betrieb und bei der Arbeitnehmerüberwachung durch technische Einrichtungen (wie sie etwa bei Social Media Monitoring vorkommen kann) nach Betriebsverfassungsgesetz ein Mitbestimmungsrecht besitzt.

Umfang, Detaillierung und Strukturierung von Social Media Policies
Nach einer Studie von Socialmediagovernance.com haben die meisten Social Media Policies einen Umfang von rund 500 bis 2.000 Wörtern. Nur wenige fassen sich mit weniger als 300 Wörtern extrem kurz (siehe dazu auch die Beispiele in diesem Buch). Rekordhalter im Umfang ist – nach der oben genannten Studie – das U. S. Army Corps of Engineers mit rund 28.000 Wörtern (nicht im Buch behandelt, da nicht relevant).
Klar ist, dass die Lesbarkeit unter einer Überfülle an Text leidet. Empfehlenswert ist daher – soweit sich längere Texte nicht vermeiden lassen – eine Zusammenfassung der wichtigsten Punkte etwa in Form von „Sieben goldene Regeln für …". Sinnvoll sind auch zweckorientierte Policies, die im jeweiligen Kontext aufbereitet sind. Auch eine Strukturierung nach Mitarbeiter-Skills ist vorstellbar.
Was das Dokument selbst angeht, so findet man häufig einen Aufbau, bestehend aus einem Rahmendokument mit der Verlinkung auf weitere Elemente, die Einzelregelungen, etwa für einzelne Dienste, enthalten. In jedem Fall sollte eine Möglichkeit des Kontakts zu Verantwortlichen, an die sich der Mitarbeiter in Zweifelsfällen wenden kann, integriert werden.
Interessant ist auch die Frage, inwieweit die Policy auf bestimmte Dienste eingehen sollte

oder es für bestimmte Dienste wie Twitter, Facebook, Xing, Wikis oder LinkedIn eigene Policies geben sollte.

Betrachtet man die Übersicht über gängige Policies in diesem Buch, dann haben nur wenige Organisationen tatsächlich Regelungen für einzelne Dienste, und wenn, dann sind das in den meisten Fällen gewachsene Policies, die – etwa ausgehend von der Welle der Unternehmens-Blogs ab etwa 2004/2005 – Regelungen dafür erlassen und diese später verallgemeinert oder erweitert haben.

Bei auf bestimmte Online-Dienste zugeschnittenenen Policies sollte stets bedacht werden, dass die Halbwertszeit der erfolgreichen Anbieter durchaus gering ist – wer nutzt heute noch aktiv Myspace? – und neue Dienste ständig entstehen. Um hier einen laufenden Zwang zur Ergänzung beziehungsweise Überarbeitung der Policy zu vermeiden, sollte diese möglichst allgemein gültig realisiert werden.

Weitere wichtige Aspekte sind die Ausgestaltung von Accounts. Grundlegend denkbar sind persönliche Accounts und sogenannte Organizational Accounts. Nutzt der Mitarbeiter Social Media, ohne Beauftragter des Unternehmens zu sein, so liegt es auf der Hand, dass es sich um eine persönlich identifizierbare Nutzung handelt. Die damit entstehende Problematik, dass auch private Äußerungen auf das Unternehmen zurückstrahlen können, wurde bereits hinreichend diskutiert. Die wesentlichen Fragen lauten hier: Dürfen private Accounts während der Arbeitszeit beziehungsweise mithilfe von Firmen-Equipment genutzt werden?

Anders liegt der Fall bei Mitarbeitern, die im Rahmen ihrer offiziellen Aufgaben Social-Media-Aktivitäten für das Unternehmen planen und durchführen. Hier besteht grundsätzlich eine Wahlmöglichkeit, ob man diese etwa mit „Twitter-Team Firma XYZ" oder „Sandra Meier Firma XY" firmieren lässt.

Hintergrund der Organisations-Accounts ist natürlich, dass unter Umständen mehrere Mitarbeiter diese gemeinschaftlich verwenden.

In jedem Fall benötigen die auch „Social Media Account Manager" genannten Mitarbeiter die Autorität, Nachrichten in ihrem Einsatzgebiet, das auf bestimmte Themenstellen begrenzt sein kann, ohne weitere Bewilligung verfassen und versenden („posten") oder auf gepostete Nachrichten entsprechend reagieren zu können. Mit Blick auf die Sicherheit, insbesondere die Zuordenbarkeit der Aussagen, ist es empfehlenswert, die Anzahl der Nutzer pro Organisations-Account zu beschränken und auf eine Absicherung gegen unbefugte Nutzung (Passwörter etc.) zu achten. Außerdem ist eine laufende Überwachung derartiger Accounts notwendig. Insbesondere selten genutzte Accounts sollten überwacht werden, um zu vermeiden, dass diese durch Dritte missbraucht werden.

Für die Ausgestaltung der Kommunikation gilt das bereits oben Gesagte:
- Höflichkeit ist wesentlich.
- Ironie und Sarkasmus sollte vermieden werden (Gefahr des Missverständnisses!).
- Es gibt einen Unterschied zwischen Meinung und Fakten – dies ist zu berücksichtigen.
- Das Erleben der Nutzer ist nicht immer so exakt wie die Faktenlage, deswegen gilt dennoch: „Der Kunde/Nutzer hat recht."

[…]

Weitere Implikationen von Social-Media-Richtlinien

Denkt man weiter über Social-Media-Richtlinien nach, so stellt man fest, dass die darin enthaltenen Regeln in ihren Auswirkungen nachhaltig auf das Unternehmen zurückstrahlen können. Dies gilt nicht nur in den Außenwirkungen wie Reputation, Wahrnehmung, Werte, Realität und Wahrheit, sondern auch im Innenverhältnis, strahlt ein per Social Media Guideline verhängter Maulkorb doch auf die Mitarbeiter zurück. Selbst jene, die keinen oder noch keinen Bezug haben, werden mit Regelungen konfrontiert, die das Menschenbild des Unternehmens berühren.

Dies tritt insbesondere bei der häufig zu findenden Frage nach den privaten Aktivitäten des Mitarbeiters zutage:

- Welche Aktivitäten verfolgt er?
- Welchen Clubs und Gruppen gehört er an?
- Welche Meinungen vertritt er?

Diese treten im Rahmen eines Social-Media-Monitorings ganz selbstverständlich zutage, wenn sie nicht ohnehin bereits Gegenstand des Recruiting-Prozesses waren oder sind (auf den in diesem Buch nicht weiter eingegangen wird). Einige Social Media Policies versuchen daher, dem Mitarbeiter auch im Privatleben Regeln aufzugeben, die seine individuelle Freiheit tangieren. Dass dies auf – wohl überwiegend berechtigten – Widerstand stoßen wird, ist abzusehen. Auch die Frage nach den Aktivitäten des Partners kann so ins Licht der Unternehmensregelungen rücken, etwa mit: „Wir haben festgestellt, dass Ihr Partner folgende Vorstellungen hat …". Auch hier sind Konflikte programmiert. Die Vorstellung, mit Social-Media-Richtlinien alles regeln zu wollen, was irgendwie die Außenwirkung des Unternehmens tangieren könnte, greift spätestens hier ins Leere.

Ähnliches gilt bei international agierenden Unternehmen. Hier sind kulturelle Gepflogenheiten wie auch rechtliche Rahmenbedingungen unter Umständen von Land zu Land derart unterschiedlich, dass eine einheitliche Richtlinie nur eine Art Schnittmenge sinnvoll regeln kann. In Summe ist sowohl bei der Regelungsbreite als auch bei der Regelungstiefe ein gesundes Augenmaß gefragt – zum Wohl des Unternehmens wie auch des Mitarbeiters.

Die Empfehlungen im folgenden Abschnitt und die im Folgekapitel zusammengestellten Policies sollen hier beispielhaft zeigen, was möglich und für welche Branchen sinnvoll ist.

Das „Fünf x Fünf" der Social Media Policies

Unternehmen lassen sich vielfach eingruppieren, ob Hersteller, Dienstleister oder Händler, B-to-B oder B-to-C, nationaler oder internationaler Player, ob forschungsorientierter Spezialist oder „Me-too"-Generalist, hier sind vielfältige Einstufungen möglich. Auch Faktoren wie staatliche Regulierung versus freier Markt oder Gemeinnützigkeit versus Profitorientierung können helfen, Unternehmen und andere Organisationen in verschiedene Schubladen zu sortieren. Die Möglichkeiten der Eingruppierung sind schier unerschöpflich.

Sucht man aber nach für Social Media relevanten Charakteristiken, so kann man die Unternehmen insgesamt – mit Blick auf die Ausgestaltung der Social Media Guidelines – in fünf dominierende Gruppen zusammenfassen:

- „Erfolgreicher Markenartikler"
- „Forschungsorientiertes High-Tech-Unternehmen"
- „Internetaffines Unternehmen"
- „Staatlich regulierte oder in der Öffentlichkeit kritisch gesehene Organisation"
- „Gemeinnützige Organisation"

Für diese werden jeweils nachfolgend Empfehlungen für die Social-Media-Nutzung und Policy-Erstellung abgeben – mit folgender Einteilung in fünf Bereiche:
- Herangehensweise an Social Media: aktiv/passiv
- Fokussierung der Policy: Risiken vermeiden/Status quo absichern/Chancen suchen
- Involvement Mitarbeiter: wird ausgeschlossen/toleriert/gefördert
- Definition spezieller Social-Media-Rollen: nein/ja
- Erstellung Policy empfehlenswert durch: Wiki/Workshop

Die Empfehlungen lauten entsprechend für

„Erfolgreicher Markenartikler"
- Herangehensweise an Social Media: aktiv
- Fokussierung der Policy: Chancen suchen
- Involvement Mitarbeiter: gefördert
- Definition spezieller Social-Media-Rollen: ja
- Erstellung Policy empfehlenswert durch: Workshop

Der Markenartikler steht mitten drin im Social Web. Ob er will oder nicht, sein Produkt und seine Leistung sind längst Gegenstand der öffentlichen Debatte. Hier empfiehlt es sich, aktiv einzusteigen und die Chancen zu nutzen. Dazu zählt nicht nur, dass man gezielt Social-Media-Protagonisten einsetzt, sondern es kann auch hilfreich sein, alle interessierten Mitarbeiter zu motivieren, am Aufbau und an der Pflege der eigenen Reputation aktiv mitzuwirken.

Forschungsorientiertes High-Tech-Unternehmen
- Herangehensweise an Social Media: passiv
- Fokussierung der Policy: Risiken vermeiden
- Involvement Mitarbeiter: wird ausgeschlossen
- Definition spezieller Social-Media-Rollen: nein (ja)
- Erstellung Policy empfehlenswert durch: Workshop

Bei Hochtechnologieunternehmen klassischer Prägung wie Maschinenbauern oder Autozulieferern hat der Schutz des geistigen Eigentums absolute Priorität. Hier können explizite Verbote der Beteilung an Social-Media-Aktivitäten wirkungsvoll sein, kann ein Wettbewerber oder böswilliger Angreifer doch allein aus den persönlichen Angaben und den Beziehungen der Mitarbeiter Rückschlüsse für mögliche Social-Engineering-Angriffe ziehen.

Internetaffines Unternehmen
– Herangehensweise an Social Media: aktiv
– Fokussierung der Policy: Chancen suchen
– Involvement Mitarbeiter: wird gefördert
– Definition spezieller Social-Media-Rollen: nein (jeder ist Botschafter)
– Erstellung Policy empfehlenswert durch: Wiki

Ist man selbst Anbieter von Internetdiensten oder in Branchen mit direktem Bezug dazu tätig, ist eine aktive, chancenorientiere, Policy-Gestaltung Pflicht. Die Mitarbeiter sind meist ohnehin stark involviert. Daher empfiehlt sich auch eine gemeinschaftliche Erstellung derselben – etwa mittels Wiki.

Staatlich regulierte oder in der Öffentlichkeit kritisch gesehene Organisation
– Herangehensweise an Social Media: passiv oder vorsichtig aktiv
– Fokussierung der Policy: Risiken vermeiden/Status quo absichern
– Involvement Mitarbeiter: toleriert
– Definition spezieller Social-Media-Rollen: ja
– Erstellung Policy empfehlenswert durch: Workshop

Steht man – wie etwa Anbieter im Gesundheitswesen, im Finanzwesen oder in ähnlich stark regulierten Branchen – unter Druck oder wird das eigene Unternehmen in der Öffentlichkeit kritisch wahrgenommen, so empfiehlt es sich, Social-Media-Aktivitäten nur sehr vorsichtig und kontrolliert wahrzunehmen – stets mit dem Blick auf mögliche Risiken. Ein aktives Monitoring ist Pflicht.

Gemeinnützige Organisation
– Herangehensweise an Social Media: aktiv
– Fokussierung der Policy: Chancen suchen
– Involvement Mitarbeiter: gefördert
– Definition spezieller Social-Media-Rollen: nein (jeder ist Botschafter)
– Erstellung Policy empfehlenswert durch: Wiki

Für eine gemeinnützige Organisation ist Öffentlichkeitsarbeit ein wesentlicher Erfolgsfaktor zur Spendenakquise. Social Media kann dabei helfen, die „Freiwilligen" zu aktivieren und Image wie Finanzsituation auf Dauer positiv zu beeinflussen. Eine Social-Media-Richtlinie für eine gemeinnützige Organisation sollte dies entsprechend widerspiegeln.

Selbstverständlich sind die hier gegebenen Empfehlungen nur ein erster Anhaltspunkt für die Erstellung und sollten jeweils individuell – idealerweise auch „mit Seitenblick" auf die nachfolgend vorgestellten Social Media Guidelines aus verschiedenen Branchen – im Workshop oder Wiki erarbeitet und von der Rechtsabteilung überprüft werden.

Beispielhafte Social Media Guidelines

Die nachfolgende alphabetische Liste gibt einen Überblick über Social Media Guidelines aus verschiedenen Branchen sowohl von deutschen als auch von internationalen Unternehmen.

Alle hier zusammengetragenen Informationen wurden auf Anfrage von den Unternehmen bereitgestellt oder stammen aus öffentlich zugänglichen Quellen. Ein Großteil der hier dokumentierten Richtlinien ist in deutscher Sprache, der Rest in englischer Sprache abgefasst. Viele Unternehmen haben – auch wenn sie in Deutschland tätig sind – nur Policies in englischer Sprache. Soweit die Policies nur in Englisch vorliegen, wurde auf eine Übersetzung verzichtet, um Übersetzungsfehler oder -unschärfen zu vermeiden.

1&1

Zum Unternehmen: Die 1&1 Internet AG ist die Keimzelle der United-Internet-Unternehmensgruppe und wurde über Webhosting-Angebote und DSL-Anschlussvermarktung bekannt. Das Unternehmen sieht sich mit nach eigenen Angaben 9,5 Millionen Kundenverträgen als einen der führenden Internet-Provider in Deutschland. Neben Hosting und DSL werden inzwischen auch Mobilfunkverträge vermarktet.

Im April 2010 hat 1&1 seine Social Media Guidelines auf dem Unternehmens-Blog veröffentlicht (http://blog.1und1.de/2010/04/16/die-social-media-guidelines-von-11/): „Unsere Guidelines wurden im Social-Media-Team entworfen und dann mit der Pressestelle, der Personalabteilung und unserer größten Kommunikationsabteilung – dem Kundenservicebereich mit über 2.000 Mitarbeitern, die täglich im Unternehmensauftrag kommunizieren – abgestimmt."

Social Media Guidelines

Immer mehr Kolleginnen und Kollegen bewegen sich privat wie auch geschäftlich auf Social-Media-Plattformen wie Twitter, Facebook oder Xing, schreiben eigene Blogs, beteiligen sich an Foren-Diskussionen und nutzen weitere Web-2.0-Plattformen.

Auch 1&1 ist aktiv im Web 2.0 unterwegs. Das Mitmach-Web ist für uns ein wichtiger neuer Kanal für die Kommunikation mit Kunden, Multiplikatoren und der Öffentlichkeit allgemein. Für die Steuerung und Koordinierung aller Web-2.0-Aktivitäten des Unternehmens ist das Team Social Media Communications (PR SMC) innerhalb der Pressestelle verantwortlich.

Mit den folgenden Social Media Guidelines wollen wir euch einige Verhaltensrichtlinien für die richtige Kommunikation im Web 2.0 an die Hand geben. Für Äußerungen im Web 2.0, in denen es um eure Arbeit oder euer Unternehmen geht, sind diese Richtlinien bindend:

1. Das Unternehmen begrüßt ausdrücklich, wenn ihr euch im Web 2.0 engagiert. Insbesondere sind alle Mitarbeiter eingeladen, sich aktiv als Autoren an unseren eigenen Plattformen wie dem 1&1 Blog zu beteiligen. Wenn Fachabteilungen eigene Web-2.0-Angebote planen, werden diese mit dem Social-Media-Communications-Team abgestimmt.

2. Gegenüber der Öffentlichkeit sprechen ausschließlich Vorstände, Mitarbeiter der Presse-stellen oder anderweitig autorisierte Mitarbeiter im Namen des Unternehmens. Dies gilt ins-besondere für den Bereich Customer Care, dessen Kernaufgabe die direkte Kommunikation mit unseren Kunden ist. Support-Mitarbeiter, die das Unternehmen in Web-2.0-Angeboten vertreten (z. B. Blog, Support-Forum), werden separat benannt. Für alle offiziellen Verlaut-barungen gelten auch im Web 2.0 die Richtlinien zur Unternehmenskommunikation.

3. Offizielle Web-2.0-Angebote des Unternehmens (z. B. abteilungsbezogene Twitter-Accounts, Blogs, Facebook-Fan-Seiten etc.) müssen mit dem Social-Media-Team abgestimmt werden.

4. Wenn ihr euch ohne einen dienstlichen Auftrag in sozialen Medien äußert, macht stets deutlich, dass ihr eure persönliche Meinung vertretet und nicht für das Unternehmen sprecht. Verwendet daher Formulierungen wie „ich", statt „wir".

5. Weder Firmengeheimnisse noch urheberrechtlich geschütztes Material dürfen nach außen kommuniziert werden. Es gelten die arbeitsrechtlichen Bestimmungen. Die Veröffentlichung von Insider-Informationen kann den Aktienkurs beeinflussen und gegen börsenrechtliche Vorschriften verstoßen. Fragt im Zweifelsfall euren Vorgesetzten, die Presseabteilung oder die Abteilung Investor Relations in der United Internet AG.

6. Wenn ihr euch zu eurem direkten Arbeitsgebiet äußern wollt, stimmt dies im Vorfeld mit eurem direkten Vorgesetzten ab.

7. Seid ehrlich und transparent. Wenn ihr euch privat zu einem Thema rund um eure Arbeit oder euren Arbeitgeber äußert, müsst ihr, z. B. in einem Disclaimer, deutlich offenlegen, dass ihr bei 1&1 bzw. der entsprechenden Marke arbeitet. Dies gilt insbesondere für Antworten in Foren oder Blog-Kommentaren. Postet ihr als autorisierter Mitarbeiter im Firmenauftrag, ist dies ebenfalls zu kennzeichnen, z. B. durch eine entsprechende Unterschrift „Vorname Nachname, 1&1 Internet AG".

8. Wenn ihr im Netz auf sachliche Kritik am Unternehmen oder konkrete Probleme von Kunden stoßt, ist das zentrale Beschwerdemanagement oder das Social-Media-Team in der Presseabteilung der richtige Ansprechpartner für euch. Wenn ihr eine Kundenfrage selbst beantworten könnt, solltet ihr dem Kunden selbstverständlich helfen.

9. Beachtet bei sämtlichen Veröffentlichungen die möglichen Folgen, argumentiert sachlich, beleidigt niemanden und zeigt Respekt im Umgang mit Dritten. Die beste Richtschnur hierfür sind noch immer die Regeln der „Netiquette", die ihr hier nachlesen könnt.

10. Diskreditiert keine Mitbewerber oder deren Produkte – und natürlich auch nicht das eigene Unternehmen.

11. Antwortet nicht im Affekt, sondern denkt über eure Kommentare gründlich nach. Und denkt immer daran: Das Netz vergisst nichts.

12. Bei Fragen hat das Social-Media-Team oder eure Pressestelle immer ein offenes Ohr.

Diese Richtlinien werden kontinuierlich weiterentwickelt.

Interessant ist hierbei insbesondere Punkt 6, der bereits wenige Tage nach der Veröffentlichung in einem Blog-Kommentar dazu von einem Nutzer offen kritisiert wird:
„Sorry, aber ihr nehmt euren Mitarbeitern jegliche Möglichkeit, wirklich in einen DIALOG mit den Kunden zu treten. Aussagen wie „Wenn ihr euch zu eurem direkten Arbeitsgebiet äußern wollt, stimmt dies im Vorfeld mit eurem direkten Vorgesetzten ab." sind doch der absolute Motivationskiller für jeden Mitarbeiter, noch irgendwo überhaupt erwähnen zu wollen, wo er arbeitet. Ihr behandelt eure „mehr als 4.000 Mitarbeiter" wie ein potenzielles Risiko für das geschlossene Markenbild und nicht als potenziell 4.000 Multiplikatoren und Markenbotschaftern, und aus euren Guidelines spricht nur die Angst vor einer ‚echten' Kommunikation mit dem Kunden …"

Worauf 1&1 wie folgt antwortet:
„Hallo Herr Jorberg, wir wissen, dass viele unserer Kollegen bereits selbst aktiv Web-2.0-Medien wie Twitter, Xing, Facebook o. ä. nutzen. Daher möchten wir sie auch ermuntern, selbst zu Botschaftern unserer Marke im Social Web zu werden. Öffentliche Äußerungen müssen natürlich auch dort gewissen Regeln unterliegen. Egal ob man nun in einem kleinen Betrieb oder einem großen Konzern arbeitet, muss man doch darauf achten, keine internen Prozesse oder ‚Betriebsgeheimnisse' sorglos im Web 2.0 zu veröffentlichen. Unsere Social Media Guidelines sollen unseren Mitarbeitern, also den potenziellen Multiplikatoren, demnach Richtlinien bieten, um sich sicher und ohne Bedenken als Mitarbeiter unserer Marke in sozialen Netzwerken bewegen zu können. Der Dialog mit unseren Kunden wird so keinesfalls behindert, sondern angeregt.
Viele Grüße
Sarah Dederichs"

American Red Cross
Die amerikanische Rotkreuz-Organisation (http://www.redcross.org) veröffentlicht sowohl Guidelines für eigene Mitarbeiter als auch ein weiterführendes „Handbuch" für lokale Rotkreuz-Einheiten. Im Bereich Social Media ist man auf vielfältige Weise aktiv, u. a.:
– Diverse Weblogs (national, lokal und jugendorientierte Angebote)
– Disaster Online Newsroom (http://newsroom.redcross.org) – ein speziell auf aktuelle Katastrophen, bei denen das American Red Cross Hilfe leistet, fokussierter Weblog
– Flickr
– Twitter (national wie lokal)
– Facebook (mehrere Seiten)

American Red Cross Online Communications Guidelines

This is a living document and will continue to provide guidance over time. There are lots of great gadgets, software programs and Web 2.0 tools out there for you to use. You can be a powerful voice in telling your stories and those of the American Red Cross.

Use Disclaimers
Make it clear that the views you are expressing are yours alone and not necessarily those of the Red Cross.

Be Accurate
If you discuss the Red Cross, then you have a duty to disclose your role within the organization.
If you are creating an online space for a specific chapter or region, use the entire chapter/region name and lock-up. Social networks function well as smaller communities. Representing your community will increase activity from supporters in your community.
National Headquarters is responsible for creating national Red Cross online presences. Please contact us if you have suggestions for new national online presences.

Be Transparent
If you discuss the Red Cross, then you have a duty to disclose your role within the organization.
If you are creating an online space for a specific chapter or region, use the entire chapter/region name and lock-up. Social networks function well as smaller communities. Representing your community will increase activity from supporters in your community.
National Headquarters is responsible for creating national Red Cross online presences. Please contact us if you have suggestions for new national online presences.

Be Accurate
Even though your blog posts may be primarily made up of personal opinion, do your research well and check that your facts are accurate. Make sure you have permission to post any copyrighted or confidential information (e.g., images) to your blog, and be careful about posting or linking to items that may contain viruses.

Be Considerate
Remember that anyone, including your colleagues, may be actively reading what you publish online. In choosing your words and your content, it's a good practice to imagine that your supervisor and your family are reading everything you post. It's all about judgment: using your Weblog to bash or embarrass the Red Cross, our clients, our donors or your co-workers isn't smart or professional. If you have suggestions for improvements at the Red Cross, please state them constructively or better yet, go through the proper channels to air your concerns and share your suggestions.
If you witness illegal, unsafe or unethical conduct by a Red Cross employee or volunteer, we

would prefer that you not discuss this in your blog. Instead, for example, you can call the Red Cross Ombudsman (contact details forthcoming) or the Red Cross Concern Connection Line (888-309-9679), which is the 24-hour, confidential and anonymous toll-free line that provides American Red Cross employees, volunteer and members of the public a way to report issues like the following:
– Theft, fraud or any other dishonest conduct
– Discrimination or harassment
– Waste or abuse of Red Cross resources
– Conflicts of interest
– Unsafe situations
– Mismanagement
– Any actions that violate the Red Cross Code of Conduct
Reporting issues like those above in a blog may do more harm than good; worse yet, problems may not get to the attention of the people who can correct them. The Red Cross wants to hear your concerns and has a unit that vigorously follows up and investigates the issues.

Don't Reveal Confidential Information
If you do blog about the Red Cross, by all means talk about your good work and make meaningful connections with your readers, but you must accomplish this while respecting the privacy and confidentiality of clients and communities. When making decisions about your online content, refer often to the following documents you agreed to when you became an employee or volunteer:
– Code of Conduct
– Confidential Information and Intellectual Property Agreement
Clients and stakeholders should not be cited or obviously referenced without their approval. Never identify a client or partner by name without permission, and never discuss the confidential details of a client. It is acceptable to discuss general details and to use non-identifying pseudonyms so long as the information provided does not violate any non-disclosure agreements that may be in place with the client or make it easy for someone to identify the client. Be sensitive to matters of civic pride when discussing specific localities, especially during disasters. You should be careful to protect the dignity of clients by refraining from discussions that reflect negatively on them, even if they are not named.

Respect Copyright Laws
Show proper respect for the laws governing copyright and fair use of copyrighted material owned by others, including the Red Cross's own copyright and trademarks. For reference see: http://fairuse.stanford.edu/

Tell us about your blog
National headquarters does not intend to "police" the blogging community. Quite the contrary: we want to aggregate all the powerful stories Red Crossers are telling and showcase your individual contribution to the overall missionand gather links in a page at Redcross.org. If you have a blog and you intend to discuss the Red Cross, please contact Wendy Harman

at (202) 303-4080 or at HarmanW@usa.redcross.org, for questions, concerns or general guidance on how to engage the blogosphere.

Be Generous
The Internet is all about connecting with links, so if you see something interesting, valuable or relevant, link to it! The more you link to relevant material, the more contacts you will make and the more popular your own blog will become.

Be a Good Blogger
We're lucky; we are part of a humanitarian organization that provides relief to victims of disaster and helps people prevent, prepare for and respond to emergencies. This means we are likely to have something interesting to add online. Since being interesting is one of the cornerstones of "successful" blogging, we're off to a good start. That said, writing captivating online content is hard work and a commitment. We suggest if you decide to jump into the blogosphere, do so with a commitment to post regularly and well; link to others and show your unique personality. Make it interesting and have fun!

Respect Work Commitments
Please remember that blogging and other social networking activities are personal and should be done on your own time unless you have specifically been assigned to perform an online activity related to your Red Cross responsibilities as an employee or volunteer.

Uphold the Fundamental Principles
As a Red Crosser, you have already made a commitment to abide by the Fundamental Principles of the Red Cross and Red Crescent Movement. Please follow these principles in your online communications. If you choose to share your political or religious stances online, be certain you are representing yourself and not the organization as a whole.

Social Media Handbook for Local Red Cross Units

Introduction
This handbook is meant for all Red Crossers interested in how social media can help us deliver our mission critical services.

This information will familiarize you with our national social media philosophy, invite you to find, join, and participate in our national social media presence, and guide you in creating your own local social media presence.

You'll find steps to adopting a social media strategy, best practices from your fellow Red Cross units as well as from outside experts, and an explanation of various social media tools. We've included a powerpoint presentation for you to use however you'd like. Feel free to use the whole thing, cut it up, and/or rearrange it. It's meant to be a tool both for you to learn from and for you to teach others.

We love building online communities using social media tools, but make no mistake, adopting a social media strategy at your local unit is a significant commitment of your time both daily and long term.

We think it's worth it, but plan accordingly!

Frequently Asked Questions

How do I balance my personal and professional lives online?

You need to determine your own comfort level in discussing work in your personal communications.

If you choose to talk about your Red Cross work via your personal online accounts, please disclose your relationship with the Red Cross and be responsible.

Remember that the NHQ social media team will see all mentions of the Red Cross and may contact you to praise your discussion, invite you to contribute to our corporate online spaces, or to give you guidance about how to talk about your work responsibly. Always follow our Fundamental Principles.

Should I respond to comments or mentions I see on other blogs?

Your national social media team often responds to mentions you see in the NHQ daily social media update. When needed, we seek the counsel of subject matter experts here and at the chapter level to help us get the right information to people talking about us. You are also welcome to respond to these mentions, but please let us know when you do. If the mention deals with a local chapter issue we consult with the chapter to decide if they want to respond directly or if the NHQ team should assist.

Should I use social media platforms to fundraise?

Many people enjoy social media communities simply because they are free from corporate marketing machines. Our goal is to offer value in these spaces rather than to offer our marketing solicitations. Social marketing/fundraising is a tricky beast so tread carefully here. Once you build an online community, offer tools that make it easy for your supporters to do the fundraising for you. For example, offer web banners and widgets that link to online fundraising portals.

Most successful social media fundraising events are hosted by individual supporters of the organization they're supporting. Be inspiring and make it easy for your individual donors to take on a fun(draising) campaign.

What if people leave mean comments on our Red Cross blog, Facebook page, Twitter account, Flickr photos, etc?

If you're following the guidelines and our philosophy, this won't happen very often.

Social Networking sites such as Facebook, MySpace, Flickr, and YouTube don't currently allow you to moderate comments before they're published, so you will need someone dedicated to checking in with your sites each day. If you receive a negative comment, evaluate whether it's constructive. If it is constructive, don't be afraid to engage the person who left it. Even if you don't have all the right answers, try to find them together. If the comment is not constructive and does not align with the fundamental principles, you can remove it.

If you have a blog, you can usually moderate your comments before they're published to your site. Again, if the comment is constructive you should use it as an opportunity to discuss, clear up the misunderstanding, or otherwise work through whatever issue the person is having. If you'd like to moderate your comments, you can use this lawyer-approved language: "Remember, we encourage you to comment on this blog. All viewpoints are welcome, but please be constructive. We reserve the right to make editorial decisions regarding submitted comments, including but not limited to removal of comments. The comments are moderated, so you may have to be a tiny bit patient in waiting to see them. We will review and post them as promptly as possible during regular business hours (Monday through Friday, 8:30 – 5:30)."

Contact
Please contact Wendy Harman, Manager of Social Media, with any inquiries, comments, suggestions, or questions.
SocialMedia@usa.redcross.org
Listen to the Existing Conversation
Learn to Listen to the Existing Conversation
Daily Social Media Update
NHQ does most of the reputation management and listening for you
We read and respond to the 400+ daily mentions of the Red Cross on various blogs and social networking sites
We distribute a daily email that contains the most relevant mentions
ACTION ITEM: Sign up to receive NHQ's daily social media update via email
Email socialmedia@usa.redcross.org
Subject line: Please add me to the social media update list
Learn the Culture of Social Media
We recommend following these steps in sequential order when you're first creating a strategy. After that, use this handbook and these steps as a reference when you adapt, expand, and sharpen your strategy.

Getting Familiar with Social Media
Get Social Media Savvy
Initiate personal social media use:
Explore the tools you'd like to adopt by using them in your personal life first. It's easier to understand the culture behind tools like Facebook and Twitter when you spend some time posting your own pictures and experiences.
Follow the personal online communications guidelines
Resources
CommonCraft
Beth's Blog for Nonprofits and Social Media
Participate in Our National Social Media Presence
Learn National's Social Media Philosophy
Our Red Cross social media philosophy:

To use social media to execute the American Red Cross mission of helping people prevent, prepare for, and respond to emergencies

Our Red Cross social media goals:
To create an empowered online community of Red Cross supporters to:
Reenergize the brand
Raise awareness of our services and mission
Provide critical information to the public during emergencies
Engage our employees, volunteers, and supporters in a two way conversation that enhances the mission
Engage and Participate in National Social Media Presence
Familiarize yourself with our national social media presence
Take specific action [link to PDF called Step4CrossNet here] for each platform national is using
Create Your Social Media Strategy
Study what other Red Cross chapters are doing with their Social Media Presence
Use these links to find chapter/blood region social media projects
Find local blogs
Find local Twitter accounts
Find local Facebook accounts: pages, groups, and causes
Find local YouTube accounts (list coming soon)
Find local Flickr accounts (list coming soon)

Evaluate best practices
Take cues from the successes and challenges of your colleagues
Talk to one another to share information and collaborate
We encourage you to share each other's content, but please properly attribute the content by disclosing its origin and linking back to the original source
Evaluate your chapter's overall goals
Think about what you want to achieve
What are your mission critical services?
These are the services you should concentrate on providing to your local stakeholders online
For example, we use Twitter to provide reliable real time information and tips during disasters
What are your public relations goals?
Evaluate how you currently correspond with local media, stakeholders, volunteers, donors, and the public
What are your community goals?
Evaluate how you're currently mobilizing volunteers
Evaluate how you're currently engaging with your donors

Strategy and Tactics
Evaluating and reviewing your organizational goals, strategy and tactics will inform how you choose to use social media

Adopt a local social media philosophy
You are encouraged to follow the national philosophy
If you'd like to create your own philosophy, please consult the social media team

Create your social media goals
Write down the goals you hope to achieve by using social media
Analyze whether your goals make sense and work with your chapter's strategic plan or other goals

Create your social media strategy
Write down the reasons your social media use will complement your chapter's overall strategic plan
Write down the types of content you'll provide and the types of content you'll solicit from your community

Create tactics
Figure out how you'll execute the strategy to achieve your goals
Who will be responsible?
What tools will you use?
See detailed strategy plans for 5 of the most common social media tools in the navigation buttons above

How will you develop content?
How will you engage with your audience?
How often will you be present?
What steps will you take to reach your desired outcome?

Implement Your Social Media Strategy
Tell us what you're doing and how you are doing it
Now that you've done the hard work of tying your social media goals to your organizational goals, picking the right tools for you, and creating a strategy, you're ready to tell us!

We're interested in cataloguing your:
– Strategy
– Chosen Tools
– Links to your activities

We will do the following with this information:
– List you on our aggregated national sites
– Cull your strategy for best practices. We hope this will bring you additional fame and glory

Ask us about any hesitation or issues you encounter
That's what we're here for. To help you. Email socialmedia@usa.redcross.org

Implement Your Plan
Have a short term and long term implementation plan
Devise a communication plan for your community where you announce that you're now available in social media spaces
Consider linking to your social media activities from your main web site
Stick to your commitments, but be ready to be flexible and make adjustments as you encounter successes and challenges along the way
Remember that we're here to support you and ready to help at any time.

Measure Your Successes and Challenges
ROI of Your Social Media Strategy
Define the "R" – what are your expected results?
Define the metrics – what you want to become
Determine what you are benchmarking against
Document your challenges and successes on your chosen tools
Analyze results, glean insight, take action, measure again

Documentation
If you've documented your activities as you progress through these steps, you've got a great baseline starting point to measure:
The impact your social media strategy has in your community
Whether you are able to achieve your original goals
Write down everything that happens in the beginning so you have a multitude of qualitative and quantitative results to analyze

Evaluation
In the beginning, give yourself room to learn and gain insight before you tie yourself to a traditional ROI analysis
Adopt a "listen, learn, adapt" measurement strategy
After you've tried your strategy for a while, ask yourself what you've learned and how you can improve for the next iteration or try.

ROI Resources
Beth Kanter Social Media Metrics and ROI for nonprofits
Katie Paine Social Media Measurement Blog
David Armano
Send your links and measurement data to national
You're doing it! You're really doing it!
Make sure we know what you're up to so we can toot your horn from a national platform
We strive to be a leader in how nonprofits utilize the social web – you all are a huge part of this goal so don't be shy about sharing with us
Together, we are bringing the mission of the American Red Cross into the 21st Century – Congratulations!

Social Media Tools: Blogging

Evaluate whether blogging is right for your Red Cross unit

– You'll need a handful of employees and volunteers who are willing to share their personal Red Cross stories regularly. They don't have to be (and shouldn't be) professional writers, just good story tellers. They also need to have good judgment and willing to uphold the good name and reputation of the Red Cross online.
– You'll need enough capacity to commit to updating your blog regularly (at least once every few days)
– You'll need one or more people to act as editors or keepers of the blog, making sure your contributors update regularly or otherwise providing content
– Explore content that works
– Be creative: [example]
– Engage your audience – invite readers to get involved by posing questions or inviting them to share photos and personal stories
– Tell important stories [example]
– Share your process – how your chapter carries out the mission
– Share successes and challenges
– Be impactful: action oriented posts
– Link to interesting local news
– Find your niche
– Be a subject matter expert
– Be conversational – write like you'd talk to your neighbor
– Feel free to use the first person

One small Alabama chapter, Covington County, uses a blog as their web presence. This is something you might consider if you have a small chapter. It's free and easy to update with multimedia content.

Follow these technical requirements

Wordpress platform

Use the Wordpress blogging platform-it's FREE!

We recommend using the Digg 3 Wordpress theme

Name

Call your blog a blog

We know there's a desire to have a clever blog name, but 500 different clever Red Cross blog names dilutes our brand. Keep it simple.

Masthead (header)

Show some creativity with your header

Please follow brand standards

Please use your chapter lockup or otherwise state the name and location of your chapter/ blood region in your header

Learn from these excellent local Red Cross examples:
Oregon Trail Chapter
Greater Chicago
St. Louis

Social Media Tools: Facebook Page
More than 200 million people are now on Facebook, making it a prime opportunity to offer Red Cross services to a wide audience. We hope to achieve the following with our collective Facebook presence:
– provide information to help people prevent, prepare for, and respond to emergencies
– mobilize our existing volunteers
– inspire new volunteers and donors
– provide an engagement point for supporters
We encourage you to create a personal Facebook account before you create a presence for your chapter or blood unit. It's important to take this step so you understand how the platform works, how the culture works, and how you can be effective.
No matter how you choose to use Facebook for your local Red Cross unit, please remember to follow the fundamental principles and remember that we are a 501(c)(3) nonprofit so your chapter must not join any political or religious advocacy groups, pages, or causes.

Background Information
Pages work just like personal profiles.
– you can make friends
– you can update your status
– you can upload videos, photos, and articles
– you can create events

Decide if a Facebook is right for your chapter/blood region

Is your local audience on Facebook?
Do a little research (search your area within Facebook)
Ask your constituents if they use Facebook

Decide whether you have the time to update your page with valuable content?
If you choose to launch a Facebook page, you'll need to update it daily
You'll need someone to be responsible for your page and make sure they have a few minutes each day to concentrate on updating it

Determine whether you have the capacity or desire to interact with your fans on a daily basis here?

Not only will you need to update your status, post news items, and offer other types of timely content on your page, you'll need to acknowledge and engage your fans here each day. Please assign someone to be responsible for these activities

Determine whether you can offer local content focused on your local stakeholders? Please list your local events, volunteer opportunities, classes, and mission-related news in your area.
Share it with people who care about you.
Set out a clear goal that your Facebook page will help you achieve

If you can answer yes to all of the above questions, you are ready to set up a Facebook page.

If you can't answer yes to all of the above questions, please join our national page and let your stakeholders know they can find Red Cross there.

What are the rules?
Name your page after your chapter name or blood region name
Use your chapter lockup or otherwise identify the name and location of your chapter or blood region in your profile image
Please host only 1 Facebook page. Below we'll explore ways you can highlight all you do and your action items with Causes.

Social Media Tools: Facebook Cause

Background Information

Causes are basically online fundraisers
You can set up multiple causes for your campaigns or current issues
Since we all share a single EIN number, the cause you create will benefit American National Red Cross.

Is a Facebook Cause right for you?
Don't get too excited. You're probably not going to overflow the coffers with a Cause, but you might just be able to get your passionate supporters to carry your campaign messages for you.

How to create an effective cause
– Get the name right: the name of your cause should use an active verb and grab attention, like, "Fight the Malaria Bite!" Causes is where you can show some creativity and get people passionate about what you do rather than your official name
– Turn your cause into a campaign: Set an achievable goal – like raising $1,000 – and find a creative way to engage people to invite their friends. The "Power of 10" campaign asked 10 people to invite 10 other people to send $10 each.

- You can strive to always have a fundraiser up on Causes in addition to any generic fan page you may have set up for your chapter or blood region.
- Consider an incentive, like a drawing to attend a free CPR class, a free downloadable CD, etc.
- Use the announcements feature and keep followers in close touch. Make the content different each time (and short)
- Engage your super users. Keep them encouraged and make sure you acknowledge their work.
- Don't be afraid to try different campaigns here. If one idea doesn't work very well, shut it down and try something different!

Tools: Flickr

Background Information
Flickr is a photo sharing website that allows you to post digital pictures publicly. You can tag and categorize them so they're easy to find.

Set up a personal account first
We encourage you to set up a personal Flickr account so that you understand how awesome Flickr is.
Decide for yourself how you'd like to present yourself publicly. For example, if you don't want photos of your children to be accessible to everyone, post them only for friends & family or not at all. Otherwise, have fun and show your personality!
You are welcome to post photos you have taken for or about the American Red Cross to your personal photo stream, and we encourage you to add these photos to our group.
Your local chapter may also have a Flickr group. You'll want to add appropriate photos there, too.
Participate or start Red Cross discussions in the comments of the group.

Is a Flickr photostream right for your chapter/blood region?
Photos are a powerful way to tell your story.
Do you have an open mind about sharing your photos with the public?
Will you be happy if your local news outlets use your photos?
Do you have the ability to obtain releases for the photos you post online?

Is a Flickr group right for you?
A group is a place where your supporters can add their own photos.
Do you have offline events where people take photos? If so, Flickr is a great way to invite these people to contribute to your chapter/blood region. Ask them to add their photos to your group.
Do you have the capacity to manage and support a Flickr group? We estimate this takes a few minutes each day.

How to set up a Flickr account:
Directions for creating a Flickr account
First, upload your digital photos to your computer and store them wherever you normally would.
Go to http://www.flickr.com
Click "sign up"
Register. Please use your chapter or blood region name
Go to the page marked "You."
Click on "Upload Photos"
Find the photos you want to share on your hard drive
Tag the photos: American Red Cross and any additional tags (or keywords) you wish to identify your work
Directions for creating a Flickr group:
Sign in to Flickr
Click "Groups"
Click "Create a new group"
Follow the step-by-step guide to create a group for your needs
Directions for adding your photos to your group:
Go to your group's URL
Click "Join this group"
Go back to your photos
Click on the photo you wish to add to the group
On top of the photo you will see a button that says, "Send to Group" – click that.
You should see the name of your group in a pop-up window – click it
You're done! You've added your photo to the pool. Congratulations!

What are the rules?

Profile Image
As with all social media tools, we stress that you use your chapter lockup or other image clearly identifying your location and name

Account Name
As with all social media tools, please choose a username that clearly states who you are. For example, "Chicago Red Cross."

Tools: YouTube

Is a YouTube channel right for you?
Do you create video often?
Do you have events that can be captured by your employees and volunteers on digital and/ or flip cameras?

Do you have creative ideas to tell your story?
What kinds of videos work on YouTube?
Reach out: YouTube is an interactive space. Post videos, get a 2 way dialogue going and then stay in the conversation.
Ask questions
Make statements
Call people to action
Give people a chance to get involved in your work
Partner up: find your local partners on YouTube and exchange ideas and cross-promote each other's work
Keep your content fresh: a steady stream of content will keep your viewers engaged.
Your subscribers will be notified each time you upload a new video
Try developing a series of episodic videos to hook people in and then keep them coming back for more
Spread your message: YouTube is built for sharing.
Embed your videos on your other online sites.
Pass your links to your supporters
Be genuine: your videos don't have to be perfect.
Authenticity speaks volumes
This is your chance to have a visual conversation on the issues you care about, so be yourself
Have fun and experiment with different types of content

How to get started:
Visit http://www.youtube.com/nonprofits to apply for a nonprofit channel

What are the rules?
Naming your account: Please choose a name that clearly states your location and chapter or blood region name
Profile image: Please use your chapter lockup or otherwise clearly identifying image that adheres to brand standards
Channel customization: please adhere to brand standards when choosing the look and feel for your channel.

Tools: Twitter

What is Twitter?
Twitter asks the question What are you doing? and millions of people answer in 140 characters or less.

Personal Account
We recommend setting up a personal Twitter account and using it for at least a month before creating your chapter or blood region strategy.

While you're welcome to talk about your Red Cross work on your personal account in accordance with the online communications guidelines, please don't Red Cross "brand" your personal account unless it's part of your overall Twitter strategy. For example don't use a Twitter name such as "RedcrossBob" or "ARCJane" for your personal account.

Is Twitter right for my chapter/blood region?
Are you ready to offer mission-based value to your local supporters?
Have you read the entirety of this article and its supplemental links?
Do you have at least one person dedicated to spending a few minutes per day tweeting, engaging and responding to supporters?

What works on Twitter?
Lots of stuff works. Here are a few examples of chapters we think are doing a bang up job of providing valuable information to people who want it:
– Tampa Red Cross
– Southeastern Wisconsin Red Cross
– Hawaii Red Cross

What are the rules?
Naming your Twitter account:
Choose a name that clearly indicates your local affiliation.
Keep your name as short as possible. You only have 140 characters to type, so the less your name takes up, the better for retweeting.

Your profile image
Twitter's image machine is tiny. It's difficult to adhere to brand standards on this one, but you must! If you're having trouble, please contact us at national and we'll help you devise an appropriate image

Your Twitter design
You have the flexibility to design a background image for your Twitter account. Please follow brand standards if you choose to do this.

Audible.de

Audible ist einer der führenden Anbieter von Hörbuch-Downloads. Derzeit stehen nach Unternehmensangaben mehr als 40.000 Titel in fünf Sprachen von über 800 Verlagen zur Verfügung – darunter die größte Auswahl an ungekürzten Hörbüchern. Audible ist weltweit exklusiver Hörbuch-Partner des Apple iTunes Store.

Audible.de hat seine Social-Media-Richtlinien auf http://www.slideshare.net/Audible/social-media-richtlinien-von-audiblede veröffentlicht.

Social-Media-Richtlinien – Audible.de

Als Social Media werden Plattformen im Internet bezeichnet, auf denen man sich als Person bewegt und in Austausch mit anderen treten kann.

Wir beteiligen uns bereits heute als Privatpersonen, Mitarbeiter und als Unternehmen im Internet an Gesprächen rund um die Welt der Hörbücher. Wir verstärken unser Engagement als Unternehmen aktiv, speziell auf Facebook & Twitter. Wir rufen zusätzlich einen Blog ins Leben, um unser Wissen und unsere Freude an Hörbüchern zu teilen, weiterzugeben und von anderen hörbuchbegeisterten Menschen zu lernen.

Die Beteiligung an diesen Gesprächen soll in erster Linie Transparenz gegenüber unseren Kunden, Geschäftspartnern, Interessierten und Hörbuchfans schaffen. Wir wollen Menschen durch unsere Leidenschaft für Hörbücher begeistern. Das Zusammenbringen von Hörbuchfans und die Teilnahme an den Gesprächen wollen wir lernen, um unsere Arbeit, unser Angebot und unseren Service zu verbessern.

Für unsere Aktivitäten als Unternehmen und als einzelner Mitarbeiter von Audible.de haben wir Richtlinien verfasst, die uns allen die Kommunikation im Internet erleichtern sollen. Die Kommunikation im Internet ist mit persönlicher, direkter Kommunikation gleichzustellen: Wir halten uns bei einem Telefonat mit einem Geschäftspartner, einer E-Mail an einen Kunden oder einem Gespräch mit einem Freund an meist ungeschriebene Regeln. Die Social-Media-Richtlinien gelten als ebensolche Regeln für den öffentlichen Austausch im Internet.

Die Teilnahme am Austausch im Internet ist freiwillig, aber wir wollen alle Mitarbeiter ausdrücklich unterstützen, sich sowohl privat als auch als Mitarbeiter von Audible.de im Netz zu bewegen, zu bloggen, zu twittern oder durch andere Plattformen an Gesprächen teilzunehmen.

1. Relevanz
Im Austausch mit anderen Hörbuchliebhabern bieten wir immer einen Mehrwert. Wir geben den Gesprächsteilnehmern mehr Einblicke und Hintergründe in die Hörbuchwelt bei Audible. de und nutzen dafür alle uns zur Verfügung stehenden Möglichkeiten. Dafür können Verweise auf Personen, Veranstaltungen oder Internetseiten zu Hilfe genommen werden. Unsere subjektiven Meinungen sind ausdrücklich erwünscht.

2. Respekt
Die Meinung jedes Gesprächsteilnehmers ist zu respektieren. Wir wollen niemandem unsere Meinung aufzwingen, machen uns über niemanden lustig oder beleidigen jemanden. Stimmen wir nicht mit der Meinung eines Gesprächsteilnehmers überein, ist eine wertschätzende Diskussion ausdrücklich erwünscht. Jeder Austausch geschieht auf Augenhöhe.

3. Spaß
Wir verlieren nie unseren Humor. Wir haben Spaß, wenn wir uns mit anderen Menschen austauschen.

4. Transparenz
Wenn wir unsere Meinung als Mitarbeiter von Audible.de vertreten, dann machen wir uns als Mitarbeiter deutlich kenntlich. Es ist wichtig für jeden zu wissen, welchen Hintergrund die anderen Teilnehmer haben, um Aussagen einordnen zu können.

5. Schnelligkeit
Wenn wir uns in ein Gespräch einbringen, reagieren wir zeitnah auf Reaktionen von anderen Gesprächsteilnehmern.

6. Gelassenheit
In Gesprächen im Internet geht es oft kontrovers zu. Jeder kann seine Meinung vertreten. Diese muss nicht immer positiv sein. Schriftlich formuliert hören sich Standpunkte oft aggressiver an, als sie in Wirklichkeit gemeint sind. Egal wie hitzig eine Diskussion von Gesprächsteilnehmern geführt wird, lautet unsere Devise: cool bleiben, Lösungen anbieten und nie den Humor verlieren.

7. Sicherheit
Das Internet erinnert sich an fast alles. Also bringen wir uns nicht in Verlegenheit. Im Zweifel stellt man sich folgende Frage: „Würde ich das, was ich hier schreibe, auch in einem Gespräch zu meinen Eltern sagen?"

8. Verbindlichkeit
Informationen, die wir aufgrund von Unternehmensrichtlinien bisher nicht kommuniziert haben, besprechen wir auch nicht im Internet.

9. Ansprechpartner
Wer über diese Richtlinien hinausgehende Fragen hat, kann sich jederzeit an Paul Fritze oder Silvia Jonas wenden. Ihr wisst ja, wo Ihr uns findet.

Australian Broadcasting Corporation (ABC)
ABC ist der öffentlich-rechtliche Rundfunk Australiens. Er produziert sowohl nationale als auch regionale Radio- und TV-Programme und bietet darüber hinaus verschiedene Online-Services.
Die Australian Broadcasting Corporation's social media policy wird zitiert nach: http://www. socialmedia.biz/social-media-policies/australian-broadcasting-corporations-social-media-policy/ und ist bemerkenswert für ihre Kürze und Prägnanz:

1. Do not mix the professional and the personal in ways likely to bring the ABC into disrepute.
2. Do not undermine your effectiveness at work.
3. Do not imply ABC endorsement of your personal views.
4. Do not disclose confidential information obtained through work.

Basecom

Basecom ist eine deutsche Online-Agentur mit dem Fokus auf Online-Communities, d. h. das Unternehmen betreibt selbst Communities und liefert auch Software für den Betrieb von Online-Communities an Unternehmen.

Die Sozial Media Policy von Basecom „11 Kommunikationsrichtlinien" wurde zitiert nach http://www.community-management.de/2009/09/social-media-guidelines-best-practise-beispiel-basecom/

Die 11 Kommunikationsrichtlinien

1. Sprich dich aus ...
Nimm an der Internet-Community teil und nutze sie! Sei aktiv und tausche dich mit anderen aus, teile deine Gedanken und lass dich von anderen inspirieren. Die freiwilligen Mitarbeiter und am Produkt interessierten Nutzer sind auf deine Ansichten gespannt.

2. ... aber nicht zu allem
Bitte achte penibel darauf, Geheimnisse geheim und Internas intern zu belassen (z. B. Neu-entwicklungen und Finanzzahlen). Wenn wir ein Produkt offiziell ankündigen, darf darüber natürlich öffentlich geredet werden. Um rechtliche Belange und Presseanfragen sollten sich jedoch nur die zuständigen Mitarbeiter kümmern.

3. Du bist Profi
Professionalität und Höflichkeit im Umgang mit deinen Gesprächspartnern sind für dich eine Selbstverständlichkeit. Wen du respektvoll behandelst, der wird dir denselben Respekt entgegenbringen.

4. Gesunder Menschenverstand
Manche Menschen haben von Respekt noch nicht viel gehört: Aber lass dich bitte nicht provozieren und provoziere selber auch nicht! Provokationen, die du als Teammitglied von Nutzern bekommst, richten sich gegen das Produkt, nicht gegen dich persönlich. Bleib cool und sachlich.

5. Unsere Freunde sind deine Freunde
Auch wenn du das Gefühl hast, dass manche Partner und Kunden dich nur nerven wollen, und du dich über sie ärgerst: Tu das bitte niemals in der Öffentlichkeit! Unsere Geschäfts-partner und vor allem unsere Kunden sind wichtig – ohne sie geht gar nichts. Beachte dies in allen deinen Veröffentlichungen.

6. Unser Produkt ist dein Produkt
Du musst nicht alles an unseren Produkten mögen, aber du musst nach außen voll dahin-terstehen. Wenn dir etwas missfällt, dann sprich es unbedingt intern an – Verbesserungsvor-schläge sind ausdrücklich erwünscht!

7. Du bist das Team!

Wo auch immer du unterwegs bist, Außenstehende werden dich zuerst als Teammitglied ansehen. Sei dir dessen bei deinen Einträgen bewusst. Mache deutlich, wenn du als Privatperson schreibst, behalte aber immer im Hinterkopf, dass der Nutzer dich auch weiterhin als Teammitglied ansehen könnte und wird.

8. Pass auf deine und auf fremde Daten auf

Respektiere den Wunsch deiner Umgebung nach Privatsphäre und gönne sie dir selbst auch. Eine Handynummer im Internet kann einem so manche Nacht versauen.

9. „Vir sprächen deutsh"

Auch wenn man es eigentlich nicht erwähnen muss: Saubere Rechtschreibung und Grammatik machen oft den ganzen Unterschied zwischen einer ernst zu nehmenden und einer zweifelhaften Aussage aus.

10. Es entgleitet dir alles?

Fehler sind menschlich. Wenn du merkst, dass du Mist gebaut hast, stehe dazu. Ändere Einträge nicht einfach unkommentiert, sondern korrigiere deine Fehler proaktiv.

11. Fragen, Fragen, Fragen

Wenn du nicht mehr weiterweißt oder unsicher bist, was du veröffentlichen darfst, rede mit deinem Ansprechpartner in der Abteilung. Hinterfrage auch dich selber vor jedem Absenden noch einmal und lese das Geschriebene erneut durch. Ein Text sollte dir keine Bauchschmerzen machen oder Zweifel aufkommen lassen.

BBC

Im Rahmen seiner Editorial Guidelines (http://www.bbc.co.uk/guidelines/editorialguidelines/guidance) veröffentlicht der öffentlich-rechtliche Rundfunkanbieter des Vereinigten Königreichs auch mehrere Richtlinien, die Social Media betreffen und detaillierte Regelungen und Verhaltensanweisungen enthalten. Diese sind damit praktisch der Gegenentwurf zu den Richtlinien der australischen Kollegen (Hinweis: Regelungen deutscher Rundfunkanbieter konnten – auch auf Anfrage – nicht bis Redaktionsschluss bereitgestellt werden, daher wird hier auf ABC und BBC referenziert).

Zu den Regelungen der BBC zählen:
- Social Me Networking, Microblogs and Other Third Party Websites: BBC Use (http://www. bbc.co.uk/guidelines/editorialguidelines/page/guidance-blogs-bbc-summary)
- Social Me Networking, Microblogs and Other Third Party Websites: Personal Use
- Social Media and Third Party Websites: Use of Pictures from

Social Me Networking, Microblogs and Other Third Party Websites: BBC Use – Summary of Main Points

- It should be clear to users whether a site is a "BBC" page or a "personal" page.

- The overall parameters, purpose and benchmarks of any project should be discussed with the relevant Interactive Editor or senior editorial figure, as well as the relevant Head of Marketing.
- You may put BBC branding on a third party site, but the associated content should bring credit to the brand.
- When the BBC joins a third party site, we should "go with the grain" and not alienate existing users by giving the impression of seeking to impose ourselves on them and their space.
- Before a site/profile/page is launched, you should decide what level of engagement you want, what resources you need to achieve it and over what time-frame.
- We should not seek to duplicate measures of protection and intervention already established by a particular social networking site. There will, however, be times when the BBC may implement "light touch" intervention.
- You should check online "friends" before approving them and review their comments regularly once approved.
- We should not give users the impression that a particular site will have a longer life than is planned. In some circumstances, it may be appropriate to "hand over" a BBC page to an online community.
- Any proposal to use a chat room, message board, microblog or social networking site to find contributors must be referred to the relevant Divisional representative or, for indies, to the Commissioning Editor.
- When forwarding or "retweeting" messages, care should be taken that it does not appear that the BBC is endorsing a particular opinion.
- When on social media, you should always link back to BBC Online, to encourage users to consume more BBC content.
- Sites aimed at teens should be suitable for that audience. If in doubt, the Home Office Task Force Good Practice Guidance on Social Networking may be consulted.
- We should be sensitive to the minimum age requirements on different social networking sites. This is often set at 13.
- Advertisements on BBC-branded social networking pages should be monitored to check that they are appropriate.
- Before uploading BBC material onto a social networking site, you should make sure that you are aware of, and comfortable with, the site's own terms and conditions.
- The closure or mothballing of a site should be carefully managed to ensure that it does not remain BBC-branded but neglected.

Social Me Networking, Microblogs and Other Third Party Websites: Personal Use – Summary of Main Points

- The personal use of the internet by BBC staff must be tempered by an awareness of the potential conflicts that may arise.
- There should be a clear division between "BBC" pages and "personal" pages.
- On Social Networking sites, you should be mindful that the information you disclose does not bring the BBC into disrepute.

– For example, editorial staff should not indicate their political allegiance. Non-editorial staff should make their role clear if they wish to engage in political activity
– It may not be appropriate to share BBC-related photographs, comments and videos. Offensive comment about BBC colleagues may be deemed a disciplinary offence
– BBC staff are free to edit online encyclopaedias (such as Wikipedia) but should be transparent about doing so. You may respond to legitimate criticism of the BBC but not remove it
– Blogs, microblogs and other personal websites which do not identify the author as a BBC employee, do not discuss the BBC and are purely personal would fall outside this guidance
– New and existing blogs, microblogs and other personal websites which do identify the author as a BBC employee should be discussed with your line manager to ensure that due impartiality and confidentiality is maintained.

Social Media and Third Party Websites: Use of Pictures from

– Don't assume that pictures from the internet show what or who they purport to show – verify them to ensure due accuracy.
– The ease of availability of pictures on social media and personal websites does not remove our responsibility to consider the sensitivities in using them, balancing these with any public interest the pictures may serve.
– What was the original intention in publication? The publication of a picture on a personal website or social networking site does not necessarily mean the owner of that picture intended it to be available for all purposes and circumstances – or understood that it could be.
– Is it likely that the individuals in the picture will have consented, either explicitly or tacitly, to its publication and public accessibility on the internet?
– We have a responsibility to consider the impact our re-use of a picture to a much wider audience may have on those in the picture, their family or firends – particularly when they are grieving or distressed.
– We should take care that photos taken from social media and personal websites do not assume another, possibly incorrect, meaning or imply unfounded suggestions when lifted from those websites and shown in the context of a particular news story.
– When pictures or video show illegal/anti-social activity, we should avoid becoming simply a stage on which lawbreakers can perform.
– The re-use of material from the internet can raise legal issues of privacy and copyright. Advice is available from BBC Lawyers.

Introduction

New technology has presented new opportunities for journalists and programme makers, offering an unprecedented ease of access to potential content. But it also presents a range of new challenges: we seek to meet the demands and expectations of audiences who now have the ability to seek out a similar range of content directly on the internet as and when it becomes of interest – whilst simultaneously paying due regard to any privacy or other ethical considerations if we choose to re-publish that content to large audiences.

Most notably, the internet has provided a source of pictures of private individuals that can be imported into news coverage, as and when those individuals become involved in news events. Where in the past, journalists might have had to visit friends and relatives to request photographs of those who become the subject of news stories, a trawl of social networking sites such as Facebook and Myspace, or other personal websites, can frequently provide a ready source of such pictures.

However, ease of availability of pictures does not remove our responsibility to consider the sensitivities in using them.

The growth of social media has undoubtedly created a generation of people who are willing to make personal information about themselves available online, and much of that information may be considered to have been placed in the public domain – but the fact that material has been placed in the public domain does not necessarily give us the right to exploit its existence, disregarding the consequences.

Whilst some in the media might argue that, once an individual has begun a declarative lifestyle, opening the door to their personal lives by putting private information into the public domain of the internet, they cannot expect to be able to set limits on that, people making content for the BBC should ask themselves whether a door that is only ajar can justifiably be pushed further open by the media.

Despite the fact that a generation of primarily younger people are sharing personal information and pictures on line, there is research that suggests they still place a high value on privacy. And it should be considered that the use of social media content by the BBC often brings that content to a much wider public than a personal website or social media page that would only be found with very specific search criteria.

Consequently, when the opportunity arises to use pictures from social media and personal websites, without first seeking the consent of those concerned, we should pay due regard to the context in which it was originally made available online and media responsibilities in its re-use – balancing our considerations with any public interest the pictures may serve. Inevitably, this will require a decision on re-use to be made on a case-by-case basis, but the checklist in this guidance can help programme makers and content producers to think through the relevant issues.

Checklist

Authenticate
Like much user content, accuracy is always a concern. Don't assume that pictures show what or who they purport to show – verify them to ensure due accuracy.

User or Publisher Intentions

Consider the original intention in publication. The publication of a picture on a personal website or social networking site does not necessarily mean the owner of that picture intended it to be available for all purposes and circumstances – or understood that it could be.

There are many people who take advantage of the internet and social networking to lead a declarative lifestyle, attempting to make aspects of their life open to the widest possible audience. However, for many others, social media tools are just an effective means of sharing personal content with a relatively small group of friends or family – material that makes no attempt to be discovered in the wealth of social media content online and is, effectively, hidden in the open. The context in which the pictures are displayed, including the surrounding content, can often provide a good clue to the publisher's original intentions.

However, whilst it is advisable to give thought to the publisher's intentions, that must be balanced against the responsibility of the user to ensure appropriate levels of security are applied to material they would not want to be republished elsewhere (for example, by broadcasters or newspapers). As privacy settings become more sophisticated and awareness of how to use them increases, along with understanding of the potential consequences of leaving content in a public space, the more the availability of the content may be considered a matter of the user's responsibility.

Consent

Whose site does the picture appear on? If the picture features one or more individual who is not the owner/user of the site (or is published by an unknown uses on a video sharing sites such as YouTube), we should consider whether the individuals in the picture are likely to have consented – either explicitly or tacitly – to its publication and public accessibility on the internet.

Impact of Re-use

A picture available without meaningful restrictions on a website may be considered to be in the public domain and the media may consider that it has the right to exploit it – but that does not always make it the right thing to do. We have a responsibility to consider the impact our re-use to a much wider audience may have on those in the picture, their family or friends – particularly when they are grieving or distressed. For example, it may be inappropriate to use a picture from a social networking site of a particularly happy event (such as a wedding) or a favourite family picture if it is to be associated with reporting of a tragic event. Neutral pictures may be more acceptable to friends and relatives.

Is the Re-use Misleading?

We should take care with the choice of photos taken from social media and personal websites so that they do not assume another, possibly incorrect, meaning when lifted from those websites and shown in the context of a particular news story. Changing the context in which the pictures are seen may sometimes mislead the audience by implying unfounded suggestions and could be unfair to those in the pictures – for example, pictures of an individual laughing when used in connection with a tragic event, or pictures of someone looking particularly vampish at a fancy dress party when used in connection with reports of a sex attack.

Badge of Honour

When pictures or video is being lifted from social networking sites to illustrate either specific or general illegal/anti-social behaviour, we should take care that our broadcasting it to a much wider audience does not become a 'badge of honour' for the perpetrators. We should ensure that the use of the material achieves a public interest purpose and avoid becoming simply a stage on which lawbreakers can perform.

Legal Issues

The re-use of material from the internet can raise legal issues of privacy and copyright. A strong public interest reason for using a photograph can help justify re-use without permission, but you should not automatically assume that pictures or video you are seeking to include can be used under 'fair dealing'. Advice is available from BBC Lawyers.

Die Guidelines für „BBC use" im Langtext:

Introduction
Scope
Hybrid Sites
Editorial Purpose
Use of the BBC Brand
Content Syndication
Social Media Representatives
Tone of Voice
Level of Engagement
Presumption Against Taking Over Responsibility on Third Party Sites
Friends
Working with the Community
Advertising for Contributors
Content Labelling
Blogs and Microblogs
Linking Strategy
Teens
Children
Advertising
Legal and Rights Issues
Site Closure
Introduction

This guidance is intended to help BBC producers implement the BBC Social Media strategy on social networking and microblogging sites. The strategy relies on the

BBC engaging with users on the sites where they go, in the conversations they are having, off bbc.co.uk as much as on bbc.co.uk, in part so that users who may consume little or no BBC content can discover for themselves and enjoy more of what we have to offer.

It assumes that, within this framework for engagement, a flexible approach is necessary, as social networking and microblogging sites continue to evolve and as we learn what approaches work best in different places.

The guidance complements the BBC Social Media strategy principles, including the following:
– With conversations, participate online: don't "broadcast" messages to users
– Don't bring the BBC into disrepute
– With moderation, only police where we have to; trust our users where we don't
– Be open and transparent in our social media dealings

Scope
This guidance is primarily designed to cover informal, non-contractual BBC presences on third party social networking and microblogging sites. These are most likely to be BBC-branded but they may simply be set up by the BBC to pursue our public purposes. The guidance is not primarily designed to cover formal, contractual BBC partnerships on social networking sites (e.g. YouTube), although some of the guidance will be relevant and useful in these circumstances.

It is not intended to apply to sites which are set up and run by users to talk about BBC content or talent.

Where the BBC already has a formal partnership, producers should normally see if the available BBC channel fits their editorial purpose before creating their own site.

Hybrid Sites
It should be clear to users whether the site they are interacting with is a BBC page run by the BBC for BBC purposes or whether this is a personal page run by an individual for their own purposes.

We should avoid creating or endorsing "hybrid" sites which contain elements of both and which are likely to cause confusion, editorial problems and brand damage. For example, a presenter's personal profile should not have a URL or username or avatar which contains a BBC brand or programme name.

A successful BBC microblog is likely to be personal in tone but it must not contain any personal views which would damage the BBC's reputation, for example over impartiality.

For guidance on personal sites of BBC staff and BBC talent, including blogs and microblogs, see the guidance note on Personal use of Social Networking and Other Third Party Websites.

(See Editorial Policy Guidance: Personal Use of Social Networking and Other Third Party Websites)

Editorial Purpose
Discuss what you want to do first with the relevant Interactive Editor or senior editorial figure, and the relevant Head of Marketing.

Key questions include:
– What is the editorial purpose? How does this fit in with your overall editorial and marketing strategy?
– Could you achieve the same effect or better on bbc.co.uk?
– Does the site appeal to a key demographic not available via bbc.co.uk? Is this the right site to engage with your audiences?
– Does anything similar already exist? If it does, would working with an existing presence be better for users and for the BBC?
– What commitment are you willing to make to the site? Do you have the resources you need to keep it refreshed and relevant? For how long?
– What is your exit strategy?
– How will you measure success? Try to set a target and a review point before you launch;
– Is your overall investment in time and/or money likely to be worth the benefit the offshore presence is likely to deliver?
– The relevant Interactive Editor/senior editorial figure will nominate a named editorial owner for the page. They will be responsible for maintaining and refreshing it;
– The relevant Social Media representative for each Division will have overall responsibility for keeping a record of any informal, non-contractual pages/profiles/sites set up by their teams on third party social networking sites. Formal, contractual BBC partnerships may be dealt with separately.

Use of the BBC Brand
You can put the brand/logo of your network, programme or event on a third party site. This has the advantage of transparency. Remember that a BBC logo is intended to give the impression that this is a genuine, authorised, BBC presence so the nature of that presence should reflect credit on the brand.
– Any logos should, where possible, contain links back to the relevant page on BBC Online. If this cannot be done technically, the link should be as close as possible to the logo;
– If you have a query about the correct use of the BBC's brands, ask the relevant Head of Marketing who may consult the Head of Brand Guardianship. If you do not use a logo, it should be clear to users that they are interacting with a BBC page run by the BBC.

Content Syndication
This guidance does not deal with what forms of content you can upload to your page/profile. For advice in this area, see the Syndication Guidelines. If in doubt, refer to Controller, Business Development, FM&T.

Social Media Representatives
New kinds of informal activity on third party sites will need to be discussed with the relevant Division's Social Media Representative. Interactive Editors/senior editorial figures should keep their Divisional Representatives informed of all relevant activity.

One reason for this is to manage risk; another is to share valuable new experience across the Divisions.

Tone of Voice
We should be sensitive to the expectations of existing users of the specific site. If we add a BBC presence, we are joining their site rather than the opposite. Users are likely to feel that they already have a significant stake in it. When adding an informal

BBC presence, we should "go with the grain" and be sensitive to user customs and conventions to avoid giving the impression that the BBC is imposing itself on them and their space.

For example, we should respect the fact that users on site X are not our users: they are not bound by the same Terms of Use and House Rules as we apply on BBC Online. Attempts to enforce our standard community rules on third party sites may lead to resentment, criticism and in some cases outright hostility to the BBC's presence.

This is not to say that behaviour likely to cause extreme offence, for example racist insults, should be tolerated by the BBC on a BBC-branded space on a social networking site. It should not. Neither should behaviour which is clearly likely to put a child or teenager at substantial risk of significant harm. But where we do decide to intervene, we will normally need to do so with a light touch, sensitive to different expectations and a different context from BBC Online.

Level of Engagement
Before the page/profile/site is launched, you will need to decide with the relevant Interactive Editor/senior editorial figure what level of engagement you want, what resources you will need to achieve it and over what period of time.

For example, a page which advertises forthcoming editions of a TV programme with clips and some background information will need regular refreshing. But you may want to offer a higher level of user engagement on the BBC-branded space.

For example,
— Will users be able to upload still, audio or video contributions? (See also Legal and Rights Issues below)
— Will users be able to add their own text comments?

If so,
— How do you plan to engage with the community? Will you offer a host presence, for example, to answer a question about when the next series is starting?
— How do you plan to protect the BBC brand? Will you need to consider some additional moderation?
— Do you have the necessary resources to do the job properly?

Presumption Against Taking Over Responsibility on Third Party Sites

The responsibility for measures of protection and intervention lies first with the social networking site itself. We should never set out to duplicate measures of protection and intervention which the social networking site already takes e.g. against illegal or against harmful and offensive content, whether by using its own staff or by working with the community to alert them to breaches of the site's terms and conditions.

In practice, different social networking sites offer different models of intervention in different areas.

For example, the photo sharing site Flickr has worked with its users to moderate the most offensive images itself quite effectively. But it does not appear to offer its own user-facing mechanism for removing the most offensive user comments. Instead, Flickr gives the right to moderate and comment on user text comments to the Administrator of each Group. BBC producers have used this facility to actively host BBC Groups and to remove some comments.

So there are some circumstances where the BBC will need to plan and implement an additional "light touch" intervention, for example to remove comments which are likely to cause extreme offence. We will need to work out how this should be done, who will do it and when. Where necessary, Editorial Policy can advise on a suitable threshold for "light touch" intervention. Recent research suggests that this approach matches audience expectations.

One problem is that while social networking sites may publish clear rules of acceptable behaviour for their users, they are often very reluctant to share much information about how they intervene or to what level. If you are not familiar with how, for example, MySpace, Facebook and Bebo deal in practice with different forms of harmful and illegal content on their sites, ask the Central Communities Team in FM&T.

Friends
You may wish to make "friends" on a third party web page. But remember that approving a "friend" may make other users of a site think they are more trustworthy.

Check all friends carefully before you approve them. Look at their profiles first. If you have any doubts about whether you should approve a friend, discuss it with your Interactive Editor/ senior editorial figure.

Review comments of "friends" regularly and remove (or do not post) any which exceed the appropriate threshold.

If you want to update your list of "friends" with a regular newsletter, make sure they are happy to receive it. Only use the list for activities on the same site or you may be in breach of the Data Protection Act.

If you want to make "friends" with an organisation (e.g. a company or a political campaign), consult your Interactive Editor/senior editorial figure first. Remember that this is likely to give the impression that the BBC is endorsing the organisation.

Once accepted, some group "friends" have changed from an innocuous group into porn or gambling spammers, so these are worth keeping an eye on.

Working with the Community
We should take care not to give users the impression that we are interested in setting up a fully interactive profile or page if that page is then neglected or abandoned after it has achieved a one-off short term purpose. This is particularly true if a community of interest has formed around the page or profile. It may be possible to hand a limited-life BBC page or profile over to the community which has grown around it, after a broadcast-led engagement has come to an end. This needs thinking about before the page is created. It may then become necessary to remove some or all of the BBC branding. It may also be useful to add a disclaimer to the effect that this site was created by the BBC but is now being run by the community.

Advertising for Contributors
Any proposal to use a chat room, message board, microblog or social networking site to find contributors must be referred to the relevant Divisional representative or for independents to the commissioning editor. Each Division will decide the level at which referrals must be made and may do so according to the particular circumstances, taking account of the experience of the BBC person who wishes to make the request, the sensitivity of the subject matter and the medium to be used.

The proposed wording of all written adverts must be referred to the same person.

The main reason for this is that there are risks in advertising for contributors whether using posters or personal adverts in newspapers, specialist publications, or the internet. The people who reply are self-selecting and may seek to appear regularly as "serial guests". We need to screen out those who are unsuitable or dishonest and those prone to exaggeration.

We should only advertise for contributors to factual and factual entertainment programmes as a last resort when other research methods have been exhausted.

When we do use adverts, we must word them carefully to avoid bringing the BBC into disrepute.

It may be appropriate for entertainment programmes to advertise for contestants and audiences. Even then all appropriate checks should be made to screen out unsuitable or untruthful contributors.

Content Labelling
Very strong BBC content, or very strong user generated content inspired by a BBC call to action, may require a short content label. This applies the same principle as on BBC Online that users should be able to take an informed decision about what content they wish to consume before they do so.

Blogs and Microblogs
BBC blogs should be published on BBC Online, and only after discussion with your Divisional Social Media representative. See s.3 and s.6 above.

The BBC does not have its own microblogging platform, so this guidance applies to BBC use of microblogging, for example on Twitter. Divisional representatives will advise.

You may wish to consider forwarding or "retweeting" a selection of a person's microblog entries/posts or "tweets". This is very unlikely to be a problem when you are "retweeting" a colleague's BBC "tweet" or a BBC headline. But in some cases, you will need to consider the risk that "retweeting" of third party content by the BBC may appear to be an endorsement of the original author's point of view.

It may not be enough to write on your BBC microblog's biography page that "retweeting" does not signify endorsement, particularly if the views expressed are about politics or a matter of controversial public policy. Instead you should consider adding your own comment to the "tweet" you have selected, making it clear why you are forwarding it and where you are speaking in your own voice and where you are quoting someone else's.

For personal use of blogs and microblogs, see the Guidance Note on personal use of social networking and other third party websites including blogs, microblogs and personal web-space.

Linking Strategy
The BBC Social Media strategy relies on the BBC engaging with users on the sites where they go, in the conversations they are having, as well as on BBC Online. This is partly so that users who may consume little or no BBC content can discover for themselves more of what we have to offer. So we should always link back to BBC Online. We can then encourage users to consume more BBC content on our site, for example by accessing long form video content on BBC iPlayer.

Links to social networking or microblogging sites should be clearly editorially justifiable, as with any other external link.

On air, we only trail BBC URLs.

On occasion, it may be appropriate to mention on air that there is a BBC presence on a social networking or microblogging site. But we must avoid undue prominence and there would need to be a strong editorial justification for doing so; this would require an active editorial presence from that programme on the site and the editorial justification should be pertinent to that broadcast.

For example, it may be appropriate for a BBC political correspondent to mention their Twitter feed connected to their BBC work during their coverage of a Party Conference. There could be one mention during their weekly programme covering that Party Conference or two mentions during a week of daily programmes covering it. If in any doubt, refer to Editorial Policy first.

Presenters of live chat shows, music and entertainment shows may sometimes refer on air, where editorially justifiable, to their personal microblogging accounts. This is where the account is used as a personal tool by the presenter; it should not be used as a normal or official means of contacting the programme but it can be used to gather instant feedback by the presenter. Presenters should not give out specific urls of their personal accounts on air.

Teens
Some social networking sites attract a significant proportion of teenagers. This makes these sites a very attractive place for the BBC to engage with this hard-to reach age group, which routinely consumes little or no BBC content.

Teenagers clearly do run risks on social networking sites, particularly some 13–15 year olds whose technical knowledge may run ahead of their social skills. They may be at risk from being bullied or from publishing sensitive personal information on their profiles or from treating anonymous online "friends" as if they were real friends and becoming targets for online "grooming".

Where a BBC brand or site is targeting teenagers, particularly 13–15 year olds, on a social networking site:

- The site should be suitable for the likely audience for the relevant BBC brand or programming;
- BBC content and user generated content inspired by a BBC call to action should be suitable for the likely audience on the site.

If you are in doubt about the suitability of the site to engage with younger teenagers, it may be worth asking whether it operates within the Home Office Task Force Good Practice Guidance on Social Networking, which is designed to protect children and young people online.

Divisional Social Media Representatives can offer more information about the likely audience for specific social networking sites. The Central Communities Team in FM&T may also be able to offer advice.

Children

We should be sensitive to the minimum age requirements on different social networking sites – often set at 13. These are intended to prevent users below the minimum age from registering for full membership and then being able to publish online. But they also give a clear indication from the site owner about what the owner considers to be a suitable minimum age for casual visitors, even though the site owner may not be able to enforce this.

We should check minimum ages carefully. If we were to post BBC content specifically designed for 6–12 year olds on a site whose stated minimum age is 13, we would run the risk of appearing to encourage visits by 6–12 year olds to a site where contact and content rules and standards are designed to suit teenagers but not children. This might also give the impression that we were encouraging 6–12 year olds to lie about their age in order to interact with that content.

Once uploaded, content clearly unsuitable for 6–12 year olds could very easily be placed right next to BBC content specifically designed for children – and we would in effect have encouraged 6–12 year olds to go there to see it.

Advertising

Users generally appear to accept that advertisements on areas of BBC-branded social networking pages which are not under our editorial control (e.g. banner ads) are not our responsibility and are not connected with BBC content. But you should keep an eye on the full range of advertisements which appear on BBC-branded pages and you should alert your Interactive Executive/senior editorial figure immediately if clearly inappropriate advertisements for example involving pornography appear on the same pages. For the time being, we should not allow

BBC Online video content uploaded by the BBC to contain pre-roll, mid-roll or postroll advertising if the advertisements are visible from within the UK.

Legal and Rights Issues

Before we upload BBC material or invite users to upload their user generated content to a page on a social networking site, we should make sure that we are aware of, and comfortable with, the site's own terms and conditions. This is because by uploading our content, it is likely that we are agreeing to be bound by its terms.

For example:
- We need to make sure we have the necessary rights to any content we put on third party sites – not only to ensure we do not breach our agreements with rights holders but also because we are likely to be liable to the site itself if we post uncleared material;
- Some sites' terms and conditions covering uploaded content only allow "personal" reuse and do not allow any "commercial" reuse of content or envisage any reuse on radio or TV. If you want to reuse uploaded content on radio or TV, you should first consult Legal and Business Affairs to get the necessary consents;
- Some sites' terms and conditions state that the site is for personal use only and not for "commercial" use – we should be aware that if we use such a site to promote BBC content, we may technically be in breach;
- Some sites will take a pretty broad licence to use BBC content and the BBC trademark; while this may be a necessary risk, BBC content and BBC brands should only be posted for as long as is necessary and be removed once they have achieved their purposes on the site.

In some cases, the BBC has managed to add additional bespoke terms to an informal arrangement, to mitigate risk and facilitate our use of the content. Legal and Business Affairs in FM&T can advise.

Site Closure

It is important to have a clear plan from the start about how long the association between the BBC and the site/profile/page will last. Our presence may be tactical, we may wish to hand the space over to the community or it may be sensible to announce closure to its users and then shut the space down. It is incumbent on the person responsible for our presence to maintain the site or to arrange an exit.

Above all, we should not leave the site BBC branded but neglected, carrying the risk to the brand without exercising any editorial control.

Die Regelungen für Personal Use im Langtext:

Introduction
Basic Principles
Hybrid Sites
Social Networking Sites
Open Access Online Encylopaedias
Blogging and Microblogging

Introduction
The Internet provides a number of benefits in which BBC staff may wish to participate. From rediscovering old school friends on Facebook to keeping up with other people's daily lives on Twitter or helping to maintain open access online encyclopaedias such as Wikipedia.

However, when someone clearly identifies their association with the BBC and/or discusses their work, they are expected to behave appropriately when on the Internet, and in ways that are consistent with the BBC's editorial values and policies.

This editorial guidance note sets out the principles which BBC staff are expected to follow when using the Internet and gives interpretations for current forms of interactivity. It applies to blogs, to microblogs like Twitter and to other personal webspace.

The Internet is a fast moving technology and it is impossible to cover all circumstances. However, the principles set out in this document should always be followed.

The intention of this note is not to stop BBC staff from conducting legitimate activities on the Internet, but serves to flag-up those areas in which conflicts can arise.

Basic Principles
The BBC's reputation for impartiality and objectivity is crucial. The public must be able to trust the integrity of BBC programmes and services. Our audiences need to be confident that the outside activities of our presenters, programme makers and other staff do not undermine the BBC's impartiality or reputation and that editorial decisions are not perceived to be influenced by any commercial or personal interests.

To this end when identified as a BBC staff member or BBC talent, people:
– Should not engage in activities on the Internet which might bring the BBC into disrepute;
– Should act in a transparent manner when altering online sources of information;
– Should not use the Internet in any way to attack or abuse colleagues;
– Should not post derogatory or offensive comments on the Internet.

Even if they are not identified as a BBC staff member, editorial staff and staff in politically sensitive areas should not be seen to support any political party or cause.

Any online activities associated with work for the BBC should be discussed and approved in advance by a line manager.

(Note that 'editorial staff' includes any member of staff who may influence our editorial output from researchers in News and Current Affairs or factual programming to members of the Executive Board. Being 'identified as a BBC staff member' includes at its most obvious, for example, displaying a bbc.co.uk e-mail address or joining the BBC Network on Facebook (which displays the words "British Broadcasting Corporation" after the person's name).

Hybrid Sites
It should be clear to users whether the site they are interacting with is a BBC page run by the BBC for BBC purposes or whether this is a personal page run by an individual for their own purposes.

We should avoid creating or endorsing "hybrid" sites which contain elements of both and which are likely to cause confusion, editorial problems and brand damage. For example, a presenter's personal profile should not have a URL or username or avatar which contains a BBC brand or programme name.

For guidance on BBC use of third party sites, see the separate Guidance note below.
(See Guidance: BBC use of Social Networking and Other Third Party Websites)

Social Networking Sites
Social networking sites provide a great way for people to maintain contact with friends. However, through the open nature of such sites, it is also possible for third parties to collate vast amounts of information.

For example, The Shawshank Redemption was the most popular film amongst the 11,899 members of the BBC network on Facebook in February 2008 and 8 % listed their political views as "liberal". (Note: information from www.facebook.com on 25 February 2008).

All BBC staff should be mindful of the information they disclose on social networking sites. Where they associate themselves with the Corporation (through providing work details or joining a BBC network) they should act in a manner which does not bring the BBC into disrepute.

When a staff member is contacted by the press about posts on their social networking site that relate to the BBC they should talk to their manager before responding. The relevant BBC press office must be consulted.

Political Activities on Social Networking sites
Editorial staff and staff in politically sensitive areas should never indicate a political allegiance on social networking sites, either through profile information or through joining political groups. This is particularly important for all staff in News and Current Affairs, Nations and Regions and factual programming and applies regardless of whether they indicate that they are employed by the BBC or not.
Any rare exception to this must be agreed in advance by a line manager. For instance, it may be appropriate to join Facebook groups related to political causes for reasons of political research. Where this is agreed we should be transparent and should consider how membership of the group can be balanced.
For example, if a Political Correspondent were to join the Facebook group "Labour History" it may also be appropriate also to join "Conservative History" and the equivalents for the

Liberal Democrats and the Nationalists. In such circumstance, the specific post held at the BBC should be given in the work details on the Facebook profile.

Editorial staff and staff in politically sensitive areas should also be careful about joining campaigning groups. They should discuss this in advance with their line manager.

Non-Editorial Staff are free to engage in political activity, in line with the Section 15 of the Editorial Guidelines on Conflicts of Interest. However, on social networking sites, when they identify themselves as BBC staff members they must make clear that they are not a member of editorial staff. This can be achieved by stating the position (or type of position) they hold at the BBC in their work details. If non-Editorial Staff associate themselves with the BBC and do not make clear they have no editorial input then this could give rise to questions about the Corporation's impartiality.

Consideration towards other members of staff when using social networking sites
Social networking sites allow photographs, videos and comments to be shared with thousands of other users. However, it may not be appropriate to share work-related information in this way.

For example, there may be an expectation that photographs taken at a private BBC event will not appear publicly on the Internet, both from those present and perhaps those not at the event. Or the BBC may have objections. Staff should be considerate to their colleague in such circumstance and should not post information when they have been asked not to. They should also remove information about a colleague if that colleague asks them to do so.

Under no circumstance should offensive comments be made about BBC colleagues on the Internet. This may amount to cyber-bullying and could be deemed a disciplinary offence.

Open Access Online Encylopaedias
In the course of BBC work, staff may find errors in online encyclopaedias. If staff members edit online encyclopaedias at work the source of the correction will be recorded as a BBC IP address. The intervention may therefore look as if it comes from the BBC itself. BBC staff should therefore act in a manner that does not bring the BBC into disrepute and should not post derogatory or offensive comments on any online encyclopaedias.

When correcting errors about the BBC, we should be transparent about who we are. We should never remove criticism of the BBC. Instead, we should respond to legitimate criticism. We should not remove derogatory or offensive comments but must report them to the relevant administrators for them to take action.

Before editing an online encyclopaedia entry about the BBC, or any entry which might be deemed a conflict of interest, BBC staff should consult the house rules of the site concerned and, if necessary, ask permission from the relevant wikieditor. They may also need to seek advice from their line manager.

Blogging and Microblogging

Many bloggers, particularly in technical areas, use their personal blogs, and increasingly their microblogs like Twitter, to discuss their BBC work in ways that benefit the BBC, and add to the "industry conversation".

This editorial guidance note is not intended to restrict this, as long as confidential information is not revealed.

Blogs, microblogs or other personal websites which do not identify the blogger as a BBC employee, do not discuss the BBC and are purely about personal matters would normally fall outside this guidance.

Staff members who already have a personal blog, microblog or website which indicates in any way that they work at the BBC should discuss any potential conflicts of interest with their line manager.

Similarly, staff members who want to start blogging or microblogging, and wish to say that they work for the BBC, should discuss any potential conflicts of interest with their line manager.

If a blog makes it clear that the author works for the BBC, it should include a simple and visible disclaimer such as "these are my personal views and not those of the BBC".

Unless there are specific concerns about the nature of their role (for instance because they are a member of editorial staff), staff members are free to talk about BBC programmes and content on their blogs or microblogs. If in doubt, staff members should consult their line manager.

Personal blogs, microblogs and websites should not reveal confidential information about the BBC. This might include aspects of BBC policy or details of internal BBC discussions. If in doubt about what might be confidential, staff members should consult their line manager.

Personal blogs, microblogs and websites should not be used to attack or abuse colleagues. Staff members should respect the privacy and the feelings of others.

Remember also that if they break the law on a blog or microblog (for example by posting something defamatory), they will be personally responsible.

If a staff member thinks something on their blog, microblog or website gives rise to concerns about a conflict of interest, and in particular concerns about impartiality or confidentiality, this must be discussed with their line manager.

If a staff member is offered payment to produce a blog or microblog for a third party this could constitute a conflict of interest and must be discussed with their line manager.

When a staff member is contacted by the press about posts on their blog or tweets on their microblog that relate to the BBC they should talk to their line manager before responding. The relevant BBC press office must be consulted.

Staff members are allowed to update their personal blog or microblog from a BBC computer at work, under the BBC's Acceptable Use Policy for Internet and Email (see here. Link only available to internal BBC users)

Guidance for Managers on Blogging and Microblogging
(Under this Guidance Note, managers in each area will decide what is appropriate).

They should not adopt an unnecessarily restrictive approach. Managers should ensure that any special instructions on blogging or microblogging are reasonable and explained clearly to staff.

Managers should bear in mind concerns about impartiality, confidentiality, conflicts of interest or commercial sensitivity. In some cases individuals may be dealing with matters which are so sensitive that rules may have to be set on what they can and cannot talk about on their personal blog or microblog.

Those involved in editorial or production areas must take particular care to ensure that they do not undermine the integrity or impartiality of the BBC or its output on their blogs or microblogs. For example those involved in News and Current Affairs or factual programming should not advocate a particular position on high profile controversial subjects relevant to their areas.

Managers can consult Section 15 of the Editorial Guidelines on Conflicts of Interest Guidelines and the BBC's Acceptable Use Policy for Internet and Email (see here. Link only available to internal BBC users.)

News and Current Affairs Staff, Blogging and Microblogging
Impartiality is a particular concern for those working in News and Current Affairs. Nothing should appear on their personal blogs or microblogs which undermines the integrity or impartiality of the BBC. For example, News and Current Affairs staff should not:
– advocate support for a particular political party;
– express views for or against any policy which is a matter of current party political debate;
– advocate any particular position on an issue of current public controversy or debate.

If News and Current Affairs staff are in doubt, they should refer immediately to their line manager.

If News and Current Affairs staff are asked to blog or tweet for commercial gain this could constitute a conflict of interest. Managers should consult the Guidance Note on "Off Air Activities for Presenters and Editorial Staff in BBC News, Global News and Nations and Regions".

BGLT – Berchtesgadener Land Tourismus GmbH

Die „Social Media"-Richtlinie der Berchtesgadener Land Tourismus GmbH für Mitarbeiter wurde vom Unternehmen in Form eines PDFs (1 Seite) zur Verfügung gestellt und ist nachfolgend vollständig wiedergegeben.

BGLT-Social-Media-Ziele:

Wir verfolgen im Social-Media-Marketing das Primär-Ziel Kundenbindung: Verjüngung und Bindung bestehender Zielgruppen in den strategischen Produktsäulen Naturerlebnisse und Gesundheit.

Daraus ergeben sich folgende **strategische Sekundärziele:**
- BGLT-Branding, Neukundengewinnung, Verkaufsförderung
- Glaubwürdige, authentische Gäste-Kommunikation; Gäste-Feedback/Marktforschung
- Konzentration auf die wichtigsten Plattformen: BGLT-Blog, Facebook, YouTube, Holidaycheck; Keine Abhängigkeit von nur einer Plattform, der BGLT-Blog ist unsere Social-Media-Zentrale
- Online-Reputation-Management für das BGL und seine Gastgeber (TrustYou, Holidaycheck)
- Social-Media-Vorreiterrolle ausbauen: Im Südbayern-Tourismus die größte Facebook-Fanseite bleiben. Themenführerschaft im Bereich Wandern erreichen.
- Regionsinternes Marketing; Alle BGLT-Mitarbeiter sammeln Erfahrung im Social Marketing; Wissen um Social Media an unsere BGL-Partner weitergeben.

§ 1 Vereinbarungen kennen und beachten
Wie jede aktive Marketingorganisation muss die Berchtesgadener Land Tourismus GmbH auf allen wichtigen Kommunikationsplattformen präsent sein (auch in den wichtigsten Sozialen Medien) und dem Gästewunsch nach neuen Kommunikations- und Bewertungsformen entgegenkommen.
Mitarbeitern des Unternehmens ist die Nutzung von Social Media zu geschäftlichen Zwecken (eingeschränkte Privatnutzung siehe § 4) nach einer Einschulung ausdrücklich gestattet. Die Verwendung der Unternehmens-E-Mail-Adresse zur Registrierung in sozialen Netzwerken zum Zweck der geschäftlichen und privaten Nutzung ist Mitarbeitern gestattet.
Die Mitarbeiter des Unternehmens halten sich bei allen Aktivitäten an die Gesetze und arbeitsrechtlichen Verpflichtungen sowie die vorliegenden BGLT-Kommunikations-Richtlinie. Darüber hinaus achten sie auf gute Umgangsformen.

§ 2 Rechtliche Rahmenbedingungen
Mitarbeiter halten sich an geltendes Recht und berücksichtigen bei allen Veröffentlichungen insbesondere Urheber-, Persönlichkeits- und Markenrechte wie auch Datenschutzbestimmungen.

§ 3 Beachten Sie die Geheimhaltungsverpflichtung
Vertrauliche Informationen über Ihr Unternehmen oder über Dritte dürfen nicht kommuniziert werden. Im Zweifel holen Sie die Erlaubnis der Unternehmensleitung zur Veröffentlichung ein.

§ 4 Nutzung während der Arbeitszeit
Mitarbeiter dürfen Social Media in ihrer Arbeitszeit grundsätzlich nur zu geschäftlichen Zwecken nutzen (max. 60 Min. pro Tag, abgesehen von den Social-Media-Verantwortlichen). Die private Nutzung ist eingeschränkt (nicht mehr als 10 Min. täglich) erlaubt, wenn damit indirekt geschäftliche Zwecke verfolgt werden (z. B. „Gefällt-mir"-Klicks etc.). Allerdings darf die eigentliche Aufgabe des Mitarbeiters nicht beeinträchtigt werden.

§ 5 Persönliche Verantwortung jedes Mitarbeiters für eigene Veröffentlichungen
Mitarbeiter veröffentlichen überlegt, schützen ihre eigene Privatsphäre und respektieren die der anderen.

§ 6 Öffentliche Kritik am Unternehmen ist tabu
Das eigene Unternehmen sowie Partner, Kunden und Lieferanten des Unternehmens werden öffentlich nicht kritisiert. Probleme werden intern diskutiert und geklärt.

§ 7 Toleranz und respektvoller Umgang mit anderen
Mitarbeiter der Berchtesgadener Land Tourismus GmbH akzeptieren die Meinungsfreiheit in Social Media (Kommentare durch Gäste, Fans etc.) und veröffentlichen keine beleidigenden oder diskriminierenden Inhalte.

§ 8 Umgang mit Fehlern, Irrtümern und anderen Krisen
Mitarbeiter geben Fehler und Irrtümer ohne Umschweife zu und korrigieren diese zeitnah. Auch auf öffentliche Kritik wird rasch reagiert. Fehlerhafte oder kritische Meldungen werden nicht kommentarlos gelöscht, sondern richtiggestellt. Lediglich destruktive, unsachliche oder beleidigende Kommentare werden gelöscht.

§ 9 Kontinuierliches Engagement
Mitarbeiter, die sich in Social Media engagieren, kommunizieren regelmäßig und reagieren auf Kommentare, Fragen und Kritik.

Cirquent

Die Selbstdarstellung des IT-Beratungsunternehmens liest sich laut Website wie folgt: „Cirquent gehört zu den Top Ten im Ranking der führenden IT-Beratungs- und System-integrations-Unternehmen Deutschlands (Quelle: Lünendonk-Liste 2010). Mit mehr als 35 Jahren Erfahrung bietet Cirquent Consulting entlang der gesamten Wertschöpfungs-kette für Banken, Versicherungen, Fertigungs- und Telekommunikationsunternehmen. Ende September 2008 übernahm der in Tokio börsennotierte IT-Konzern NTT Data, eine Tochtergesellschaft der Nippon Telegraph and Telephone Corporation (NTT), 72,9 Prozent der Cirquent-Anteile. Die BMW Group bleibt mit 25,1 Prozent an der Cirquent GmbH beteiligt.

Cirquent veröffentlicht seine Richtlinien u. a. im eigenen Blog:
http://www.cirquent-blog.de/ueber-mich/social-media-guidelines/

Social Media Guidelines

In der künftigen Wirtschaftsgesellschaft besteht die wichtigste Aufgabe nicht darin, Informationen zu verwalten, sondern komplexe Probleme zu lösen. Komplexe Probleme löst niemand allein. Darum werden Kooperations- und Kommunikationsfähigkeit zu Schlüsselkompetenzen für die Wettbewerbsfähigkeit der Zukunft. Mit der rasanten Verbreitung neuer Online-Medien und -Plattformen in den sogenannten Social Media eröffnen sich für Unternehmen und ihre Mitarbeiter in dieser Hinsicht völlig neue Möglichkeiten – intern wie extern.

Viele Mitarbeiterinnen und Mitarbeiter von Cirquent nutzen bereits aktiv Social Media wie Facebook, Xing, Blogs oder Twitter, um sich mit anderen auszutauschen – privat und geschäftlich. Für Cirquent stecken in dieser Entwicklung enorme Chancen!

Diejenigen, die im Social Web aktiv sind, geben der Marke beziehungsweise dem Unternehmen ein Gesicht. Mitarbeiter werden so immer mehr zu Botschaftern und Multiplikatoren unseres Unternehmens – mit ihren persönlichen Erfahrungen, Ansichten und ihrem speziellen Know-how.

Es liegt im Interesse von Cirquent und unseres Mutterkonzern NTT Data Group, an diesem Informationsaustausch teilzuhaben und aktiv mitzuwirken. Daher haben wir Richtlinien für unsere Mitarbeiterinnen und Mitarbeitern zusammengestellt – als Orientierung beim Umgang mit dem Social Web.

1. Transparenz ist wesentlich
Manche äußern sich lieber anonym oder unter einem Pseudonym, wenn sie im Internet unterwegs sind. Sofern ihr über eure Arbeit bei Cirquent auf Blogs, in Foren oder in Communities sprecht, schreibt im eigenen Namen, in der ersten Person und erwähnt auch eure Rolle bei Cirquent. Dadurch wird deutlich, wer ihr seid und dass ihr eure persönliche Meinung kundtut.

2. Verantwortung übernehmen
Grundsätzlich gilt: Jeder schreibt in eigener Verantwortung mit eigenem Namen. Denkt daran, dass das Internet nichts vergisst. Was einmal im Internet steht, ist für viele Jahre auffindbar. In jedem sozialen Netzwerk lässt es sich individuell einstellen, wer mitlesen darf.

3. Austausch bringt Mehrwert
Der soziale Austausch im Netz sollte allen Beteiligten nützliche Informationen bieten. Nicht nur aus Statements, sondern auch aus Feedback kann man lernen. Kommentiert Artikel anderer, um ihnen Mehrwert zu bieten.

4. Kunden, Partner, Lieferanten und Shareholder schützen
Erwähnt Kunden, Partner oder Lieferanten nur mit deren Zustimmung. Vertrauliche Informationen dürfen auf keinen Fall herausgegeben werden. Wichtig ist auch, das Urheberrecht von

Artikeln, Bildern und Videos anderer zu beachten. Und: Wer zweifelhafte Inhalte weiterverbreitet, kann dafür belangt werden.

5. Respekt vor anderen Teilnehmern
Social Media leben von der Meinungsvielfalt. Es gibt kein richtig und falsch. Habt keine Angst, ihr selbst zu sein (authentisch zu sein), aber tut dies respektvoll. Hinzu kommt: Kennzeichnet eure Meinung als solche und trefft keine Aussagen, die keine andere Meinung gelten lassen.

6. Diskussion suchen, Streit meiden
Für den Fall, dass ein Sachverhalt einmal negativ oder fehlerhaft dargestellt wird, könnt ihr die Sachlage selbstverständlich aus eurer Sicht darstellen. Wichtig: Orientiert euch dabei immer an den Fakten, argumentiert nicht auf der persönlichen Ebene, bleibt höflich.

7. Auf Fehler reagieren
Fehler passieren. Reagiert so schnell wie möglich darauf. Bei Blog-Beiträgen etwa besteht die Möglichkeit, auf Fehler in einem früheren Post hinzuweisen und diese zu berichtigen.

Noch Fragen?
Mit allgemeinen oder ganz konkreten Fragen zum Verhalten im Social-Media-Umfeld könnt ihr euch gerne an diese E-Mail-Adresse wenden: Social.Media@cirquent.de.

Cisco Systems: „Cisco's Internet Postings Policy"
Cisco Systems ist der weltweit führende Netzwerkausrüster mit (nach Unternehmensangaben) rund 70.000 Mitarbeitern und 40 Milliarden US-Dollar Umsatz weltweit.
Seit 2008 ist die Regelung für Internet Postings bei Cisco in Gebrauch (http://blogs.cisco.com/news/ciscos_internet_postings_policy/):

With the rise of new media and next generation communications tools, the way in which Cisco employees can communicate internally and externally continues to evolve. While this creates new opportunities for communication and collaboration, it also creates new responsibilities for Cisco employees. This Internet Postings Policy applies to employees who use the following:
– Multi-media and social networking websites such as MySpace, Facebook, Yahoo! Groups and YouTube
– Blogs (Both Cisco Blogs and Blogs external to Cisco)
– Wikis such as Wikipedia and any other site where text can be posted

All of these activities are referred to as "Internet postings" in this Policy Please be aware that violation of this policy may result in disciplinary action up to and including termination. Common sense is the best guide if you decide to post information in any way relating to Cisco. If you are unsure about any particular posting, please contact the Cisco "Internet postings" email alias for guidance. For instance, if you are writing about Cisco business where you have responsibility, you may wish to make sure your manager is comfortable with your taking that action.

Your Internet postings should not disclose any information that is confidential or proprietary to the company or to any third party that has disclosed information to Cisco. If you comment on any aspect of the company's business or any policy issue in which the company is involved and in which you have responsibility, you must clearly identify yourself as a Cisco employee in your postings or blog site(s) and include a disclaimer that the views are your own and not those of Cisco. In addition, Cisco employees should not circulate postings they know are written by other Cisco employees without informing the recipient that the author of the posting is a Cisco employee. Your Internet posting should reflect your personal point of view, not necessarily the point of view of Cisco. Because you are legally responsible for your postings, you may be subject to liability if your posts are found defamatory, harassing, or in violation of any other applicable law. You may also be liable if you make postings which include confidential or copyrighted information (music, videos, text, etc.) belonging to third parties. All of the above mentioned postings are prohibited under this policy.

When posting your point of view, you should neither claim nor imply you are speaking on Cisco's behalf, unless you are authorized in writing by your manager to do so. If you identify yourself as a Cisco employee on any Internet posting, refer to the work done by Cisco or provide a link on a Cisco website, you are required to include the following disclaimer in a reasonably prominent place: "the views expressed on this post are mine and do not necessarily reflect the views of Cisco." Your Internet postings should not include Cisco's logos or trademarks, and should respect copyright, privacy, fair use, financial disclosure, and other applicable laws. Cisco Blogs (located on http://blogs.cisco.com) are blogs requiring corporate approval in which employees may blog about Cisco and our industry. Only Cisco Blogs may include the company's logo. Cisco Blogs may also include links back to Cisco web destinations. All Cisco Blogs must include a legal disclaimer stating that all posts by the author, guest author and visitors reflect personal thoughts and opinions which are not necessarily those of the company.

Cisco may request that you avoid certain subjects or withdraw certain posts from a Cisco Blog if it believes that doing so will help ensure compliance with applicable laws, including securities regulations. Cisco reserves the right to remove any posted comment on Cisco Blog site(s) that is not appropriate for the topic discussed or uses inappropriate language. Cisco also reserves the right to post particular communications on a Cisco Blog. If a member of the news media or blogger contacts you about an Internet posting that concerns the business of Cisco, please refer that person to Cisco public relations, see: http://tools.cisco.com/newsroom/contactSearch/jsp/prSearch.jsp Your Internet postings should not violate any other applicable policy of Cisco, including those set forth in the Employee Resource Guide and the Code of Business Conduct. You agree that Cisco shall not be liable, under any circumstances, for any errors, omissions, loss or damages claimed or incurred due to any of your Internet postings. Cisco reserves the right to suspend, modify, or withdraw this Internet Postings Policy, and you are responsible for regularly reviewing the terms of this Internet Postings Policy.

Coca-Cola

The Coca-Cola Company ist ein weltweit führender Getränkeanbieter, der in über 200 Ländern mehr als 3.500 Getränkesorten anbietet (Unternehmensangaben). Unter: http://www.thecoca-colacompany.com/socialmedia/ finden sich die Cocal Cola Online Social Media Principles, als Teil des Bereiches „Reporting und Policies", der folgende Bereiche insgesamt umfasst:

Reporting & Policies
CEO Water Mandate
Global Reporting Initiative
Global School Beverage Guidelines
Millennium Development Goals
Online Social Media Principles
Political Contributions Policy
Responsible Marketing
Sustainability Reports
UN Global Compact

Die Online Social Media Principles sind unterteilt in Hinweise für alle Mitarbeiter und „Online Spokespeople". Sie lesen sich wie folgt:

Every day, people discuss, debate and embrace The Coca-Cola Company and our brands in thousands of online conversations.

We recognize the vital importance of participating in these online conversations and are committed to ensuring that we participate in online social media the right way. These Online Social Media Principles have been developed to help empower our associates to participate in this new frontier of marketing and communications, represent our Company, and share the optimistic and positive spirits of our brands.

The vision of the Company to achieve sustainable growth online and offline is guided by certain shared values that we live by as an organization and as individuals:
– LEADERSHIP: The courage to shape a better future;
– COLLABORATION: Leveraging our collective genius;
– INTEGRITY: Being real;
– ACCOUNTABILITY: Recognizing that if it is to be, it's up to me;
– PASSION: Showing commitment in heart and mind;
– DIVERSITY: Being as inclusive as our brands; and
– QUALITY: Ensuring what we do, we do well.

These Online Social Media Principles are intended to outline how these values should be demonstrated in the online social media space and to guide your participation in this area, both when you are participating personally, as well as when you are acting on behalf of the

Company. It is critical that we always remember who we are (a marketing company) and what our role is in the social media community (to build our brands). The same rules that apply to our messaging and communications in traditional media still apply in the online social media space; simply because the development and implementation of an online social media program can be fast, easy, and inexpensive doesn't mean that different rules apply.

The Company encourages all of its associates to explore and engage in social media communities at a level at which they feel comfortable. Have fun, but be smart. The best advice is to approach online worlds in the same way we do the physical one – by using sound judgment and common sense, by adhering to the Company's values, and by following the Code of Business Conduct and all other applicable policies.

COMPANY COMMITMENTS

The Company adheres strongly to its core values in the online social media community, and we expect the same commitment from all Company representatives – including Company associates, and associates of our agencies, vendors and suppliers. Any deviation from these commitments may be subject to disciplinary review or other appropriate action.

The Five Core Values of the Company in the Online Social Media Community
1. Transparency in every social media engagement. The Company does not condone manipulating the social media flow by creating "fake" destinations and posts designed to mislead followers and control a conversation. Every Web site, "fan page", or other online destination that is ultimately controlled by the Company must make that fact known to users and must be authorized according to applicable internal protocols in order to track and monitor the Company's online presence. We also require bloggers and social media influencers to disclose to their readers when we're associating with them, whether by providing them with product samples or hosting them at Company events, and we need to monitor whether they are complying with this requirement.
2. Protection of our consumers' privacy. This means that we should be conscientious regarding any Personally Identifiable Information (PII) that we collect, including how we collect, store, use, or share that PII, all of which should be done pursuant to applicable Privacy Policies, laws and IT policies.
3. Respect of copyrights, trademarks, rights of publicity, and other third-party rights in the online social media space, including with regard to user-generated content (UGC). How exactly you do this may depend on your particular situation, so work with your cross-functional teams to make informed, appropriate decisions.
4. Responsibility in our use of technology. We will not use or align the Company with any organizations or Web sites that deploy the use of excessive tracking software, adware, malware or spyware.
5. Utilization of best practices, listening to the online community, and compliance with applicable regulations to ensure that these Online Social Media Principles remain current and reflect the most up-to-date and appropriate standards of behavior.

COMPANY AND AGENCY ASSOCIATES' ONLINE SOCIAL MEDIA ACTIVITIES

The Company respects the rights of its associates and its authorized agencies' associates to use blogs and other social media tools not only as a form of self-expression, but also as a means to further the Company's business. It is important that all associates are aware of the implications of engaging in forms of social media and online conversations that reference the Company and/or the associate's relationship with the Company and its brands, and that associates recognize when the Company might be held responsible for their behavior.

Our Expectations for Associates' Personal Behavior in Online Social Media
There's a big difference in speaking "on behalf of the Company" and speaking "about" the Company. This set of 5 principles refers to those personal or unofficial online activities where you might refer to Coca-Cola.
1. Adhere to the Code of Business Conduct and other applicable policies. All Company associates, from the Chairman to every intern, are subject to the Company's Code of Business Conduct in every public setting. In addition, other policies, including the Information Protection Policy and the Insider Trading Policy, govern associates' behavior with respect to the disclosure of information; these policies are applicable to your personal activities online.
2. You are responsible for your actions. Anything you post that can potentially tarnish the Company's image will ultimately be your responsibility. We do encourage you to participate in the online social media space, but urge you to do so properly, exercising sound judgment and common sense.
3. Be a "scout" for compliments and criticism. Even if you are not an official online spokesperson for the Company, you are one of our most vital assets for monitoring the social media landscape. If you come across positive or negative remarks about the Company or its brands online that you believe are important, consider sharing them by forwarding them to the internal email address that you have been provided.
4. Let the subject matter experts respond to negative posts. You may come across negative or disparaging posts about the Company or its brands, or see third parties trying to spark negative conversations. Unless you are a certified online spokesperson, avoid the temptation to react yourself. Pass the post(s) along to our official in-market spokespersons who are trained to address such comments, at the internal email address that you have been provided.
5. Be conscious when mixing your business and personal lives. Online, your personal and business personas are likely to intersect. The Company respects the free speech rights of all of its associates, but you must remember that customers, colleagues and supervisors often have access to the online content you post. Keep this in mind when publishing information online that can be seen by more than friends and family, and know that information originally intended just for friends and family can be forwarded on. Remember NEVER to disclose non-public information of the Company (including confidential information), and be aware that taking public positions online that are counter to the Company's interests might cause conflict.

Our Expectations for Online Spokespeople

Just as with traditional media, we have an opportunity – and a responsibility – to effectively manage the Company's reputation online and to selectively engage and participate in the thousands of online conversations that mention us every day. The following 10 principles guide how our Certified Online Spokespeople should represent the Company in an online, official capacity when they are speaking "on behalf of the Company:"

1. Be Certified in the Social Media Certification Program. All associates who wish to officially represent the Company online must complete the Social Media Certification Program prior to beginning or continuing these activities.

2. Follow our Code of Business Conduct and all other Company policies. Our Code of Business Conduct provides the foundation for these Online Social Media Principles: "As a representative of [the Company], you must act with honesty and integrity in all matters." This commitment is true for all forms of social media. In addition, several other policies govern your behavior as a Company spokesperson in the online social media space, including the Information Protection Policy and the Insider Trading Policy.

3. Be mindful that you are representing the Company. As a Company representative, it is important that your posts convey the same positive, optimistic spirit that the Company instills in all of its communications. Be respectful of all individuals, races, religions and cultures; how you conduct yourself in the online social media space not only reflects on you – it is a direct reflection on the Company.

4. Fully disclose your affiliation with the Company. The Company requires all associates who are communicating on behalf of the Company to always disclose their name and their affiliation. It is never acceptable to use aliases or otherwise deceive people. State your relationship with the Company from the outset, e.g., "Hi, I'm John and I work for The Coca-Cola Company ...." This disclosure is equally important for any agency/vendor/partner/third party who is representing the Company online. They must disclose that they work "with The Coca-Cola Company."

5. Keep records. It is critical that we keep records of our interactions in the online social media space and monitor the activities of those with whom we engage. Because online conversations are often fleeting and immediate, it is important for you to keep track of them when you're officially representing the Company. Remember that online Company state-ments can be held to the same legal standards as traditional media communications. Keep records of any online dialogue pertaining to the Company and send a copy to the internal email address that you have been provided.

6. When in doubt, do not post. Associates are personally responsible for their words and actions, wherever they are. As online spokespeople, you must ensure that your posts are completely accurate and not misleading, and that they do not reveal non-public information of the Company. Exercise sound judgment and common sense, and if there is any doubt, DO NOT POST IT. In any circumstance in which you are uncertain about how to respond to a post, send the link to the internal email address that you have been provided.

7. Give credit where credit is due and don't violate others' rights. DO NOT claim authorship of something that is not yours. If you are using another party's content, make certain that they are credited for it in your post and that they approve of you utilizing their content. Do

not use the copyrights, trademarks, publicity rights, or other rights of others without the necessary permissions of the rightsholder(s).

8. Be responsible to your work. The Company understands that associates engage in online social media activities at work for legitimate purposes and that these activities may be helpful for Company affairs. However, the Company encourages all associates to exercise sound judgment and common sense to prevent online social media sites from becoming a distraction at work.

9. Remember that your local posts can have global significance. The way that you answer an online question might be accurate in some parts of the world, but inaccurate (or even illegal) in others. Keep that "world view" in mind when you are participating in online conversations.

10. Know that the Internet is permanent. Once information is published online, it is essentially part of a permanent record, even if you "remove/delete" it later or attempt to make it anonymous. If your complete thought, along with its context, cannot be squeezed into a character-restricted space (such as Twitter), provide a link to an online space where the message can be expressed completely and accurately.

Daimler

Mit 260.000 Mitarbeitern und fast 100 Milliarden Euro Umsatz (2010) zählt das von den Erfindern des Automobils gegründete Unternehmen auch 125 Jahre später zu den globalen Schwergewichten im Automobilsektor.

Daimler nutzt vielfältige Möglichkeiten des Social Web, unter anderem:
– Facebook (offizielle Karriere-Seite)
– Blogs (DaimlerBlog, Car2Go-Blog)
– Twitter (mehrere Accounts)
– YouTube

Zusätzlich gibt es noch weitere Social-Media-Aktivitäten der einzelnen Marken.

Die Daimler Social Media Policy ist hier: http://www.daimler.com/Projects/c2c/channel/documents/1895106_Social_Media_Leitfaden_Final.pdf veröffentlicht.

Daimler AG – Social-Media-Leitfaden
Das Internet ist aus unserer Gesellschaft nicht mehr wegzudenken. Zurzeit gewinnt vor allem die Nutzung von Social-Media-Angeboten mehr und mehr an Bedeutung. Unter dem Begriff „Social Media" werden Plattformen und Netzwerke zusammengefasst, bei denen die Nutzer die Möglichkeit haben, beispielsweise Fotos und Videos, aber auch Erfahrungsberichte oder Meinungen auszutauschen. Dazu zählen unter anderem Blogs, Wikipedia, YouTube, Facebook oder auch Twitter.
Die wachsende Beliebtheit von Social Media ist auch für Unternehmen von großer Bedeutung: Nutzer sprechen im Internet über Firmen, diskutieren über neue Technologien und empfehlen Produkte – oder eben nicht. Wer diese Diskussionsplattformen ignoriert, der ignoriert auch einen äußerst wirksamen Kommunikationskanal. Social-Media-Engagement kann helfen,

Trends frühzeitig zu erkennen, auf Kritik zu reagieren oder eigene Themen anzustoßen. Und wer könnte das Unternehmen und seine Vielfalt in der Öffentlichkeit besser darstellen als die Mitarbeiter? Mit Ihrem Expertenwissen können Sie Diskussionen im Internet bereichern oder nützliche Anregungen für Ihre Arbeit finden. Es ist daher im Interesse von Daimler, Ihr Engagement im Bereich Social Media zu fördern. Allerdings stellen wir auch immer wieder fest, dass es im Umgang mit diesen Kommunikationsformen noch viele Unsicherheiten gibt. Um Sie über die Möglichkeiten und Risiken der beruflichen Nutzung zu informieren, haben wir die folgenden Hinweise zusammengestellt. Soweit es dabei nicht um gesetzlich vorgeschriebene Dinge geht, handelt es sich ausdrücklich nicht um Gebote, sondern um Empfehlungen, die Ihnen beim Umgang mit Social Media helfen sollen.

10 Tipps zum Umgang mit Social Media

1. Es geht immer um Konversation. Wenn Sie Social Media nur für Einbahnstraßenkommunikation nutzen, reden Sie bald gegen eine Wand. Nur wer aktiv das Gespräch sucht, sich in Diskussionen zu Wort meldet und auf Fragen antwortet, wird im Web ernst genommen.
2. Achten Sie auf Qualität. Es ist einfach, im Internet schnell und viel Aufmerksamkeit zu erhalten. Langfristige, intensive und wertvolle Konversationen lassen sich aber nur mit qualitativ hochwertigen Inhalten anstoßen bzw. bereichern.
3. Seien Sie ehrlich. Lügen haben im Internet besonders kurze Beine. Informationen sind im Netz sofort nachprüfbar. Falschaussagen oder auch nur Weglassungen werden umgehend aufgedeckt. Legen Sie Ihre Quellen offen; das zeugt von Respekt dem Urheber gegenüber, und Sie gewinnen an Glaubwürdigkeit.
4. Bleiben Sie höflich. Eine Konversation kann nur wertvoll sein, wenn sich alle Beteiligten respektvoll begegnen. Vermeiden Sie Provokationen und Beleidigungen und brechen Sie Gespräche ab, wenn der Gesprächspartner beleidigend wird.
5. Berichtigen Sie eigene Fehler. Viele Nutzer im Web sind schnell verärgert, verzeihen aber auch rasch. Geben Sie eigene Fehler oder Irrtümer zu und berichtigen Sie diese. Es empfiehlt sich, diese Änderungen zeitnah und nachvollziehbar vorzunehmen, um Missverständnisse oder Irritationen zu vermeiden. Weisen Sie gegebenenfalls auf Fehler in Beiträgen, die Ihr Arbeitsgebiet betreffen, sachlich und höflich hin.
6. Seien Sie auch als Privatperson professionell. Auch wenn Sie Social Media „nur" privat nutzen, kann es vorkommen, dass Sie auf berufliche Kontakte stoßen oder mit Fragen zu Ihrem Beruf konfrontiert werden. Dann ist es gut, wenn Ihnen Privates nicht peinlich sein muss. Einmal Veröffentlichtes lässt sich nur schwer wieder vollständig aus dem Netz entfernen. Durch einfaches Suchen und Verknüpfen der Ergebnisse lassen sich beispielsweise Rückschlüsse auf persönliche Beziehungen, berufliche Zuständigkeiten oder Einstellungen zu bestimmten Themen ziehen.
7. Trennen Sie Meinungen und Fakten. Um Missverständnisse zu vermeiden, sollten Sie deutlich machen, welche Teile Ihrer Aussagen Meinungen und welche Fakten darstellen. Zudem sollten Sie darauf hinweisen, ob Sie Ihre persönliche oder die Unternehmensmeinung vertreten.
8. Seien Sie ganz Sie selbst. Vertrauen und Glaubwürdigkeit sind die Grundpfeiler sozia-

ler Netze. Verstellen Sie sich nicht, sondern zeigen Sie, wer und wie Sie sind. Zur offenen Kommunikation im Web zählt auch, dass Sie Ihren Hintergrund offenlegen. Wenn Sie für Daimler im Internet aktiv sind bzw. Daimler-Interessen vertreten, stehen Sie dazu! Transparenz können Sie beispielsweise durch einen Hinweis (Disclaimer) sicherstellen, der an den Diskussionsbeitrag angehangen wird. Beispiel: „Ich bin Mitarbeiter von Daimler und vertrete hier meine eigene Meinung."

9. Behandeln Sie Vertrauliches vertraulich. Seien Sie sorgsam im Umgang mit Firmeninformationen. Vertrauliche Informationen, die Sie im Rahmen Ihrer Anstellung erhalten, dürfen Sie nicht verbreiten. Wenn Sie unsicher sind, ob Sie eine bestimmte Information veröffentlichen dürfen, fragen Sie bei Ihrem Vorgesetzten, Ihrem Informationssicherheitsbeauftragten (ISO) oder der Unternehmenskommunikation nach. Im Zweifelsfall verzichten Sie auf die Veröffentlichung. Wahren Sie auch den Datenschutz. Veröffentlichen Sie nichts über Dritte, ohne es vorher mit den betroffenen Personen abgesprochen zu haben.

10. Achten Sie das Gesetz. Veröffentlichen Sie keine verleumderischen, beleidigenden oder anderweitig rechtswidrigen Inhalte. Stellen Sie keine Inhalte ohne entsprechende Urheberverweise ins Netz, beachten Sie Copyrights und respektieren Sie das Recht am eigenen Bild. Halten Sie unternehmensbezogene Informationen geheim, die sich auf den Börsenpreis von Daimler-Wertpapieren auswirken könnten. Solange Sie Zugang zu solchen öffentlich nicht bekannten Informationen haben, dürfen Sie keinem anderen den Kauf oder Verkauf von Daimler-Wertpapieren empfehlen oder andere Personen in sonstiger Weise dazu verleiten.

Um die Einhaltung geltender Rechtsvorschriften in Ihrem eigenen sowie auch im Interesse der Daimler AG sicherzustellen, setzen Ihr Arbeitsvertrag, die Verhaltensrichtlinie (Integrity Code) sowie die Richtlinie zum Umgang mit Informationen verbindliche Grenzen. Das gilt insbesondere für den Umgang mit vertraulichen unternehmens- und personenbezogenen Informationen sowie jedes Verhalten, das Sie einem Interessenkonflikt aussetzen kann.
Jörg Howe
Leiter Unternehmenskommunikation, Daimler AG

Daimler ergänzt diesen Leitfaden um weitere Dokumente und veröffentlicht sogar einen eigenen Kommentarleitfaden für den Unternehmens-Blog (http://blog.daimler.de/kommentar-richtlinien):

Kommentarrichtlinien

Wir freuen uns über Kommentare. Bitte beachten Sie dabei folgende allgemeine Grundregeln:

Die Blog-Kommentarfunktion soll eine sachliche Diskussion ermöglichen. Um dies zu gewährleisten, behält sich die Redaktion vor, Beiträge zu löschen, die einer solchen Diskussion nicht förderlich sind und sich nicht auf die Beiträge beziehen. Es besteht kein Anspruch auf Veröffentlichung.
Die E-Mail-Adresse wird nicht veröffentlicht und nur im Zusammenhang mit dem Kommentar gespeichert.

Dieses Blog ist ein Webtagebuch von Daimler-Mitarbeitern, in dem wir gerne mit Ihnen diskutieren. Falls Sie aber Fragen, Irritationen oder Anregungen zu Ihrem Fahrzeug oder unserem Service haben oder einen Service in Anspruch nehmen möchten, wenden Sie sich bitte direkt an die Ansprechpartner auf dieser Seite.
http://www.daimler.com/dccom/kontakt

Umgangston und Netiquette

Behandeln Sie andere Nutzer so, wie Sie selbst behandelt werden möchten. Denken Sie immer daran, dass Sie es mit Menschen und nicht mit virtuellen Persönlichkeiten zu tun haben. Argumentieren Sie hart in der Sache, aber nie mit persönlichen Angriffen oder Argumenten, die sich auf die Person beziehen. Beleidigungen, sexuelle Anspielungen und sexistische oder rassistische Äußerungen sind untersagt.
Jeder hat das Recht auf seine eigene Meinung. Versuchen Sie deshalb nie, Ihre Meinung anderen aufzuzwingen.

Nachfolgendes führt zur Löschung des Kommentars beziehungsweise zur Sperrung der IP-Adresse für weitere Kommentare:
– Der Missbrauch als Werbefläche für Webseiten oder Dienste
– Das maschinelle Hinterlassen von Kommentaren
– Das kommerzielle oder private Anbieten von Waren oder Dienstleistungen
– Rassismus und Hasspropaganda
– Aufforderungen zu Gewalt gegen Personen, Institutionen oder Unternehmen
– Pornografie
– Beleidigungen und Entwürdigungen von Personen in jeglicher Form
– Verletzungen von Rechten Dritter, auch und insbesondere von Urheberrechten
– Aufruf zu Demonstrationen und Kundgebungen jeglicher politischer Richtung
– Kommentare, die nicht in deutscher oder englischer Sprache verfasst sind
– Kommentare, die sich nicht auf den kommentierten Beitrag beziehen

Diese Regeln gelten auch für die Verwendung von Benutzernamen.
Verstöße gegen diese Richtlinien werden wir nicht dulden: Wir behalten uns vor, Beiträge oder Kommentare zu bearbeiten, zu verschieben oder zu löschen und gegebenenfalls die Kommentarfunktion zu schließen.
Jeder Nutzer ist für die von ihm publizierten Beiträge selbst verantwortlich.
Allgemein gilt: Interne, vertrauliche oder geheime Informationen gehören nicht ins Netz! Weitere Hinweise dazu finden Sie in unserem Social-Media-Leitfaden.

Ausschlussklausel für Haftung
Die Kommentare zu unseren Beiträgen spiegeln allein die Meinung einzelner Leser wider. Für die Richtigkeit und Vollständigkeit der Inhalte übernimmt die Daimler AG keinerlei Gewähr.

Datev

Der Dienstleister für Deutschlands Steuerberater nutzt auf vielfältige Weise Social Media und hat dafür hinsichtlich Umfang und Verständlichkeit vorbildliche Guidelines entwickelt. (http://www.datev.de/portal/ShowPage.do?pid=dpi&nid=108237)

Social Media Guidelines in Kürze

1. Verantwortung: Sie sind für das, was Sie in Social Media tun, selbst verantwortlich.
2. Persönlichkeit: Sprechen Sie für sich.
3. Transparenz: Sagen Sie, wer Sie sind.
4. Mehrwert: Bieten Sie Nutzen.
5. Rechtliche Rahmenbedingungen: Halten Sie Gesetze und Ihren Arbeitsvertrag ein.
6. Verhaltenskodex: Achten Sie den Datev Code of Business Conduct.
7. Urheberrecht: Verwenden Sie nur eigene Inhalte.
8. Private Nutzung: Achten Sie auf die Datev-Bestimmungen zur privaten Nutzung des Internets.
9. Privatsphäre und Sicherheit: Schützen Sie sich und Ihre privaten Daten.
10. Öffentlichkeit: Halten Sie, wo nötig, Kontakt zur Datev-Pressestelle.
11. Besonnenheit: Bewahren Sie einen kühlen Kopf.

Neben dieser Kurzform, die nur aus elf Stichpunkten besteht, gibt es ein Interview mit dem Vorstandsvorsitzenden und dem Personalvorstand, ein Glossar, weiter Anleitungen für die Benutzung von Xing, Facebook und Twitter (jeweils hier nicht wiedergegeben) sowie einen Verweis auf einen privaten Weblog des Online-Kommunikationsbeauftragten, in dem dieser die Entwicklung der Guidelines zusammenfasst (http://buggisch.wordpress.com/2010/12/06/einfuhrung-von-social-media-guidelines-ein-praxisbericht/):

[...]

Am Anfang stand, wie so oft, die Einsicht in die Notwendigkeit. Es gab immer mehr Anfragen von Mitarbeitern zum Thema Social Media, die letztlich gezeigt haben: Es gibt Bedarf an Hilfestellung und Orientierung. Die Fragen reichten von ganz allgemeinen Themen („Ist es nicht besser, auf Social-Media-Plattformen anonym unterwegs zu sein?") bis hin zu speziellen Problemen („Was mache ich, wenn ein Kunde mit mir auf Facebook ‚befreundet' sein will?").

Bereichsübergreifendes Projekt
Um den Mitarbeitern die nötige Orientierung bieten zu können, reifte daher im Sommer der Entschluss, dem Vorbild vieler anderer Firmen und Institutionen zu folgen und Social Media Guidelines bei Datev einzuführen. Federführend war die Abteilung Zentrales Marketing (in der auch mein Team beheimatet ist), da wir uns in den letzten Jahren am intensivsten mit Social Media beschäftigt haben. Die notwendigen Beteiligten waren relativ schnell gefunden – es waren Kollegen aus

– dem Bereich Presse- und Öffentlichkeitsarbeit,
– der Personalabteilung,
– der Rechtsabteilung und
– dem Bereich Business Development.

Außerdem hatten wir uns entschlossen, auch über den Datev-Tellerrand hinauszublicken und das Know-how einer externen Agentur (Text100 aus München) zu beanspruchen, die bereits Erfahrungen mit der Erstellung von Social Media Guidelines gesammelt hatte und uns hervorragend unterstützt hat.

Aufklären, ermutigen, auf Regeln hinweisen
In den Projekttreffen und dem Workshop mit Text100 konnten wir relativ schnell Einigung darüber erzielen, was die Social Media Guidelines bei Datev leisten müssen. Nämlich vor allem Folgendes:
– Aufklären: Informationen zu Social Media bereitstellen; Ansprechpartner bei Datev nennen
– Ermutigen: Unsicherheit abbauen; die Mitarbeiter ermuntern, den vorhandenen Handlungsspielraum zu nutzen
– Regeln nennen: Hinweise auf die relevanten Passagen der verbindlichen Regelwerke wie Arbeitsvertrag und Code of Business Conduct geben

Die Festlegung der Inhalte, die Ausformulierung der Guidelines und die finale Abstimmung zwischen allen Beteiligten gingen dann wirklich flott und war innerhalb weniger Wochen abgeschlossen. Die Freigabe erfolgte durch den Datev-Vorstand.

Kommunikation an die Mitarbeiter
Fehlte nur noch die Kommunikation an die Mitarbeiter. Wir haben uns für eine zweistufige Kommunikation entschieden: Die Guidelines selbst wurden zusammen mit der Mitarbeiterzeitschrift an alle Mitarbeiter verteilt. In derselben Ausgabe gab es begleitend ein Interview mit unserem Vorstandsvorsitzenden und dem Personalvorstand, die Sinn und Zweck der Guidelines erläutern.

Das Interview und natürlich auch die Guidelines finden sich ebenfalls in Intranet und Internet, aber angereichert um hilfreiche Zusatzinformationen, zum Beispiel um Datenschutzhinweise oder Schritt-für-Schritt-Anleitungen zum Einstieg in die bekanntesten Social-Media-Plattformen. Anfang 2011 gibt es zudem Info-Veranstaltungen, auf denen ich die Guidelines interessierten Mitarbeitern vorstellen und Fragen dazu beantworten werde.

Feedback natürlich erwünscht
Denn natürlich sind die Guidelines nun nicht in Stein gemeißelt – sie sollen leben, wachsen und gedeihen, insbesondere durch Anregungen derjenigen, denen sie letztlich helfen sollen.
[…]

Außerdem wird ausdrücklich auf den Datev-Arbeitsvertrag verwiesen und dieser in Auszügen wiedergegeben:

Kapitel 11: Verschwiegenheitspflicht
Der Schweige- und Geheimhaltungspflicht des Mitarbeiters unterliegen auch über das Ende des Arbeitsverhältnisses hinaus insbesondere:

Geschäfts- und Betriebsgeheimnisse;
Tatsachen oder Informationen – insbesondere über die geschäftlichen Verhältnisse –, die dem Mitarbeiter in Ausübung oder bei Gelegenheit seiner Tätigkeit über Datev, ihre Mitglieder und Geschäftspartner sowie andere Mitarbeiter bekannt werden;
Angelegenheiten, die geeignet sind, dem Unternehmen zu schaden oder sein Ansehen zu verletzen.

Der Mitarbeiter ist über die Geschäftsverhältnisse der Mandanten von Datev-Mitgliedern zur Verschwiegenheit im gleichen Umfang verpflichtet wie die Mitglieder selbst. Diese haben über alle ihnen anvertrauten oder bekannt gewordenen Verhältnisse ihrer Mandanten von Gesetzes wegen Stillschweigen zu bewahren.

Kapitel 12: Verpflichtung auf das Datengeheimnis
Der Mitarbeiter verpflichtet sich, die nachstehenden Regelungen einzuhalten:
1. Es ist untersagt, geschützte personenbezogene Daten unbefugt zu einem anderen als zu dem zur jeweiligen rechtmäßigen Aufgabenerfüllung gehörenden Zweck zu erheben, zu verarbeiten, bekannt zu geben, zugänglich zu machen oder sonst zu nutzen. Dies gilt auch über die Beendigung des Arbeitsverhältnisses bei Datev hinaus.
2. Bestehende Vorschriften über den Umgang bzw. die Sicherung personenbezogener Daten sind zu beachten.
3. Zum Schutz personenbezogener Daten ist im Rahmen der zugewiesenen Aufgabe die notwendige Sorgfalt anzuwenden; festgestellte Mängel im Sicherungssystem sind dem Datenschutzbeauftragten oder der Führungskraft zu melden.

Hier die Datev-„Social Media Guidelines – ausführliche Version"

1. Verantwortung
Sie sind für das, was Sie in sozialen Netzwerken tun und veröffentlichen, selbst verantwortlich. Bitte gehen Sie bewusst mit dieser Verantwortung um, in Ihrem eigenen Interesse und im Interesse Ihres Arbeitgebers.

2. Persönlichkeit
Wenn Sie sich ohne einen dienstlichen Auftrag in sozialen Medien zu einem Thema äußern, machen Sie bitte deutlich, dass Sie hier Ihre persönliche Meinung vertreten und nicht für das Unternehmen sprechen. Verwenden Sie daher immer die Formulierung „ich" statt „wir".

3. Transparenz

Es ist Ihr persönlicher Beitrag, der in den sozialen Medien zählt. Daher bekennen Sie sich auch bitte immer mit ihrem Klarnamen dazu. Spitznamen, sogenannten Nicknames, begegnet man zwar immer wieder, für den Leser und auch Sie selbst ist es aber hilfreicher und angenehmer, über die Identität des Verfassers Klarheit zu haben.

4. Mehrwert

Auch in Social Media wird (wie in manch anderem Medium) viel redundantes und nutzloses Wissen produziert und reproduziert. Fragen Sie sich also am besten vor jedem eigenen Beitrag, ob er dem Leser wirklich einen Mehrwert bietet. Falls nicht, seien Sie bitte so höflich und verschonen Sie ihn damit. Wenn Sie sich im Rahmen Ihrer Fachkompetenz in den Social Media zu einem Thema äußern wollen und unsicher sind, stimmen Sie sich am besten im Vorfeld mit Ihrem Vorgesetzten ab.

5. Rechtliche Rahmenbedingungen

Machen Sie sich bewusst, dass Sie mit der Nutzung von sozialen Netzwerken keinen rechtsfreien Raum betreten – Sie unterliegen hier ebenso den Gesetzen und Verträgen, zu denen Sie sich bekannt haben, wie wenn Sie an Ihrem Schreibtisch sitzen, im Zug oder in der Kneipe. Davor schützt Sie auch kein Nickname. Auch haben viele Netzwerke eigene Nutzungsbedingungen; mit deren Anerkennung bei der Registrierung werden diese verbindlich.

Wichtige Regeln, die auch verbindlich gelten, während Sie sich in den sozialen Netzwerken bewegen, finden sich in Ihrem Arbeitsvertrag. Vor allem die Kapitel 11 und 12 sind hier relevant: Kapitel 11 behandelt die Verschwiegenheitspflicht und besagt, dass Sie keine Interna nach außen geben dürfen, also vor allem Betriebsgeheimnisse, Wissen über andere Mitarbeiter oder Angelegenheiten, die dem Unternehmen schaden oder sein Ansehen verletzen könnten. Kapitel 12 bescheinigt, dass Datev-Mitarbeiter zum Datengeheimnis verpflichtet sind. Das heißt, geschützte, personenbezogene Daten dürfen nicht zu einem anderen als „zu dem zur jeweiligen rechtmäßigen Aufgabenerfüllung gehörenden Zweck" bekannt oder zugänglich gemacht werden.

6. Der Datev-Verhaltenskodex

Das zweite wichtige Regelwerk, das für Sie verbindlich ist, wenn Sie sich im dienstlichen Auftrag an Social Media beteiligen, ist der allgemeine Verhaltenskodex von Datev, der sogenannte „Code of Business Conduct". Wenn Sie sich nicht sicher sind, wie Sie sich im Sinne von Datev in den Social Media richtig verhalten, finden Sie hier vor allem in den Artikeln 2 (Datenschutz und Datensicherheit), 4 (Integrität), 5 (Arbeitsschutz, Betriebliche Mitbestimmung, Kollegialität, Menschenwürde), 6 (Produktinnovation, Produktsicherheit, Umweltschutz) und 7 (Wettbewerb) eine erste Orientierung. Wie Sie sicher wissen, werden hier Verhaltensweisen beschrieben, von denen wir annehmen, dass sie auch allgemein dem gesunden Menschenverstand entsprechen.

7. Urheberrecht

Ein wichtiger Punkt des Verhaltenskodex betrifft das Urheberrecht: Social Media verleiten nicht selten dazu, Inhalte von anderen einfach zu kopieren. Das ist nach dem Urheberrecht nicht erlaubt. Kopieren Sie also in Ihren Beiträgen kein Material von anderen und geben Sie es nicht als Ihr eigenes aus. Wenn Sie auf fremde Inhalte verweisen, nutzen Sie Links. Vermeiden Sie auch lange Zitate. Laden Sie nur Bilder oder Videos ins Internet hoch, wenn Sie die nötigen Rechte besitzen, weil Sie zum Beispiel über die Zustimmung der Fotografen oder des Filmemachers und auch der abgebildeten Personen verfügen.

8. Die private Nutzung
Die Social-Media-Nutzung bringt es mit sich, dass häufig private und dienstliche Nutzung ineinander übergehen. Was die private Nutzung während der Arbeitszeit betrifft, so ist diese innerhalb des Unternehmens in der Gesamtbetriebsvereinbarung über die Nutzung der Kommunikationseinrichtungen geregelt. Nutzen Sie erforderlichenfalls die Zeitkorrektur-Buchungen im personalwirtschaftlichen Self-Service.

9. Privatsphäre und Sicherheit
Eine der größten Sorgen der Menschen beim Umgang mit dem Internet im Allgemeinen und den sozialen Medien im Besonderen ist, dass aufgrund von Pannen, krimineller Energie oder schlicht Unwissen persönliche und vertrauliche Daten offen für jedermann sichtbar werden. Ein weiteres Problem können Viren und Hacker sein. Diese Risiken sind jedoch überschaubar, wenn man bestimmte Grundsätze beherzigt und etwa die Einstellungen für die Privatsphäre der gängigen Online-Plattformen kennt. Aus diesem Grund haben wir für Sie die wichtigsten Einstellungen der beliebtesten Plattformen erklärt.

10. Öffentlichkeit
Auch Journalisten und andere Berufsgruppen, die die Öffentlichkeit vertreten, nutzen verstärkt Social Media bei ihren Recherchen. Hier gilt die Regel, dass nur Mitarbeiter der Datev-Pressestelle oder anderweitig autorisierte Mitarbeiter im Namen des Unternehmens sprechen dürfen. Wenn Sie also im Zuge Ihres Social-Media-Engagements auf Anfragen vonseiten der Medien treffen, leiten Sie diese bitte an die Pressestelle (presse@datev.de, Telefon 1210) weiter.

11. Besonnenheit
Denken Sie immer daran, dass Ihre Beiträge öffentlich sind – und das unter Umständen sehr lange bleiben. Bewahren Sie also auch in hitzigen Debatten einen kühlen Kopf und lassen Sie sich zu nichts hinreißen. Unterdrücken Sie im Zweifelsfall den Impuls, sich zu äußern, auch wenn Sie sich im Recht sehen. Argumentieren Sie also immer sachlich, beleidigen Sie niemanden, seien Sie respektvoll im Umgang mit Ihren Dialogpartnern. Halten Sie sich am besten an die Datev-Netiquette.

Dell

Dell ist weltbekannt als Anbieter von PCs, Notebooks und Serversystemen. Im Social-Media-Umfeld ist Dell vielfach aktiv – unter anderem mit der Ideastorm-Website (http://www.ideastorm.com), die als eine der ersten großen Implementationen von Social Media im Bereich der Marktforschung und Produktentwicklung gilt. Die Website wurde weithin bekannt, da zahlreiche unzufriedene Dell-Kunden die Plattform nutzten, um Beschwerden anzubringen. Dennoch hält Dell bis heute daran fest. Daneben nutzt das Unternehmen auch andere Kanäle, etwa Facebook und Twitter, setzt auf Social-Media-Monitoring durch Einrichtung eines eigenen „Kontrollzentrums" (siehe: http://www.wuv.de/nachrichten/digital/social_media_bei_dell_jeder_mitarbeiter_soll_mit_eingebunden_werden) und schult regelmäßig Mitarbeiter im Umgang mit Sozialen Medien.

Bei Dell ist die „Global Social Media Policy" Teil der umfassenden „Terms of Sale, License Agreements & Policies" (http://www.dell.com/content/topics/global.aspx/policy/en/policy?c=us&l=en&s=corp&~section=019&redirect=1).

Dell's Global Social Media Policy

Scope
This Global Policy on Social Media (Policy) is a Corporate Compliance Policy and applies to all Dell employees, employees of any Dell subsidiary, assigned workers, as well as to third parties performing services on Dell's behalf (hereinafter collectively referred to as "You"). For employees, compliance with this Policy is an expectation of employment (subject to local legal requirements). For assigned workers and third parties, compliance with this Policy is a condition of access to Dell facilities and resources, and of being permitted to perform services for Dell.
Definitions for capitalized terms used in this Policy may be found at the end of the Policy.

Purpose
Dell recognizes that Social Media tools such as blogs, micro-blogs, online forums, content-sharing websites and other digital channels established for online interaction and connection are increasingly used to: Promote Dell to colleagues, customers, the media and other Dell stakeholders; and/or
Share personal opinions and participate in online dialogue as individuals.

The purpose of this Policy is to establish standards and expectations regarding any Dell-related use of Social Media. Dell's commitment to being direct supports open communications provided such communications adhere to this Policy.

Policy Statement
You must adhere to the following when engaging in Social Media:
Appropriate Use of Information Technology Resources. Dell's Information Technology (IT) resources are company property dedicated to achieving Dell's business objectives.

Inappropriate use is not acceptable. This includes, but is not limited to, using Dell IT assets to post offensive material on content-sharing websites, publish defamatory remarks about colleagues or customers on web forums or blogs, and leaking Confidential Information.

Speaking On Behalf of Dell. Blogging and other online dialogue are far-reaching forms of communication; distribution is meant for a vast public audience. Information purported to be published by Dell contained within blogs and other websites could have a negative impact to Dell and our stakeholders, with potential legal implications. Unless You have successfully completed Dell's Social Media training courses and have been certified to speak on behalf of the company via Social Media, You shall never claim to be speaking on behalf of Dell or expressing an official company position in such communications.

Ethical Conduct. You shall not conduct activities that are illegal or contrary to Dell's Code of Conduct, Privacy Statement Regarding Customer and Online User Information, or other Dell policies. Always respect the dignity and privacy of colleagues, customers, other Dell stakeholders, and Dell competitors. Harassing, intimidating, offensive, abusive, threatening, menacing or hostile content communicated through blogs and other online communications is prohibited. Data related to others, including, but not limited to, personal details and pictures, shall only be posted with that party's consent.

Transparency of Origin. You shall disclose Your connection to Dell in all communications with customers, the media or other Dell stakeholders when speaking on behalf of Dell (if authorized to do so) or discussing or recommending Dell or its products or services (even when doing so in Your personal capacity). You must also provide Your Dell contact information upon request. Unless you are certified to speak on behalf of Dell, You should make it clear that the opinions are Yours alone and do not necessarily reflect Dell's views or positions.

Accurate Information. Never knowingly communicate information that is untrue or deceptive. Communications shall be based on current, accurate, complete and relevant data. Dell will take all reasonable steps to assure the validity of information communicated via any channel but it is Your responsibility to assure accuracy in the first instance. Anecdotes and opinions shall be identified as such.

Protection of Confidential Information. You shall protect Confidential Information as such information represents one of Dell's most important assets. It is never appropriate to share, post, publish, or otherwise disclose Confidential Information unless You are explicitly authorized to do so. You must respect securities and financial disclosure laws, and must not post or otherwise comment in any capacity on Confidential Information that may be considered financial information (such as earnings, future business performance, business plans or prospects).

Accountability. You will be held accountable for the information You share in online activities. Be careful what You share, publish, post, or otherwise disclose. You are personally responsible for what You share and should remember that anything You post may be public for an indefinite period of time (even if You attempt to modify or delete). Try to ensure Your online communications reflect Dell's brand attributes of openness, responsiveness, integrity and optimism.

Procedures and Training
Dell has adopted training materials to assist You in complying with this Policy. Dell's Social Media & Communities (SMaC) Team will deliver role-appropriate training.

Asking Questions
You are encouraged to ask any questions You may have about this Policy. To learn more about how to use Social Media in accordance with this Policy, contact Dell's Social Media & Communities (SMaC) Team at social@dell.com. You may also ask Your leader, or Human Resources representative, or contact the Global Ethics & Compliance Office at ethics@dell.com, or the Legal Department.

Reporting and Investigation
It is very important that You immediately report any suspicious behavior regarding Dell employees or Dell third parties. To report known or suspected violations of this Policy, contact your leader or another member of management, your Human Resources representative, an Ethics & Compliance team member, or call the Ethics Helpline, a confidential toll-free, third party-operated telephone service, You may also submit a report via the Ethicsline, a confidential web-based online reporting vehicle. Reports made via the telephone Helpline or the web-based Ethicsline may be made anonymously where permitted by local law. Anyone reporting a suspected or actual violation of this Policy is protected from retaliation under Dell's Code of Conduct. All good faith allegations of violations of this Policy will be fully and confidentially investigated pursuant to Dell's Global Policy on Raising and Investigating Potential Ethics & Compliance Violations. You are required to cooperate with all investigations of alleged Policy violations.

Discipline and Other Consequences
Employees who violate this Policy will be subject to appropriate disciplinary action or other remedial measures up to and including termination of employment if warranted under the circumstances and permissible under applicable law. Assigned workers and third parties who violate this Policy are subject to being denied access to Dell facilities, personnel and assets, and permission to perform services on Dell's behalf.

Waivers
The provisions of this policy cannot be waived. Dell management does not have the authority to approve waivers to this Policy.

Revision and Revocation
This Policy is not a contract between Dell and any employee, assigned worker, or third party. This Policy may be revised or revoked by Dell at any time, without advance notice or cause.

Local Policies and Procedures
Dell operates in many countries and it is Dell's intention to comply with all applicable legal requirements. Accordingly, if a provision of this Policy conflicts with applicable local legal requirements, Dell will follow the local legal requirement (provided the local requirement does not conflict with U. S. law). In addition, Dell may adopt regional or country-specific policies on this subject to accommodate local conditions or legal requirements, and will inform employees in the applicable region or country of the terms of any such policy.

Definitions
Confidential Information – Important or valuable business information that is not available to the public. It includes trade secrets and other intellectual property that has been developed, licensed or acquired by Dell. It can also include information of customers, business partners or others that has been disclosed to Dell under obligations of confidentiality. Examples include unannounced financial information, strategic business plans, unannounced product or services and solutions offerings, planned or contemplated mergers or acquisitions, lawsuits and other legal proceedings, product design and technical knowledge, customer and team member personal information.

Social Media – Web-based technologies used to broadcast messages and participate in dialogues. Examples of Social Media software applications on the Internet include social networking applications such as Facebook; video-sharing applications such as YouTube; microblogging applications such as Twitter; collaboration applications such as Wikipedia; and Dell's official corporate blog, Direct2Dell. Examples of Social Media applications used within Dell are Dell's internal blog, One Dell Way, and Dell's internal networking tool, Yammer.

Global Policy on Social Media Effective Date: August 5, 2010

Deutscher Knigge Rat
Keine Social Media Guidelines im eigentlichen Sinne dieses Buches, aber dennoch lesenswert sind die Empfehlungen des Deutschen Knigge Rates (www.knigge-rat.de), der sich als Verein zur Förderung der „guten Umgangsformen" verschrieben hat:

Freundschaft auf den ersten Klick?
Stilvolle Kontaktpflege durch soziale Medien
von Rainer Wälde für den Deutschen Knigge Rat

Wählen Sie Ihre favorisierten Netzwerke sorgsam aus
Überlegen Sie kritisch, welche Netzwerke für Sie geeignet sind. Kriterien sind Kosten, Datenschutzbestimmungen, Popularität und Image des Netzwerks, Funktionen und Angebote sowie Ihr persönlicher Nutzen durch den Beitritt. Entscheidend ist, ob Sie die Plattform beruflich oder privat nutzen möchten. Vermeiden Sie eine Mischung aus beiden Bereichen und die Freigabe allzu vertraulicher Informationen.

Bleiben Sie authentisch
Bauen Sie keine fiktive Identität auf. Nicht nur Freunde, auch potenzielle Geschäftspartner und Arbeitgeber recherchieren im Internet. Ihre Glaubwürdigkeit und Reputation leiden, wenn das Gesamtbild nicht stimmig ist. Hilfreich ist es zum Beispiel, wenn Sie in allen Netzwerken das gleiche Foto verwenden.
Vermeiden Sie es außerdem, innerhalb eines Netzwerkes mit zwei Profilen zu agieren. Das stiftet Verwirrung.

Meiden Sie plumpe Vertraulichkeiten
Überlegen Sie sich vorab, welche Kontakte Sie über welches Netzwerk pflegen möchten. Ihre Kunden sind nicht unbedingt Ihre „Freunde" und empfinden diese Bezeichnung vielleicht als unpassend oder zu intim.

Prüfen Sie außerdem Ihre individuellen Sicherheitseinstellungen sorgfältig. Manch ein Nutzer ist verwundert, dass seine Party- und Bikinifotos vom letzten Urlaub ungeschützt und für jeden zugänglich sind.

Lehnen Sie unerwünschte Anfragen ab
Haben Sie keine Scheu davor, unerwünschte Kontaktanfragen abzulehnen. Eine taktvolle Rückmeldung, dass Sie nur persönlich bekannte Personen als Freunde bestätigen, vermeidet Missverständnisse und gehört zum guten Ton. Vorsicht ist insbesondere vor jenen geboten, die virtuelle Kontakte wie Trophäen sammeln. Dies ist kein Zeichen von Qualität, sondern eher für Oberflächlichkeit und Geltungssucht.

Belästigen Sie Ihre Kontakte nicht
Belästigen Sie Ihre „Freunde" nicht mit nervenden Spielen und Anwendungen. Wenn Sie Ihre Kommunikation nur auf spielerische Anfragen beschränken, werden Sie schnell ignoriert.

Bleiben Sie freundlich
Wahren Sie die Formen der Höflichkeit. Auch wenn alle Netzwerkpartner als „Freunde" angezeigt werden, kommt ein unvermitteltes Duzen zwischen Geschäftspartnern nicht stilvoll an. Eine korrekte Anrede und ein höflicher Abschiedsgruß gehören bei Kontaktanfragen dazu und steigern Ihre Chancen, akzeptiert zu werden.

Reagieren Sie humorvoll
Löschen Sie keine unbequemen Einträge von Ihrer Pinnwand, denn Zensuren sind den meisten Menschen suspekt. Reagieren Sie humorvoll statt verbissen. Entscheidend ist nicht der Eintrag, sondern Ihre Reaktion.

Halten Sie den Dialog lebendig
Überprüfen Sie regelmäßig Ihre Nachrichten und kommunizieren Sie mindestens einmal pro Woche mit Ihren Netzwerkpartnern. Nur wenn Sie direkt auf Einträge reagieren, bleibt der Dialog lebendig.

Behalten Sie den Weitblick
Überlegen Sie vor jedem Eintrag, ob er auch später noch gut für Ihre Reputation ist. Das Internet vergisst nie. Stellen Sie sich die Frage: Möchte ich, dass meine Meldung auch in zwei Jahren gefunden und gelesen werden kann? Achten Sie auf Ihre „innere Stimme" und löschen Sie lieber direkt impulsive Einträge, die Ihnen selbst oder anderen schaden könnten. Bedenken Sie, dass etliche Firmen die Netzwerkeinträge potenzieller Bewerber prüfen.

Schließen Sie Trolle aus
Lassen Sie sich nicht von unangenehmen Zeitgenossen zu unüberlegten Reaktionen verleiten. Die sogenannten „Trolle" sind nicht am eigentlichen Thema interessiert, sondern wollen nur Menschen in Misskredit bringen oder Diskussionen sabotieren. Blockieren Sie diese Personen in Ihrer Kontaktliste.

Extra-Tipps fürs Geschäftsleben

Business-Tipp: Geben Sie Empfehlungen
Nutzen Sie Ihr Netzwerk, um kurz über interessante Filme, Bücher oder Produkte zu schreiben. Wie im realen Leben dürfen Sie zwischendurch auch mal auf eigene Projekte hinweisen. Die Abwechslung ist entscheidend.

Business-Tipp: Aufdringliche Werbung ist tabu
Belasten Sie „Freundschaften" nicht mit aggressiver Werbung. Wenn Sie nur verkaufen wollen, werden Sie schnell ignoriert. Denken Sie langfristig und vermeiden Sie es, als „nervender Nachbar" ausgegrenzt zu werden.

Deutsche Post DHL
Deutsche Post DHL ist (nach Unternehmensangaben) der weltweit führende Post- und Logistikkonzern. Unter: https://www.dp-dhl.com/content/dam/presse/social_media/dpdhl_social_media_guidelines_de.pdf sind die Guidelines der ehemaligen Deutschen Bundespost abrufbar.

SOCIAL MEDIA GUIDELINES
Social-Media-Portale wie Facebook, YouTube oder Twitter bieten uns neue Chancen, um Meinungen, Gedanken und Erfahrungen mit anderen Nutzern, Freunden, Kollegen oder Kunden auszutauschen – und das weltweit.
Täglich wird auch über unser Unternehmen im Web intensiv diskutiert. Jeder, der sich online über Deutsche Post DHL äußert, prägt damit das Bild des Unternehmens in der Öffentlichkeit.
Wenn auch Sie sich in Blogs, Foren oder sozialen Netzwerken über Deutsche Post DHL austauschen, möchten wir Sie bitten, die folgenden Punkte zu beachten:

1 Beachten Sie unsere Unternehmenswerte.
Respekt, Toleranz, Ehrlichkeit und Offenheit sowie Integrität gegenüber Kollegen und Kunden sind in unserem Code of Conduct festgeschrieben – und gelten natürlich auch im Internet.

2 Sprechen Sie nur für sich selbst.
Offizielle Statements, Erklärungen und Publikationen von Deutsche Post DHL werden auch im Internet nur von autorisierten Mitarbeitern veröffentlicht.

3 Seien Sie authentisch und transparent.
Wenn Sie sich zu Deutsche Post DHL äußern, dann sagen Sie offen, dass Sie für unser Unternehmen tätig sind. Schreiben Sie jedoch immer in der Ich-Form und machen Sie so deutlich, dass es sich um Ihre private Meinung handelt und nicht um die des Unternehmens.

4 Behalten Sie vertrauliche Informationen für sich.
Besonders wichtig: Internes bleibt intern. Behandeln Sie alle geheimhaltungsbedürftigen Informationen und Betriebsgeheimnisse unseres Unternehmens, unserer Partner und Lieferanten streng vertraulich.

5 Schützen Sie Ihre Privatsphäre und auch die Ihrer Kinder.
Was Sie veröffentlichen, ist häufig für alle sichtbar. Auch wenn Sie Inhalte korrigieren oder löschen, alles hinterlässt Spuren im Internet. Achten Sie also sehr genau darauf, was Sie preisgeben.

6 Handeln Sie verantwortlich.
Für das, was Sie veröffentlichen, tragen Sie die Verantwortung. Sollten Sie in Einzelfällen nicht sicher sein, stellen Sie sich die Frage, ob Sie die Inhalte Ihrem Arbeitskollegen, Vorgesetzten oder Geschäftspartner auch direkt mitteilen würden.

7 Halten Sie sich an geltendes Recht.
Bestehende Gesetze gelten natürlich auch im Internet. Vor allem auf die Einhaltung von Copyright wird streng geachtet. Veröffentlichen Sie deshalb nur Inhalte, Bilder und Videos, die von Ihnen stammen, und respektieren Sie die Rechte anderer Nutzer.

8 Behandeln Sie andere mit Respekt.
Achten Sie darauf, wie Sie etwas formulieren. Handeln Sie respektvoll, bleiben Sie höflich und sachlich. Vorsicht mit Humor, Ironie und Sarkasmus – ohne Mimik und Gestik sind diese oft schwer zu verstehen.

9 Unterstützen Sie uns.
Wenn Sie im Internet auf Lob, Kritik oder Humorvolles stoßen und dies mit uns teilen oder diskutieren wollen, können Sie uns hier erreichen: socialmedia@dhl.com oder socialmedia@deutschepost.de.

10 Nutzen Sie interne Plattformen.
Social-Media-Aktivitäten werden in zunehmendem Umfang auch im Corporate Intranet ermöglicht. Benutzen Sie für alle internen Zwecke, wie z. B. Diskussionen mit Kollegen, die zur Verfügung stehenden internen Plattformen.

Unter socialmedia@dhl.com oder socialmedia@deutschepost.de haben wir immer ein offenes Ohr für Ihre Fragen, z. B. wenn Sie bei der Umsetzung der oben genannten Punkte Hilfe benötigen.
Mehr Informationen zu Social Media sowie detaillierte Erläuterungen zu diesen Guidelines finden Sie im Corporate Intranet unter: http://quicklink.intra.dpwn.net/socialmedia.

Deutsche Post DHL
Zentrale
Global Media Relations
53250 Bonn
Deutschland

DMEautomotive

DMEautomotive ist ein Anbieter von Direktmarketingleistungen für den Automobilvertrieb. Entsprechend nutzt das Unternehmen nicht nur für sich Social Media (u. a. auf Facebook, Twitter, YouTube, LinkedIn und mit eigenem Unternehmens-Blog), sondern bietet Social-Media-Marketing im Rahmen seines Produktportfolios seinen Kunden – überwiegend große Autohandelsketten – an.

DMEautomotive's Corporate Social Media Guidelines

DMEautomotive recognizes that social media has fundamentally changed the way we work, offering new opportunities to engage in two--way conversations with customers, colleagues, and the world at large. Additionally, we believe that getting involved in social media will grow our brand, strengthen our connection with customers, and will act as an important tool for DMEautomotive to maintain and improve its reputation as an industry-leading direct-marketing company. Therefore, we encourage our employees to become involved in social media networks and use these spaces to interact, engage and share.

DMEautomotive has issued the following guidelines, not in an attempt to stifle your voice, but to encourage your participation in social media and outline expectations designed to protect the interests of our employees and the company.

Representation
– Always be transparent. Be honest about who you are and any affiliations you may have. Be genuine, authentic and real.
– Add a disclaimer if you are publishing content regarding work topics outside DMEauto-

motive's website to ensure your comments aren't misconstrued as corporate policy. For example, "The opinions and positions expressed are my own and do not necessarily reflect those of DMEautomotive".
- Maintain a sense of credibility, which in turn will improve your reputation and trustworthiness.

Responsibility
- Be accountable. What you write is ultimately your responsibility.
- Be truthful. Ensure that content is factually accurate. Should there be an error, acknowledge it and correct promptly. Do not try to erase the error or be evasive. Rather, edit the post and insert a footnote that the original post was modified. Additionally, should you need to, cite original content and link sources.
- Protect confidential information and relationships. We encourage you to share company projects, lessons learned, best practices and success stories. However, do not reveal any corporate proprietary information. If you wish to mention a client by name, please obtain their permission first.
- Talk about what you know. Be the expert! Offer advice, insights and comments on topics that are within your area of expertise. For all other matters, alert those who are the relevant topic expert.

Respect
- Respect your audience. An objective of Social Media is to create dialogue and thus differences of opinion will likely arise. We encourage you to express your ideas and opinions in a respectful manner and ask that you don't resort to insults (whether personal or towards a competitor), harassment, and/or offensive language should a disagreement take place.
- Show respect for your audience's time. Add value by contributing valuable tips, insights and relevant content. Also, ask questions, respond in a timely manner and listen to what others say.

Last but certainly not least, strive for balance – though we encourage the participation in Social Media, be practical about your use and don't neglect the demands of DMEautomotive's clients and your primary job responsibilities.
Social Media is about enjoying personal interactions. Be personable, engage, interact, share and have fun!

EFF – Electronic Frontier Foundation
Die 1990 gegründete EFF – Electronic Frontier Foundation versteht sich als Bürgerrechtsorganisation, die die Freiheitsrechtsrechte in der vernetzten Welt schützt. Auch eine derartige spendenfinanzierte Non-Profit-Organisation benötigt Richtlinien für den Umgang mit Social Media. Die Besonderheiten finden sich in der Ausgestaltung, in der etwa Handlungsempfehlungen für das „anonyme Bloggen" mitgegeben werden.

"How to Blog Safely (about Work or anything else)" http://www.eff.org/wp/blog-safely=
Published April 6, 2005
Updated May 31, 2005

Blogs are like personal telephone calls crossed with newspapers. They're the perfect tool for sharing your favorite chocolate mousse recipe with friends – or for upholding the basic tenets of democracy by letting the public know that a corrupt government official has been paying off your boss.

If you blog, there are no guarantees you'll attract a readership of thousands. But at least a few readers will find your blog, and they may be the people you'd least want or expect. These include potential or current employers, coworkers, and professional colleagues; your neighbors; your spouse or partner; your family; and anyone else curious enough to type your name, email address or screen name into Google or Feedster and click a few links.

The point is that anyone can eventually find your blog if your real identity is tied to it in some way. And there may be consequences. Family members may be shocked or upset when they read your uncensored thoughts. A potential boss may think twice about hiring you. But these concerns shouldn't stop you from writing. Instead, they should inspire you to keep your blog private, or accessible only to certain trusted people.

Here we offer a few simple precautions to help you maintain control of your personal privacy so that you can express yourself without facing unjust retaliation. If followed correctly, these protections can save you from embarrassment or just plain weirdness in front of your friends and coworkers.

Blog Anonymously
The best way to blog and still preserve some privacy is to do it anonymously. But being anonymous isn't as easy as you might think.

Let's say you want to start a blog about your terrible work environment but you don't want to risk your boss or colleagues discovering that you're writing about them. You'll want to consider how to anonymize every possible detail about your situation. And you may also want to use one of several technologies that make it hard for anyone to trace the blog back to you.

1. Use a Pseudonym and Don't Give Away Any Identifying Details
When you write about your workplace, be sure not to give away telling details. These include things like where you're located, how many employees there are, and the specific sort of business you do. Even general details can give away a lot. If, for example, you write, "I work at an unnamed weekly newspaper in Seattle," it's clear that you work in one of two places. So be smart. Instead, you might say that you work at a media outlet in a mid-sized city. Obviously, don't use real names or post pictures of yourself. And don't use pseudonyms that sound like the real names they're based on – so, for instance, don't anonymize the name "Annalee"

by using the name "Leanne." And remember that almost any kind of personal information can give your identity away – you may be the only one at your workplace with a particular birthday, or with an orange tabby.

Also, if you are concerned about your colleagues finding out about your blog, do not blog while you are at work. Period. You could get in trouble for using company resources like an Internet connection to maintain your blog, and it will be very hard for you to argue that the blog is a work-related activity. It will also be much more difficult for you to hide your blogging from officemates and IT operators who observe traffic over the office network.

2. Use Anonymizing Technologies

There are a number of technical solutions for the blogger who wishes to remain anonymous.

If you are worried that your blog-hosting service may be logging your unique IP address and thus tracking what computer you're blogging from, you can use the anonymous network Tor to edit your blog. Tor routes your Internet traffic through what's called an "overlay network" that hides your IP address. More importantly, Tor makes it difficult for snoops on the Internet to follow the path your data takes and trace it back to you.

3. Use Ping Servers

If you want to protect your privacy while getting news out quickly, try using ping servers to broadcast your blog entry for you. Pingomatic http://www.pingomatic.com is a tool that allows you to do this by broadcasting to a lot of news venues at once, while making you untraceable. The program will send out notice (a "ping") about your blog entry to several blog search engines like Feedster and Technorati. Once those sites list your entry – which is usually within a few minutes – you can take the entry down. Thus the news gets out rapidly and its source can evaporate within half an hour. This protects the speaker while also helping the blog entry reach people fast.

4. Limit Your Audience

Many blogging services, including LiveJournal, allow you to designate individual posts or your entire blog as available only to those who have the password, or to people whom you've designated as friends. If your blog's main goal is to communicate to friends and family, and you want to avoid any collateral damage to your privacy, consider using such a feature. If you host your own blog, you can also set it up to be password-protected, or to be visible only to people looking at it from certain computers.

5. Don't Be Googleable

If you want to exclude most major search engines like Google from including your blog in search results, you can create a special file that tells these search services to ignore your domain. The file is called robots.txt, or a Robots Text File. You can also use it to exclude search engines from gaining access to certain parts of your blog. If you don't know how to do this yourself, you can use the "Robots Text File Generator" tool for free at Web Tool Central . However, it's important to remember that search engines like Google may choose to ignore a robots.txt file, thus making your blog easily searchable. There are many tools and tricks for making your blog less searchable, without relying on robots.txt.

6. Register Your Domain Name Anonymously

Even if you don't give your real name or personal information in your blog, people can look up the WHOIS records for your domain name and find out who you are. If you don't want anyone to do this, consider registering your domain name anonymously.

Blog Without Getting Fired

A handful of bloggers have recently discovered that their labors of love may lead to unemployment. By some estimates, dozens of people have been fired for blogging, and the numbers are growing every day.

The bad news is that in many cases, there is no legal means of redress if you've been fired for blogging. While your right to free speech is protected by the First Amendment, this protection does not shield you from the consequences of what you say. The First Amendment protects speech from being censored by the government; it does not regulate what private parties (such as most employers) do. In states with "at will" employment laws like California, employers can fire you at any time, for any reason. And no state has laws that specifically protect bloggers from discrimination, on the job or otherwise.

One way to make sure your blog doesn't earn you a pink slip is to make sure that you write about certain protected topics. Most states have laws designed to prevent employers from firing people who talk openly about their politics outside of work, for example. Be warned that laws like this do vary widely from state to state, and many are untested when it comes to blogging.

1. Political Opinions

Many states, including California, include sections in their Labor Code that prohibit employers from regulating their employees' political activities and affiliations, or influencing employees' political activities by threatening to fire them. If you blog about membership in the Libertarian Party and your boss fires you for it, you might very well have a case against him or her.

2. Unionizing

In many states, talking or writing about unionizing your workforce is strongly protected by the law, so in many cases blogging about your efforts to unionize will be safe. Also, if you are in a union, it's possible that your contract may have been negotiated in a way that permits blogging. Some states protect "concerted" speech about the workplace, which means that if two or more people start a blog discussing the conditions in their workplace, this activity could be protected under local labor laws.

3. Whistleblowing

Often there are legal shields to protect whistleblowers – people who expose the harmful activities of their employers for the public good. However, many people have the misconception that if you report the regulatory violations (of, say, toxic emissions limits) or illegal activities of your employer in a blog, you're protected. But that isn't the case. You need to report the problems to the appropriate regulatory or law enforcement bodies first. You can also complain to a manager at your company. But notify somebody in authority about the sludge your company is dumping in the wetlands first, then blog about it.

4. Reporting on Your Work for the Government
If you work for the government, blogging about what's happening at the office is protected speech under the First Amendment. It's also in the public interest to know what's happening in your workplace, because citizens are paying you with their tax dollars. Obviously, do not post classified or confidential information.

5. Legal Off-Duty Activities
Some states have laws that may protect an employee or applicant's legal off-duty blogging, especially if the employer has no policy or an unreasonably restrictive policy with regard to off-duty speech activities. For example, California has a law protecting employees from "demotion, suspension, or discharge from employment for lawful conduct occurring during nonworking hours away from the employer's premises." These laws have not been tested in a blogging context. If you are terminated for blogging while off-duty, you should contact an employment attorney to see what rights you may have.

Blog without Fear
Blogs are getting a lot of attention these days. You can no longer safely assume that people in your offline life won't find out about your blog, if you ever could. New RSS tools and services mean that it's even easier than ever search and aggregate blog entries. As long as you blog anonymously and in a work-safe way, what you say online is far less likely to come back to hurt you.

Resources
C|Net's guide to workplace blogging:
http://news.com.com/FAQ+Blogging+on+the+job/2100-1030_3-5597010.html?tag...

How Tor works:
http://tor.eff.org/overview.html

The Bloggers' Rights Blog:
http://rights.journalspace.com/

A Technical Guide to Anonymous Blogging (An Early Draft), by Ethan Zuckerman:
http://cyber.law.harvard.edu/globalvoices/?p=125

EFF's Legal Guide for Bloggers, a larger, more comprehensive look at the legal issues facing bloggers:
http://www.eff.org/bloggers/lg/

Ford

Der US-Autoriese Ford ist weltweit auch im Social Web auf vielfache Weise tätig. Geregelt sind die Social-Media-Aktivitäten bei Ford in den Digital Participation Guidelines (http://www.scribd.com/doc/36127480/Ford-Social-Media-Guidelines).

Davon abgeleitet existieren auch für Deutschland Social Media Guidelines. Obwohl diese auf Konferenzen durch Unternehmensvertreter von Ford Deutschland öffentlich diskutiert werden, konnten sie auf Anfrage nicht zur Verfügung gestellt werden („nicht öffentlich"). Hier daher die globalen Richtlinien:

Ford Motor Company's Digital Participation Guidelines

We have advised our personnel to observe these guidelines when participating in an online conversation regarding Ford or the automotive industry. These are a summary of our ethical policies. Ford personnel should refer to the more detailed information available within the Company.

Be honest about who you are
If the conversation relates to our business or our industry, you should identify yourself as working for Ford Motor Company in the content of your post/comment/other content. Not only is this the ethical thing to do, but in some countries, like the U.S., there may be personal liability under Federal Trade Commission regulations if you don't. Best practice is always to be honest about who you are without giving out detailed personal information.

Make it clear that the views expressed are yours.
Include the following notice somewhere in every social media profile you maintain: "I work at Ford, but this is my own opinion and is not the opinion of Ford Motor Company."

You speak for yourself, but your actions reflect those of Ford Motor Company.
Unless you have been authorized by Communications, you cannot speak on behalf of Ford Motor Company. Do not portray yourself as a spokesperson, even an "unofficial" spokesperson, on issues relating to Ford Motor Company. Realize that people may likely form an opinion about the Company based on the behavior of its personnel.

Use your common sense
It's good business practice for companies (and individuals) to keep certain topics confidential. Respect confidentiality. Refrain from speculation on the future of the Company and its products. Keep topics focused to matters of public record when speaking about the Company or the automotive industry. Do not disclose non-public Company information or the personal information of others.

Mind your manners
Treat past and present co-workers, other personnel, suppliers, consumers, partners, com-

petitors, Ford Motor Company, and yourself with respect. Avoid posting materials or comments that may be seen as offensive, demeaning, inappropriate, threatening, or abusive. Acknowledge ifferences of opinion. Respectfully withdraw from discussions that go off topic or become profane.

The Internet is a public space.
Consider everything you post to the Internet the same as anything you would post to a physical bulletin board or submit to a newspaper. Many eyes may fall upon your words, including those of reporters, consumers, your manager and the competition. Assume that all of these people will be reading every post, no matter how obscure or secure the site to which you are posting may seem.

The Internet remembers.
Search engines and other technologies make it virtually impossible to take something back. Be sure you mean what you say, and say what you mean.

An official response may be needed.
If you spot a potential issue and believe an official Company response is needed, bring it to the attention of a member of the Communications team or the Legal office before it reaches a crisis situation. Potential issues can often be resolved more effectively and efficiently if they are identified quickly.

Respect the privacy of offline conversations
Protect your co-workers and our partners by refraining from sharing their personal information or any conversations or statements unless you have their written permission to do so. Bringing someone else into an online conversation without their permission can be destructive to a relationship, cause misunderstandings or violate laws, commercial contracts and/or confidentiality agreements.

Same rules and laws apply: New medium, no surprise
Due to the nature of the digital medium, extra diligence is required in respecting intellectual property (such as copyright and trademark), financial disclosure laws, false advertising and the like. Also, refer people with vehicle or repair concerns to the dealer or customer relations (Contact Ford at http://www.ford.com/owner-services/customer-support/contact-ford). If anyone has a new idea for the Company, refer them to "Your Ideas" on The Ford Story.

When in doubt, ask.
If you have any questions about what is appropriate, play it smart and check with a member of the Communications team or the Legal office before posting.

Guidelines

In brief, our guidelines for engaging on the social Web consist of the following core principles:

1. Honesty about who you are
2. Clarity that your opinions are your own
3. Respect and humility in all communication
4. Good judgment in sharing only public information – including financial data
5. Awareness that what you say is permanent

These guidelines are meant to provide a simple and clear guide to online communications for Ford Motor Company personnel. For a more detailed look at the guidelines and potential implications for failing to follow them, please visit our internal resources on HR Online or FordLaw.

08/2010

Gartner
Die weltweit tätige IT-Beratungsgesellschaft nutzt selbst das Social Web mit eigener Facebook-Page, LinkedIn-Seite, eigenem Twitter-Kanal und vor allem durch umfangreiche themenspezifische Blogs.
Als Analystenfirma muss Gartner stets die Balance finden zwischen dem im Web erwarteten freien Zugang zu Informationen und dem Gartner-Geschäftsmodell, das den Verkauf des eigenen Contents in Form von Marktstudien und Reports vorsieht.

Auskunft über die erwünschten Online-Aktivitäten geben die „Gartner analyst public web participation guidelines" (http://blogs.gartner.com/?page_id=69).

The Web represents a fundamental opportunity for Gartner to evolve its means and style of interaction across its ecosystem of clients, prospects, technology providers, business leaders, media, etc., as well as expanding and deepening such interactions. In promulgating these guidelines, Gartner is building both upon longstanding policies regarding associates' personal interactions and upon the sound judgment that we expect our associates to use in their professional interactions.

Accordingly, these guidelines are simply a reflection of that expectation of sound judgment as it is applied to the concrete issues and circumstances of Web participation. These guidelines (and associated examples) will evolve as our collective experience with such participation evolves.

"Web Participation" is currently defined as all forms of public Web-based communication and expression, such as blogs, microblogs, linkblogs, wikis, bookmark sites, photo sharing sites, video sharing sites, forums, mailing lists, discussion groups, chat rooms, and social network sites.

Scope and Applicability of these Guidelines

These Guidelines apply to Gartner analysts who are registered to participate in the Gartner Blogger Network. They are expected to guide your Web Participation:

– Whenever you are participating in the Gartner Blogger Network; and/or
– Whenever you engage in Web Participation of any kind if (1) you identify yourself in the social environment as a Gartner analyst or (2) you examine or discuss topics related to information technology.

In these circumstances, you are considered to be acting in the "persona" of a Gartner analyst, and must comply with these Guidelines.

These Guidelines do not apply to official corporate communications; content published through standard research processes for clients, or internal interactions. In addition, Gartner associates, including analysts who are not registered to participate in the Gartner Blogger Network, are not covered by these Guidelines; they are, however, subject to the more restrictive policies governing public Web Participation set forth in Gartner's Blog Policy.

Gartner monitors the use of social media, including social networking sites, to ensure compliance with these guidelines.

Summary

1. All Gartner policies apply: Know and follow Gartner's policies.

2. Think before you post: Use sound judgment and think about reactions to your post before you post it.

3. Respect your audience: Avoid negative personal comments or inflammatory subjects.

4. Have productive conversations: For Gartner and its associates, the primary benefits of Web participation are for others to learn about Gartner and for Gartner to learn from others.

5. Don't "give away the farm": Don't post the kind of information and advice for which clients pay Gartner.

6. Protect and enhance the value of the Gartner brand: Present Gartner in a positive light and avoid making derogatory comments about Gartner, our products, services, management, employees, or systems.

7. Protect confidential information: Protect Gartner's and our clients' confidential information.

8. Be personable and have fun: Web participation is about enjoying personal interactions, not delivering corporate communications.

9. Be conscious of persona: Know when you are representing Gartner, are expected to post as a professional and are subject to these Guidelines.

10. Don't engage in debates defending published Gartner research: Analysts may clarify research positions but should not engage in public debates defending published Gartner research.

Detailed Discussion

1. All Gartner policies apply.
Know and follow all Gartner policies, including our Code of Conduct and Ethical Conduct Principles. See Gartner at Work for a listing of Gartner policies.

2. Think before you post.
Use sound judgment and think about reactions to your post before you post it. Remember that whatever you post may live for many years in the Web, even after you delete your copy of it. Avoid posting in the heat of the moment, especially in a discussion list that is escalating into a flame war. Ask yourself, "Is this issue better handled by another part of Gartner, such as Research management or PR?"

3. Respect your audience.
Avoid slurs, personal attacks or insults, obscenity, etc., and topics that may be considered objectionable or inflammatory – such as topics in the areas of politics and religion. Show proper consideration for others' privacy, and avoid picking fights. Be the first to correct your own mistakes, and be constructive and respectful in correcting others.

4. Have productive conversations
For Gartner and its associates, the primary benefits of Web participation are for others to learn about Gartner and for Gartner to learn from others. While it is OK to offer criticism, such criticism should be constructive and never mean-spirited, and should not involve accusations of wrongdoing or improper conduct. Find out who else is blogging on the topic, and link to them. If Gartner has relevant research on the topic, link to it (even if it is just the abstract). Try to add value. Provide worthwhile information (get your facts straight) and perspective (be constructive). Test your ideas and move research forward while avoiding direct disagreement with published research. Remember, if a posting generates a request from a technology provider for a briefing, a journalist for an interview, or a client or prospect for an inquiry, route it through normal Gartner channels.

5. Don't "give away the farm."

Don't post the kind of information and advice for which clients pay Gartner. Gartner wants clients to pay us for information and associates want Gartner to get paid for information. Associates also may want to participate in Web conversations about IT – which means exchanging information and opinion about IT. To ensure you aren't divulging too much information, be thoughtful about what information you post and how you respond to feedback. Ask yourself: "Is this the kind of information that our clients normally pay us for?" If the answer is "Yes" or even "Perhaps," then confer with other Gartner colleagues before posting. Especially with IT subjects, focus on opening a dialog around topics to enhance awareness of the topic, to gain constructive feedback from the broader IT community and to build awareness of Gartner activities and research.

6. Protect and enhance the value of Gartner's brand.

Present Gartner in a positive light and avoid making derogatory comments about Gartner, our products, services, management, employees or systems Although this is already covered by the Gartner Principles of Ethical Code of Conduct, it is worth highlighting explicitly in the context of Web participation. To minimize the risk that your individual post is perceived as a Gartner vetted research position, you should make it clear that you are posting as an individual analyst. Use a disclaimer such as: "This post is my individual opinion and does not necessarily represent a Gartner vetted research position." (A blanket disclaimer for an entire set of posts is appropriate, as long as the disclaimer is clearly visible – for example, in a blog sidebar.)

When posting about IT-related issues it is inevitable – indeed healthy – for contrary points of view to be debated and discussed. It is inevitable that an individual associate's post about an IT subject may occasionally be viewed as representing or contradicting Gartner's official position on a subject. However, it is never appropriate to intentionally disparage or contradict published Gartner research. If such a post actually generates controversy or confusion, the associate should post as quickly as possible a clarification that resolves the issue. Be careful when blogging about vendors. Do not create a new and previously unstated position(s) on a vendor, vendor action or product. This must be created through the Gartner official research process first.

7. Protect confidential information.

Protect Gartner's and our clients' confidential information. Information that we would not publicly disclose in our research due to confidentiality concerns should not be disclosed or discussed on the Web. Also, because we are a public company, don't disclose or discuss Gartner's revenues, future business plans or share price. If in doubt, gain permission prior to posting on matters that might be private or internal to Gartner. Respect copyright, fair use and financial disclosure laws.

8. Be personable and have fun.

Web participation is about enjoying personal interactions, not delivering corporate communications. Always identify yourself. Write in the first person. If your Web participation (e.g., keeping up your blog) feels like work, you're probably doing too much of it and it's likely to interfere with your work at Gartner. A big part of the Web experience is that it is more playful than most other mediums. Your Web participation should reflect this characteristic. The most successful blogs are those with an informal and humorous style. It's OK – some might say mandatory – to poke fun in Web postings, but keep in mind that such humor should always be appropriate and should stimulate discussion, not stifle it.

9. Be conscious of persona.

Persona is the role you are playing when participating on the web. In the case of Gartner analysts, you may adopt the persona of a professional IT analyst or a personal persona unconnected to your professional work life. It is important for analysts to recognize the difference, and to be careful when crossing from one persona to the other in any particular social environment. Analysts are acting in their Gartner analyst professional persona whenever they 1) identify themselves in the social environment as an analyst or 2) when they behave like an analyst, such as by discussing topics related to information technology. Whenever and wherever analysts act in their Gartner analyst persona, they must comply with these Web participation guidelines.

When posting on The Gartner Blogger Network platform, you should be acting in your Gartner analyst persona, and comply with these Guidelines. Posts that are more suited to a personal life persona belong in a social environment intended for that persona.

10. Don't engage in debates defending published Gartner Research.

Analysts are encouraged to engage in the social Web around research issues and exchange differing points of view. And analysts can also use the Gartner Blogger Network platform to promote their published research. However, if published Gartner research is disputed on the social Web, analysts should inform the Ombudsman's office and refrain from engaging in public debates. Use your best judgment in discussing and clarifying published research. While Gartner strives for transparency in our research methodologies, there are aspects of our methodologies that are proprietary and are not intended for public dissemination. Therefore, analysts should not publicly explain or clarify Gartner research methodology. This is the role of the Ombudsman's office.

General Motors

General Motors, derzeit der weltführende Autohersteller, hat – anders als andere Anbieter – nur sehr kurze Guidelines, die GM Blogger Policy (http://fastlane.gmblogs.com/about.html) als Regelung für die Unternehmensblogs des US-Autoherstellers.

1. We will tell the truth. We will acknowledge and correct any mistakes promptly.
2. We will not delete comments unless they are spam, off-topic, or defamatory.
3. We will reply to comments when appropriate as promptly as possible.
4. We will link to online references and original source materials directly
5. We will disagree with other opinions respectfully.

Grey Werbeagentur

Die international bekannte Fullservice-Werbeagentur bietet ihren Kunden unter anderem auch Social-Media-Dienstleistungen.

Für sich selbst hat man – veröffentlicht im eigenen Weblog: http://blog.grey.de/social-media-guidelines/ – folgende Guidelines entwickelt.

Die Welt spricht vom Social Web. Die Welt spricht von Social Media. Die Welt spricht von Facebook, Twitter & Co.

Wir sind mittendrin. Jeden Tag. Mit Mehrwert für unsere Kunden, für uns selbst und weil es verdammt viel Spaß macht. Wir gehen mit dem Thema Social Media offen um. Kein Mitarbeiter wird daran gehindert, sich in sozialen Netzwerken während der Arbeitszeit aufzuhalten. Im Gegenteil, der Umgang mit sozialen Medien bringt uns in den Dialog mit vielen Persönlichkeiten und birgt enormen Mehrwert für unsere tägliche Arbeit. Wir als Werbeagentur leben vom persönlichen Engagement und von den Ideen der Mitarbeiter. Die nachfolgenden Guidelines wollen Orientierung geben, um den Spirit of being Famously Effective im Social Web gemeinsam und respektvoll zu leben.

Social Media Guidelines

Tritt im Social Web als der auf, der du bist – Glaubwürdigkeit ist das A und O.

Im richtigen Leben gehst du respektvoll mit Menschen um – mach es genauso im Social Web.

Wie im richtigen Leben steht man auch im Social Web zu seinen Fehlern.

Wie im richtigen Leben trägst du die Verantwortung für dein Engagement.

Und wie im richtigen Leben hört man dir eher zu, wenn du etwas Interessantes zu erzählen hast.

Lass dich im Social Web nicht provozieren – wenn du nicht weißt, wie du reagieren sollst, bitte einen Kollegen um Rat.

Du bist Mitarbeiter von Grey – Interna bleiben Interna.

Bei Presseanfragen im Social Web an dich – leite sie einfach an die Unternehmenskommunikation weiter.

Offline beachtest du geltendes Recht, tue dies auch im Social Web, was z. B. das Urheberrecht, die Privatsphäre oder den Datenschutz angeht.

Achte darauf, dass Dein zeitliches Social-Media-Engagement in einem vernünftigen Verhältnis zu deinen Aufgaben bei Grey steht.

Harvard Law School

Auch Hochschulen stehen durch Social Media unter Zugzwang. Während in Deutschland das Thema zumeist auf Institutsebene diskutiert und bisher zumeist informell geregelt wird, haben viele amerikanische Hochschulen, wie die weltbekannte Harvard Law School, eigene Regelungen.

http://blogs.law.harvard.edu/terms-of-use/

Terms of Use

Welcome to Weblogs at Harvard Law!
We don't mean to turn you off from blogging by immediately inundating you with legalese, but we need to make clear our respective rights and responsibilities related to this service. So, the President and Fellows of Harvard College ("Harvard") offer these blogging services (the "Services") to you subject to the terms and conditions of use ("Terms") contained herein. By accessing, creating or contributing to any blogs hosted at http://blogs.law.harvard.edu/, and in consideration for the Services we provide to you, you agree to abide by these Terms. Please read them carefully before posting to or creating any blog.

1. Rights in the Content You Submit

Default Creative Commons Public License
Unless you specify otherwise, any and all works of authorship copyrightable by you and posted by you to any blog ("Content") are submitted under the terms of an Attribution-ShareAlike Creative Commons Public License. Under this license, you permit anyone to copy, distribute, display and perform your Content, royalty-free, on the condition that they credit your authorship each time they do so. You also permit others to distribute derivative works of your Content, but only if they do so under the same Attribution-ShareAlike license that governs your original Content.

[...]

If you prefer to offer your Content on more restrictive terms, you may do so as follows:

For Content you submit to your own blog, remove the Creative Commons logo from your blog template (contact us if you require instructions).

For Content you submit to a blog other than your own, label your submission with a full copyright notice, i.e., your name, the word "copyright" or symbol "©" and the year of first publication.

By posting your Content using the Services, you are granting Harvard a non-exclusive, royalty-free, perpetual, and worldwide license to use your Content in connection with the operation of the Services, including, without limitation, the license rights to copy, distribute, transmit, publicly display, publicly perform, reproduce, edit, translate and reformat your Content, and/or to incorporate it into a collective work.

Attribution
When publicly displaying, publicly performing, reproducing or distributing copies of your Content, or Content as incorporated into a collective work, Harvard will make best efforts to credit your authorship. You grant Harvard permission to use your name for such attribution purposes. You, likewise, agree to represent yourself accurately. You acknowledge that misrepresentation may lead us, in our sole discretion, to cancel your use of the Services and delete any of your Content.

2. Conduct

Posting
Those of us who are coordinating this research project believe deeply in free speech. Given our role in offering this service and our presence together as part of the extended university community, however, we must reserve the right to remove certain content that you may post. As a general matter, you may post content freely to your blog and to those of others, so long as the content is not illegal, obscene, defamatory, threatening, infringing of intellectual property rights, invasive of privacy or otherwise injurious or objectionable.

You may not use the Harvard name to endorse or promote any product, opinion, cause or political candidate. Representation of your personal opinions as institutionally endorsed by Harvard University or any of its Schools or organizations is strictly prohibited.
By posting content to any blog, you warrant and represent that you either own or otherwise control all of the rights to that content, including, without limitation, all the rights necessary for you to provide, post, upload, input or submit the content, or that your use of the content is a protected fair use. You agree that you will not knowingly and with intent to defraud provide material and misleading false information. You represent and warrant also that the content you supply does not violate these Terms, and that you will indemnify and hold Harvard harmless for any and all claims resulting from content you supply.
You acknowledge that Harvard does not pre-screen or regularly review posted content, but that it shall have the right to remove in its sole discretion any content that it considers to

violate these Terms or the terms of any other campus user agreements that may govern your use of the campus networks.

Accessing

You understand that all content posted to http://blogs.law.harvard.edu/ is the sole responsibility of the individual who originally posted the content. You understand, also, that all opinions expressed by users of this site are expressed strictly in their individual capacities, and not as representatives of any Harvard institution.

You agree that Harvard will not be liable, under any circumstances and in any way, for any errors or omissions, loss or damage of any kind incurred as a result of use of any content posted on this site. You agree that you must evaluate and bear all risks associated with the use of any content, including any reliance on the accuracy, completeness, or usefulness of such content.

Children

Collecting personal information from children under the age of 13 is prohibited. No Content should be directed toward such children without the express written permission of the Executive Director, Berkman Center for Internet & Society at Harvard Law School.

3. Disclaimer of Warranties and Limitation of Liability

This site is provided on an "as is" and "as available" basis. Harvard makes no representations or warranties of any kind, express or implied, as to the site's operation or the information, content or materials included on this site. To the full extent permissible by applicable law, Harvard hereby disclaims all warranties, express or implied, including but not limited to implied warranties of merchantability and fitness for any particular purpose. Harvard will not be liable for any damages of any kind arising from the use of or inability to use this site. You expressly agree that you use this site solely at your own risk.

4. Privacy Policy

Please be sure to read our Privacy Policy, which is incorporated herein by reference.

5. Modification of These Terms of Use

Harvard reserves the right to change, at any time, at our sole discretion, the Terms under which these Services are offered. You are responsible for regularly reviewing these Terms. Your continued use of the Services constitutes your agreement to all such Terms.

6. Copyright Complaints

Harvard respects the intellectual property of others, and requires that our users do the same. If you believe that your work has been copied and is accessible on this site in a way that constitutes copyright infringement, or that your intellectual property rights have been otherwise violated, please follow our instructions for reporting copyright infringements.

[...]

HP

Der weltbekannte IT-Dienstleister und Hardwarelieferant (PCs, Notebooks, Server, Drucker, Mobilgeräte) regelt vor allem das Thema Blogs:

HP Blogging Code of Conduct

http://www.hp.com/hpinfo/blogs/codeofconduct.html

HP blogs are written by a variety of employees at different levels and positions in the company, so you can expect many viewpoints. You can also expect the following:
1. We will strive to have open and honest dialogues with our readers.
2. We will correct inaccurate or misleading postings in a timely manner. We will not delete posts unless they violate our policies. Most changes will be made by adding to posts and we will mark any additions clearly.
3. We will disclose conflicts of interest.
4. Our Standards of Business Conduct will guide what we write about – so there are some topics we won't comment on such as information about financials, HP intellectual property, trade secrets, management changes, lawsuits, shareholder issues, layoffs, and contractual agreements with alliance partners, customers, and suppliers.
5. We will provide links to relevant material available on other blogs and Web sites. We will disclose any sources fully through credits, links and trackbacks unless the source has requested anonymity.
6. We understand that respect goes both ways – we will use good judgment in our posts and respond to you in a respectful manner. In return, we ask the same of you.
7. We trust you will be mindful of the information you share on our blogs – any personally identifiable information you share on a blog can be seen by anyone with access to the blog.
8. We will respect intellectual property rights.
9. We will use good judgment in protecting personal and corporate information and in respecting the privacy of individuals who use our blogs.

Comments:
1. Comments will be reviewed by bloggers before they are posted on our blogs.
2. We will review, post and respond to comments in a timely manner. We welcome constructive criticism. We can't respond to every comment, but will read all of them.
3. We will not post comments that are spam, inappropriate, defamatory, use profanity, or otherwise violate our policies or Terms of Use.
4. Because our blogs focus on material of general interest to all our readers, we ask that you direct customer support inquiries through our traditional customer service channels or use our IT resource center forums. Using these channels will allow you to get your issues to experienced HP support representatives in a timely manner.
5. Our bloggers will not respond to customer support issues and will not post these comments to their blogs.

IBM Social Computing Guideline

Eine der meistzitierten und ausgereiftesten Social Media Guidelines hat der vielfach im Social Web aktive Computerpionier IBM. Ursprünglich als Blogging Policy im Jahr 2005 gestartet, wurde dieses Dokument immer weiterentwickelt und so über die Jahre zum umfassenden Regelwerk für Social Media (http://www.ibm.com/blogs/zz/en/guidelines.html):

Introduction
Responsible engagement in innovation and dialogue
Online collaboration platforms are fundamentally changing the way IBMers work and engage with each other, clients and partners.

IBM is increasingly exploring how online discourse through social computing can empower IBMers as global professionals, innovators and citizens. These individual interactions represent a new model: not mass communications, but masses of communicators. Through these interactions, IBM's greatest asset – the expertise of its employees – can be shared with clients, shareholders, and the communities in which it operates.

Therefore, it is very much in IBM's interest – and, we believe, in each IBMer's own – to be aware of and participate in this sphere of information, interaction and idea exchange:

To learn: As an innovation-based company, we believe in the importance of open exchange – between IBM and its clients, and among the many constituents of the emerging business and societal ecosystem – for learning. Social computing is an important arena for organizational and individual development.

To contribute: IBM – as a business, as an innovator and as a corporate citizen – makes important contributions to the world, to the future of business and technology, and to public dialogue on a broad range of societal issues. Because our business activities provide transformational insight and high-value innovation for business, government, education, healthcare and nongovernmental organizations, it is important for IBM and IBMers to share with the world the exciting things we're learning and doing.

In 1997, IBM actively recommended that its employees use the Internet – at a time when many companies were seeking to restrict their employees' Internet access. In 2003, the company made a strategic decision to embrace the blogosphere and to encourage IBMers to participate. We continue to advocate IBMers' responsible involvement today in this rapidly growing environment of relationship, learning and collaboration.

IBM Social Computing Guidelines
1. Know and follow IBM's Business Conduct Guidelines.
2. IBMers are personally responsible for the content they publish on-line, whether in a blog, social computing site or any other form of user-generated media. Be mindful that what you publish will be public for a long time – protect your privacy and take care to understand a site's terms of service.
3. Identify yourself – name and, when relevant, role at IBM – when you discuss IBM or IBM-related matters, such as IBM products or services. You must make it clear that you are speaking for yourself and not on behalf of IBM.
4. If you publish content online relevant to IBM in your personal capacity use a disclaimer

such as this: "The postings on this site are my own and don't necessarily represent IBM's positions, strategies or opinions."

5. Respect copyright, fair use and financial disclosure laws.

6. Don't provide IBM's or another's confidential or other proprietary information and never discuss IBM business performance or other sensitive matters publicly.

7. Don't cite or reference clients, partners or suppliers without their approval. When you do make a reference, link back to the source. Don't publish anything that might allow inferences to be drawn which could embarrass or damage a client.

8. Respect your audience. Don't use ethnic slurs, personal insults, obscenity, or engage in any conduct that would not be acceptable in IBM's workplace. You should also show proper consideration for others' privacy and for topics that may be considered objectionable or inflammatory – such as politics and religion.

9. Be aware of your association with IBM in online social networks. If you identify yourself as an IBMer, ensure your profile and related content is consistent with how you wish to present yourself with colleagues and clients.

10. Don't pick fights, be the first to correct your own mistakes.

11. Try to add value. Provide worthwhile information and perspective. IBM's brand is best represented by its people and what you publish may reflect on IBM's brand.

12. Don't use use IBM logos or trademarks unless approved to do so.

Detailed Discussion

The IBM Business Conduct Guidelines and laws provide the foundation for IBM's policies and guidelines for blogs and social computing.

The same principles and guidelines that apply to IBMers' activities in general, as found in the IBM Business Conduct Guidelines, apply to IBMers' activities online. This includes forms of online publishing and discussion, including blogs, wikis, file-sharing, user-generated video and audio, virtual worlds* and social networks.

As outlined in the Business Conduct Guidelines, IBM fully respects the legal rights of our employees in all countries in which we operate. In general, what you do on your own time is your affair. However, activities in or outside of work that affect your IBM job performance, the performance of others, or IBM's business interests are a proper focus for company policy. IBM supports open dialogue and the exchange of ideas.

IBM regards blogs and other forms of online discourse as primarily a form of communication and relationship among individuals. When the company wishes to communicate publicly as a company – whether to the marketplace or to the general public – it has well established means to do so. Only those officially designated by IBM have the authorization to speak on behalf of the company.

However, IBM believes in dialogue among IBMers and with our partners, clients, members of the many communities in which we participate and the general public. Such dialogue is inherent in our business model of innovation, and in our commitment to the development of open standards. We believe that IBMers can both derive and provide important benefits from exchanges of perspective.

One of IBMers' core values is "trust and personal responsibility in all relationships." As a company, IBM trusts – and expects – IBMers to exercise personal responsibility whenever they participate in social media. This includes not violating the trust of those with whom they are engaging. IBMers should not use these media for covert marketing or public relations. If and when members of IBM's Communications, Marketing, Sales or other functions engaged in advocacy for the company have the authorization to participate in social media, they should identify themselves as such.

Know the IBM Business Conduct Guidelines. If you have any confusion about whether you ought to publish something online, chances are the BCGs will resolve it. Pay particular attention to what the BCGs have to say about proprietary information, about avoiding misrepresentation and about competing in the field. If, after checking the BCG's, you are still unclear as to the propriety of a post, it is best to refrain and seek the advice of management.

Be who you are. We believe in transparency and honesty; anonymity is not an option. When discussing topics relevant to IBM, you must use your real name, be clear who you are, and identify that you work for IBM. If you have a vested interest in something you are discussing, be the first to point it out. But also be smart about protecting yourself and your privacy. What you publish will be around for a long time, so consider the content carefully and also be judicious in disclosing personal details.

Be thoughtful about how you present yourself in online social networks. The lines between public and private, personal and professional are blurred in online social networks. By virtue of identifying yourself as an IBMer within a social network, you are now connected to your colleagues, managers and even IBM's clients. You should ensure that content associated with you is consistent with your work at IBM. If you have joined IBM recently, be sure to update your social profiles to reflect IBM's guidelines. You may not use IBM logos or trademarks as a part of your postings, including in your identity on a site, unless you are approved to do so. Speak in the first person. Use your own voice; bring your own personality to the forefront.

Use a disclaimer. Whenever you publish content to any form of digital media, make it clear that what you say there is representative of your views and opinions and not necessarily the views and opinions of IBM. For instance, in your own blog, the following standard disclaimer should be prominently displayed: "The postings on this site are my own and don't necessarily represent IBM's positions, strategies or opinions." If a site does not afford you enough space to include this full disclaimer, you should use your best judgment to position your comments appropriately. Managers and executives take note: This standard disclaimer does not by itself exempt IBM managers and executives from a special responsibility when participating in online environments. By virtue of their position, they must consider whether personal thoughts they publish may be misunderstood as expressing IBM positions. And a manager should assume that his or her team will read what is written. Public forums are not the place to communicate IBM policies to IBM employees.

Respect copyright and fair use laws. For IBM's protection and well as your own, it is critical that you show proper respect for the laws governing copyright and fair use of copyrighted material owned by others, including IBM's own copyrights and brands. You should never quote more than short excerpts of someone else's work. And it is good general blogging practice to link to others' work. Keep in mind that laws will be different depending on where you live and work.

Protecting confidential and proprietary information. Social computing blurs many of the traditional boundaries between internal and external communications. Be thoughtful about what you publish – particularly on external platforms. You must make sure you do not disclose or use IBM confidential or proprietary information or that of any other person or company in any online social computing platform. For example, ask permission before posting someone's picture in a social network or publishing in a blog a conversation that was meant to be private.

IBM's business performance and other sensitive subjects. Some topics relating to IBM are sensitive and should never be discussed, even if you're expressing your own opinion and using a disclaimer. For example, you must not comment on, or speculate about, IBM's future business performance (including upcoming quarters or future periods), IBM's business plans, unannounced strategies or prospects (including information about alliances), potential acquisitions or divestitures, similar matters involving IBM's competitors, legal or regulatory matters affecting IBM and other similar subjects that could negatively affect IBM. This applies to anyone including conversations with financial analysts, the press or other third parties (including friends). If you're unsure of the sensitivity of a particular subject, seek advice from your manager or legal team before talking about it or simply refrain from the conversation. IBM policy is not to comment on rumors in any way. You should merely say, "no comment" to rumors. Do not deny or affirm them (or suggest the same in subtle ways), speculate about them or propagate them by participating in "what if"-type conversations.

Protect IBM's clients, business partners and suppliers. Clients, partners or suppliers should not be cited or obviously referenced without their approval. Externally, never identify a client, partner or supplier by name without permission and never discuss confidential details of a client engagement. Internal social computing platforms permit suppliers and business partners to participate so be sensitive to who will see your content. If a client hasn't given explicit permission for their name to be used, think carefully about the content you're going to publish on any internal social media and get the appropriate permission where necessary. It is acceptable to discuss general details about kinds of projects and to use non-identifying pseudonyms for a client (e.g., Client 123) so long as the information provided does not make it easy for someone to identify the client or violate any non-disclosure or intellectual property agreements that may be in place with the client. Be thoughtful about the types of information that you share, which may inadvertently lead others to deduce which clients, partners and suppliers that you are working with. This might include travel plans or publishing details about your current location or where you are working on a given day. Furthermore, your blog or online social network is not the place to conduct confidential business with a client, partner or supplier.

Respect your audience and your coworkers. Remember that IBM is a global organization whose employees and clients reflect a diverse set of customs, values and points of view. Don't be afraid to be yourself, but do so respectfully. This includes not only the obvious (no ethnic slurs, personal insults, obscenity, etc.) but also proper consideration of privacy and of topics that may be considered objectionable or inflammatory – such as politics and religion. For example, if your blog is hosted on an IBM-owned property, avoid these topics and focus on subjects that are business-related. If your blog is self-hosted, use your best judgment and be sure to make it clear that the views and opinions expressed are yours alone and do not represent the official views of IBM. Further, be thoughtful when using tools hosted outside of IBM's protected Intranet environment to communicate among fellow employees about IBM or IBM related matters. Also, while it is fine for IBMers to disagree, but please don't use your external blog or other online social media to air your differences in an inappropriate manner. Add value. IBM's brand is best represented by its people and everything you publish online reflects upon it. Blogs and social networks that are hosted on IBM-owned domains should be used in a way that adds value to IBM's business. If it helps you, your coworkers, our clients or our partners to do their jobs and solve problems; if it helps to improve knowledge or skills; if it contributes directly or indirectly to the improvement of IBM's products, processes and policies; if it builds a sense of community; or if it helps to promote IBM's Values, then it is adding value. It is best to stay within your sphere of expertise, and whenever you are presenting something as fact, make sure it is a fact. Though not directly business-related, background information you choose to share about yourself, such as information about your family or personal interests, may be useful in helping establish a relationship between you and your readers, but it is entirely your choice whether to share this information.

Don't pick fights. When you see misrepresentations made about IBM by media, analysts or by other bloggers, you may certainly use your blog – or add comments on the original discussion – to point that out. Always do so with respect, stick to the facts and identify your appropriate affiliation to IBM. Also, if you speak about a competitor, you must make sure that what you say is factual and that it does not disparage the competitor. Avoid unnecessary or unproductive arguments. Brawls may earn traffic, but nobody wins in the end and you may negatively affect your own, and IBM's, reputation in the process. Don't try to settle scores or goad competitors or others into inflammatory debates. Here and in other areas of public discussion, make sure that what you are saying is factually correct.

Be the first to respond to your own mistakes. If you make an error, be up front about your mistake and correct it quickly, as this can help to restore trust. If you choose to modify content that was previously posted, such as editing a blog post, make it clear that you have done so.

Adopt a warm, open and approachable tone. Remember that much of IBM's image is developed by the public's interaction with real IBMers. We all want that image to be a positive one. Your tone, your openness and your approachability can help with that, just as they can with your own personal "brand".

Use your best judgment. Remember that there are always consequences to what you publish. If you're about to publish something that makes you even the slightest bit uncomfortable, review the suggestions above and think about why that is. If you're still unsure, and it is related to IBM business, feel free to discuss it with your manager. Ultimately, however, you have sole responsibility for what you post to your blog or publish in any form of online social media.

Don't forget your day job. You should make sure that your online activities do not interfere with your job or commitments to customers.

*Virtual worlds present a number of unique circumstances, not all of which are covered in these guidelines. Please refer to the companion, "Virtual worlds Guidelines" for additional guidelines around identity, behavior, appearance and intellectual property.

Intel

Der Chiphersteller Intel verfügt nicht nur über Richtlinien für Social Media in deutscher Sprache (http://www.intel.com/sites/sitewide/de_DE/social-media.htm), sondern auch für Anwender, die von Intel gesponsert werden (s. u.).
Hier zunächst die

Intel-Richtlinien für Social Media

Dies sind die offiziellen Richtlinien für Social Media bei Intel. Wenn Sie ein Mitarbeiter oder Lieferant von Intel sind, der Blogs, Wikis, soziale Netzwerke, virtuelle Welten oder eine andere Art von Social Media für die Kommunikation innerhalb oder außerhalb von Intel.com erstellt oder zu diesen beiträgt, dann sind diese Richtlinien für Sie bestimmt. Wir erwarten, dass alle Teilnehmer an Social Media im Namen von Intel entsprechend geschult sind und diese Richtlinien verstehen und befolgen. Andernfalls kann Ihre künftige Teilnahme infrage gestellt sein. Die Richtlinien werden ständig weiterentwickelt, wenn neue Technologien und Tools für soziale Netzwerke entstehen. Informieren Sie sich hier daher regelmäßig, um sicherzustellen, dass Sie stets über aktuelle Informationen verfügen.

Sie als Teilnehmer
Neue Plattformen für die Online-Zusammenarbeit ändern die Art, wie wir arbeiten, in fundamentaler Weise und bieten uns neue Wege für die Interaktion mit Kunden, Kollegen und der Welt insgesamt. Es handelt sich um ein neues Interaktionsmodell, und wir glauben, dass Social Computing Ihnen helfen kann, stärkere und erfolgreichere Geschäftsbeziehungen zu entwickeln. Darüber hinaus bietet es Ihnen die Möglichkeit, an globalen Diskussionen in Bezug auf die Arbeit, die wir bei Intel leisten, und die Dinge, die uns wichtig sind, teilzunehmen.

Als Teilnehmer an Social Media befolgen Sie bitte diese Richtlinien:

Halten Sie sich an Ihr Sachwissen und stellen Sie neue, individuelle Perspektiven dazu bereit, was bei Intel und in der Welt passiert.

Veröffentlichen Sie aussagekräftige Kommentare und gehen Sie mit anderen Personen respektvoll um – mit anderen Worten, veröffentlichen Sie keinen Spam und keine Bemerkungen, die nicht zum Thema gehören oder beleidigend sind.

Bevor Sie etwas veröffentlichen, überlegen Sie immer zuerst. Nichtsdestoweniger, antworten Sie auf Kommentare zeitnah und wenn eine Antwort angemessen ist.

Respektieren Sie geschützte Informationen und Inhalte sowie die Vertraulichkeit.

Wenn Sie anderer Meinung sind, antworten Sie angemessen und höflich.

Lesen und befolgen Sie den Intel Code of Conduct und die Intel-Datenschutzrichtlinien.

Regeln für die Teilnahme

Seien Sie transparent. Andere Mitglieder der Social-Media-Community finden schnell heraus, ob Sie ehrlich – oder unehrlich – sind. Verwenden Sie Ihren wahren Namen, weisen Sie darauf hin, dass Sie für Intel arbeiten, und machen Sie Ihre Rolle klar, wenn Sie einen Blog über Ihre Arbeit bei Intel verfassen. Wenn Sie ein persönliches Interesse an einem Thema haben, über das Sie diskutieren, sollten Sie der Erste sein, der darauf aufmerksam macht. Transparenz betrifft Ihre Identität und Ihre Beziehung zu Intel. Unternehmenseigene Informationen und Inhalte müssen weiterhin vertraulich behandelt werden.

Handeln Sie überlegt. Stellen Sie sicher, dass Ihre Bemühungen, transparent zu sein, nicht die Datenschutz-, Vertraulichkeits- und rechtlichen Richtlinien von Intel für die externe Kommunikation in geschäftlichen Angelegenheiten verletzen. Fragen Sie nach einer Genehmigung für die Veröffentlichung von Diskussionen oder auch Berichten über Diskussionen, wenn diese privater Art oder Intel-intern sind. Alle Aussagen müssen wahr und dürfen nicht irreführend sein. Alle Behauptungen müssen fundiert und genehmigt sein. Produkt-Benchmarks müssen für die Veröffentlichung in externen Foren durch das entsprechende Produkt-Benchmarking-Team freigegeben sein. Kommentieren Sie bitte niemals ohne entsprechende Genehmigung zu rechtlichen Angelegenheiten, Rechtsstreitigkeiten oder irgendwelchen Parteien, mit denen wir uns im Rechtsstreit befinden. Wenn Sie über den Wettbewerb schreiben möchten, stellen Sie sicher, dass Sie über das entsprechende Hintergrundwissen verfügen und die erforderliche Genehmigung haben. Denken Sie auch daran, sich selbst, Ihre Privatsphäre und vertrauliche Informationen von Intel zu schützen. Ihre Veröffentlichungen werden für eine lange Zeit zugänglich sein. Überlegen Sie sich daher sorgfältig, was Sie veröffentlichen, und handeln Sie überlegt.

Schreiben und veröffentlichen Sie nur über Themen, bei denen Sie sich auskennen, insbesondere im Hinblick auf Intel und unsere Technologie. Wenn Sie über ein Thema schreiben, das Intel betrifft, bei dem Sie aber nicht der Intel-Fachmann sind, sollten Sie dies gegenüber Ihren Lesern klarstellen. Schreiben Sie in der ersten Person. Wenn Sie Inhalte auf einer anderen als der Intel-Website veröffentlichen, verwenden Sie bitte eine Ausschlussklausel wie die folgende: „Die Veröffentlichungen auf dieser Website sind meine eigenen und stellen nicht notwendigerweise die Positionen, Strategien oder Meinungen von Intel dar." Respektieren Sie darüber hinaus bitte Gesetze zu Marken, Urheberrechten, fairem Gebrauch, Handelsgeheimnissen (einschließlich unserer Prozesse und Methodologien), Vertraulichkeit und Veröffentlichung von Finanzdaten. Wenn Sie diesbezüglich Fragen haben, wenden Sie sich an Ihren Intel-Rechtsvertreter. Denken Sie daran, dass Sie für Ihre Inhalte persönlich verantwortlich sein können.

Wahrnehmung ist Wirklichkeit. In den sozialen Netzwerken im Web sind die Grenzen zwischen öffentlich und privat, persönlich und beruflich nicht mehr eindeutig erkennbar. Indem Sie sich als Mitarbeiter von Intel identifizieren, tragen Sie bereits dazu bei, wie Intel von Aktionären, Kunden und der allgemeinen Öffentlichkeit wahrgenommen wird – und wie Sie von

Ihren Kollegen und Vorgesetzten wahrgenommen werden. Machen Sie uns alle stolz. Stellen Sie sicher, dass alle Inhalte, die mit Ihnen assoziiert sind, dem entsprechen, was Sie tun, und mit den Werten und professionellen Standards von Intel übereinstimmen.

Es ist ein Dialog. Sprechen Sie mit Ihren Lesern, wie Sie mit Kollegen in professionellen Situationen sprechen würden. Mit anderen Worten, Sie sollten eine zu pedantische oder gewählte Sprache vermeiden. Scheuen Sie sich nicht, Ihre eigene Persönlichkeit einzubringen, und sagen Sie, was Sie denken. Schreiben Sie Inhalte, die offen für den Dialog sind und zu Antworten einladen. Ermutigen Sie Ihre Leser, Kommentare zu verfassen. Sie können den Dialog auch ausweiten, indem Sie andere Personen zitieren, die zum gleichen Thema schreiben, und indem Sie gestatten, dass Ihre Inhalte gemeinsam verwendet oder syndiziert werden.

Leisten Sie einen wertvollen Beitrag zum Thema. Das Web enthält Millionen von Wörtern. Die beste Art, wie Sie Menschen dazu bringen, Ihre Beiträge im Web zu lesen, besteht darin, Inhalte zu verfassen, in denen Menschen einen Wert für sich selbst erkennen können. Soziale Kommunikation von Intel sollte für unsere Kunden, Partner und Kollegen einen Wert enthalten. Sie sollte zum Nachdenken anregen und zur Entwicklung eines Gemeinschaftssinns beitragen. Wenn sie Menschen hilft, ihr Wissen oder ihre Fähigkeiten zu verbessern, ihr Geschäft zu entwickeln, ihre Aufgaben zu erledigen, Probleme zu lösen oder Intel besser zu verstehen – dann leistet sie einen wertvollen Beitrag.

Ihre Verantwortung: Es liegt letzten Endes in Ihrer Verantwortung, was Sie schreiben. Die Teilnahme am Social Computing im Namen von Intel ist kein Recht, sondern eine Gelegenheit, die Sie bitte ernsthaft und mit Respekt behandeln sollten. Wenn Sie im Namen von Intel teilnehmen möchten, absolvieren Sie bitte die Digital IQ Schulung und wenden Sie sich an das Social Media Center of Excellence. Lesen und befolgen Sie den Intel Code of Conduct. Wenn Sie diese Richtlinien und den Intel Code of Conduct nicht befolgen, ist Ihre weitere Beteiligung an Social Media im Namen von Intel gefährdet. Weitere Informationen erhalten Sie unter social.media@intel.com. Befolgen Sie bitte ebenfalls die Nutzungsbedingungen für alle Sites von Drittanbietern.

Gestalten Sie Ihre Beiträge interessant. Als Mitglied der Geschäftswelt und der öffentlichen Gemeinschaft leistet Intel wichtige Arbeit für die gesamte Welt, die Technologie der Zukunft und für den öffentlichen Dialog über eine große Zahl von Themen. Der Schwerpunkt unserer geschäftlichen Aktivitäten liegt mehr und mehr auf hochwertigen Innovationen. Lassen Sie uns die spannenden Dinge, die wir kennenlernen und die wir tun, der Welt mitteilen – und gleichzeitig von anderen Menschen lernen.

Führen Sie Ihren Dialog. Zwischen einer konstruktiven Entgegnung und einer zornigen Reaktion kann manchmal nur eine schmale Linie gezogen werden. Setzen Sie unsere Konkurrenten oder Intel nicht herab. Genauso müssen Sie nicht auf jede Kritik oder Stichelei antworten. Formulieren Sie Inhalte nach Möglichkeit so, dass andere Menschen dazu eingeladen werden, abweichende Meinungen zu äußern, ohne Sie anzugreifen. Mit bestimmten Themen, wie

Politik oder Religion, gerät man leichter in Probleme. Seien Sie also sorgfältig und handeln Sie überlegt. Einmal veröffentlichte Inhalte können Sie nicht mehr zurückholen. Und wenn eine Diskussion einmal aufgeheizt ist, lässt sie sich nur noch schwer stoppen.

Haben Sie einen Fehler gemacht? Geben Sie zu, wenn Sie einen Fehler gemacht haben. Seien Sie offen und korrigieren Sie Ihren Fehler schnell. Wenn Sie Beiträge in einem Blog veröffentlichen, möchten Sie vielleicht einen früheren Beitrag ändern. Weisen Sie in diesem Fall jedoch deutlich darauf hin.

Nehmen Sie sich Zeit, wenn Sie sich nicht sicher sind. Wenn Sie einen Inhalt veröffentlichen wollen, bei dem Sie sich nur im Geringsten unwohlfühlen, hören Sie auf Ihr Gefühl und senden Sie ihn nicht gleich ab. Nehmen Sie sich etwas Zeit, um diese Richtlinien zu lesen. Versuchen Sie herauszufinden, was Sie stört, und beheben Sie es. Wenn Sie sich immer noch nicht sicher sind, sollten Sie den Beitrag vielleicht mit Ihrem Vorgesetzten oder einem Mitglied der Rechtsabteilung besprechen. In letzter Instanz sind Sie der Eigentümer Ihrer Veröffentlichungen – und dafür verantwortlich. Sie sollten sich also sicher sein.

Lieferanten & Empfehlungen

Intel unterstützt Transparenz. Es ist uns wichtig sicherzustellen, dass unsere Social-Media-Teilnehmer (inklusive Blogs, Twitter, Foren und alle anderen Social Media) ihre Beziehungen und Empfehlungen klar offenlegen und dass Aussagen zu Intel-Produkten wahrheitsgetreu und fundiert sind.

Bitte beachten Sie, dass alle Social-Media-Experten, die von Intel beauftragt, platziert oder anderweitig vergütet werden, die Richtlinien für Social-Media-Teilnehmer, die von Intel gesponsert, platziert oder mit Incentives kompensiert werden, befolgen müssen. Im Rahmen dieser Richtlinien müssen Sie offenlegen, dass Sie von Intel platziert oder anderweitig vergütet wurden. Ihr Blog wird auf Einhaltung unserer Richtlinien sowie wahrheitsgetreue Beschreibungen unserer Produkte und Behauptungen überwacht.

Moderationsrichtlinien

Moderation bedeutet die Überprüfung und Freigabe von Inhalten vor der Veröffentlichung auf der Site (dies betrifft Social-Media-Inhalte, die im Namen von Intel verfasst wurden, egal ob die Site auf intel.com ist oder nicht). Intel unterstützt keine Inhalte, die von Drittparteien veröffentlicht wurden (bezeichnet als „von Benutzern generierte Inhalte" oder UGC), und übernimmt auch keine Verantwortung für diese. Dazu gehören Texteingaben und hochgeladene Dateien (Video, Bilder, Audio, ausführbare Dateien, Dokumente).

Benutzer werden eindeutig zur Teilnahme ermutigt. Dabei müssen aber einige Richtlinien befolgt werden, um den Schutz für alle Beteiligten zu gewährleisten. Intel hat darüber hinaus automatische Kontrollmechanismen eingerichtet, um Spam und bösartige Inhalte zu bekämpfen. Bitte beachten Sie, dass innerhalb von Intel entstehende Inhalte nicht moderiert werden. Das bedeutet, dass die Autoren unserer Blogs ihre Beiträge direkt und ohne vorherige Genehmigung veröffentlichen, sofern sie über die entsprechende Schulung verfügen.

Vorabmoderation. Selbst wenn eine Site einen Benutzer vor der Veröffentlichung zur Registrierung auffordert, wird die Person durch einfache Angabe von Benutzername und E-Mail nicht wirklich validiert. Um daher ein Mindestmaß an Risiko und ein Höchstmaß an Schutz zu gewährleisten, verlangen wir die Moderation aller UGC-Veröffentlichungen vor ihrer Einstellung (Vorabmoderation).

Community-Moderation. Für etablierte, funktionierende Communities kann die Gruppenmoderation durch normale Benutzer eine gute Lösung sein. Dies wird gelegentlich anstatt der Vorabmoderation zugelassen, muss aber beantragt und genehmigt werden.

Ausgewogener Online-Dialog. Bei der Vorabmoderation oder Community-Moderation gelten die folgenden drei Grundsätze: das Gute, das Schlechte, aber nicht das Respektlose. Wenn die Inhalte positiv oder negativ sind und mit der Diskussion in Zusammenhang stehen, genehmigen wir die Inhalte, unabhängig davon, ob sie für Intel günstig oder ungünstig sind. Wenn die Inhalte jedoch respektlos, beleidigend, herabsetzend und in keiner Weise im Zusammenhang mit der Diskussion stehen, weisen wir die Inhalte ab.

Außerdem hat Intel ein separates Dokument für Social-Media-Teilnehmer, „die von Intel gesponsert, platziert oder mit Incentives kompensiert werden", geschaffen, das ebenfalls öffentlich über die Intel-Website zugänglich ist und sich explizit an Unternehmensexterne richtet:

Intel unterstützt Transparenz. Es ist uns wichtig sicherzustellen, dass unsere Social-Media-Teilnehmer (inklusive Blogs, Twitter, Foren und alle anderen Social Media) ihre Beziehungen und Empfehlungen klar offenlegen und dass Aussagen zu Intel-Produkten wahrheitsgetreu und fundiert sind.
Wenn Sie ein Social-Media-Teilnehmer (SMT) sind, der mit Produkten platziert oder durch Incentives kompensiert wird oder eine andere dauerhafte Geschäftsbeziehung zu Intel hat, sind diese Richtlinien für Sie verbindlich. Bei Fragen oder Unklarheiten im Zusammenhang mit diesen Richtlinien wenden Sie sich bitte an Ihren Ansprechpartner bei Intel.

Regeln für Social-Media-Teilnehmer, die von Intel gesponsert, platziert oder mit Incentives kompensiert werden

Seien Sie transparent. Intel unterstützt Transparenz in Bezug auf Ihre Identität und Ihre Beziehung zu Intel. Es ist uns wichtig sicherzustellen, dass die von uns gesponserten Social-Media-Teilnehmer (inklusive Blogs, Microblogs, Foren und alle anderen Social Media) ihre Beziehungen zu Intel, einschließlich Incentive- und Sponsoring-Aktivitäten, klar und deutlich offenlegen. Stellen Sie sicher, dass diese Informationen für die Öffentlichkeit und die Leser Ihrer Beiträge jederzeit ersichtlich sind.

Berichten Sie über Ihre Erfahrungen. Machen Sie bitte keine allgemeinen Angaben zu Produkten, sondern berichten Sie speziell über Ihre Erfahrungen.

Schreiben Sie über Themen, bei denen Sie sich auskennen. Wir empfehlen Ihnen, in der ersten Person zu schreiben, sich auf Ihr Fachgebiet zu konzentrieren und dabei die Zusammenhänge mit Technik von Intel hervorzuheben.

Ihre Verantwortung. Bitte beachten Sie, dass Sie für Ihre Beiträge verantwortlich sind und die Nichtbeachtung dieser Richtlinien Ihre Sponsoring- oder Incentive-Beziehung zu Intel gefährden kann. Befolgen Sie bitte ebenfalls die Nutzungsbedingungen aller Sites von Drittanbietern, an denen Sie teilnehmen.

Moderationsrichtlinien für Social-Media-Teilnehmer, die von Intel gesponsert, platziert oder mit Incentives kompensiert werden
Intel beobachtet und verfolgt Social Media, die in Bezug zu Intel stehen, einschließlich der Aktivitäten von Social-Media-Teilnehmern, die von Intel gesponsert, platziert oder mit Incentives kompensiert werden. Es ist uns wichtig sicherzustellen, dass Aussagen zu Intel-Produkten wahrheitsgetreu und korrekt sind.
Falls wir Behauptungen oder Aussagen finden, die falsch oder irreführend sind, werden wir uns mit der Aufforderung an Sie wenden, diese zu korrigieren. Wenn Sie als gesponserter SMT wiederholt falsche oder irreführende Aussagen zu Intel oder Produkten und Dienstleistungen von Intel machen, werden wir gegebenenfalls die Beziehung zu Ihnen beenden.
Die ausführlichen Social-Media-Richtlinien, die sich an Mitarbeiter von Intel richten, finden Sie hier.

IOC
Auch supranationale Organisationen wie das Olympische Komitee stehen vor der Herausforderung, das Social Web im Sinne der eigenen Organisation beeinflussen zu müssen, und haben daher die IOC Blogging Guidelines für „Akkreditierte Personen" zur Olympiade in Peking 2008 – http://multimedia.olympic.org/pdf/en_report_1296.pdf – herausgegeben:

These Guidelines have been developed for persons accredited ("Accredited Persons") at the Games of the XXIX Olympiad, Beijing 2008 (the "Games") who maintain personal blogs, accessible by the general public, that contain any content related to their personal experiences at, and participation in, the Games ("Olympic Content") upon the occasion of the Games, namely, from 8 days prior to the Opening Ceremony of the Games until 3 days after the Closing Ceremony of the Games. They are also applicable to Accredited Persons who post Olympic Content on the websites of others.
The IOC considers blogging, in accordance with these Guidelines, as a legitimate form of

personal expression and not as a form of journalism. Therefore, the IOC does not consider that blogs by Accredited Persons, in accordance with these Guidelines, will compromise Paragraph 3 of Bye-law to Rule 49 of the Olympic Charter which states that "Only those persons accredited as media may act as journalists, reporters or in any other media capacity".

Additionally, accredited persons at the Games must abide by the Olympic Charter.

1. Definition of a Blog

A blog is a type of website where entries are made (such as in a journal or diary), usually displayed in a reverse chronological order.

2. Personal Information

It is required that, when Accredited Persons at the Games post any Olympic Content, it be confined solely to their own personal Olympic-related experience. Without limiting the generality of the foregoing, blogs of Accredited Persons should take the form of a diary orjournal and, in any event, should not contain any interviews with, or stories about, other Accredited Persons.

Accredited Persons should not disclose any information that is confidential or private in relation to any third party including, without limitation, information which may compromise the security, staging and organisation of the Games and, where relevant, the accredited persons' respective Olympic Team or the privacy of any other Accredited Person.

In any event, blogs of Accredited Persons containing Olympic Content should at all times conform to the Olympic spirit and the fundamental principles of Olympism as contained in the Olympic Charter, and be dignified and in good taste.

3. No Sound or Moving Images of the Games

The dissemination of moving images of the Games through any media, including display on the Internet, is a part of the IOC's intellectual property rights. No sound or moving images (including sequences of still photographs which simulate moving images) of any Olympic events, including sporting action, Opening, Closing and Medal Ceremonies or other activities which occur within any zone which requires an Olympic identity and accreditation card (or ticket) for entry – e.g. competition and practice venues, Olympic Village, Main Press Centre – ("Accredited Zones") may be made available, whether on a live or delayed basis, regardless of source.

4. Still Pictures

As a general rule, blogs by Accredited Persons containing Olympic Content must not include any still picture taken within Accredited Zones at the Games. Notwithstanding the foregoing, Accredited Persons may feature still pictures taken of themselves within Accredited Zones provided that such pictures do not contain any sporting action of the Games or the Opening, Closing or Medal Ceremonies of the Games. It is the Accredited Persons' responsibility to obtain the consent of other persons appearing in any pictures which may featured in accordance with this Section.

5. Olympic Marks

The Olympic symbol, the word "Olympic" and other Olympic related words, including, but not limited to "Olympic Games", "Olympiad(s)", "Olympics" and "Olympic Team(s)" and designs (the "Olympic Marks") may be used solely for editorial purposes in conjunction with Olympic Content. Under no circumstances may the Olympic Marks be associated with any third party or any third party's products or services in any way that may give the impression that such third party or such third party's products or services have an official relationship with the IOC, the Beijing Organising Committee for the Games of the XXIX Olympiad (BOCOG), the Games, any National Olympic Committee and/or the Olympic Movement.

6. Advertising and Sponsorship

As a general rule, Accredited Persons must not include any commercial reference in connection with any Olympic Content posted on their blogs. Specifically, this means that no advertising and/or sponsorship may be visible on screen at the same time as Olympic Content. Notwithstanding the foregoing, advertising and/or sponsorship on the screen at the same time as Olympic Content is allowed only if it is of the IOC TOP Partners (listed on http://www.olympic.org/marketing). Subject to the foregoing, any advertising and/or sponsorship must not be intrusive (i.e. no pop-ups nor expandable banners) and, in any event, must not take up more than 15 per cent of the screen at any given time. In addition, the websites of BOCOG, other Organising Committees of the Olympic Games and the National Olympic Committees, as well as the websites of the official broadcast rights holders of the Games, may contain advertising and sponsorship as permitted by the IOC.

Accredited Persons may not post Olympic Content on the websites of third parties, and should take all reasonable steps to stop third parties from doing so, if there is any association being made between such third parties or other advertising and/or sponsorship and, on the other hand, the Olympic Content.

7. No Exclusivity

Accredited Persons should not enter into any exclusive agreement with any company with respect to the posting of any Olympic Content.

8. Domain Names/URLs/Page Naming

Domain Names including the word "Olympic" or "Olympics" or similar are not permitted (e.g. [myname]olympic.com would not be permitted while [myname].com/olympic would be allowed but only during the period in which these Guidelines are applicable).

9. Links

In order to facilitate access to pertinent Olympic information, Accredited Persons posting Olympic Content pursuant to these Guidelines are encouraged to "link" their blogs to various official Olympic websites including, where relevant, the website of the accredited persons' respective Olympic Team or NOC. Useful addresses include: www.olympic.org – the official website of the Olympic Movement www.beijing2008.com – the official website of the Beijing Olympic Games

10. Liability
It is brought to your attention that, when Accredited Persons choose to go public with their opinions on a blog, they are responsible for their commentary. Bloggers can be held personally liable for any commentary deemed to be defamatory, obscene or proprietary. In essence, bloggers post their blogs at their own risk and they should make it clear that the views expressed are their own.

11. Responsibility and Further Restrictions
BOCOG, the National Olympic Committees, the International Federations and other entities present at the Games (e.g. media and sponsors) are in charge of ensuring that their respective delegations (i.e. those persons to whom they grant accreditation to the Games) are informed of the content of these Guidelines and agree to fully comply with them. The above-mentioned entities may also impose upon their respective delegations more restrictive blogging guidelines relating to the Games.

12. Prior or Subsequent Agreements entered into by the IOC
Nothing in these Guidelines shall be interpreted as amending or superseding the terms and conditions set forth in any agreement entered into, or to be entered into, by the IOC.

13. Infringement of Guidelines
Violation of these Guidelines by an Accredited Person may lead to the withdrawal of such person's Olympic identity and accreditation card, as foreseen in the Olympic Charter. The IOC reserves the right to take any and all other measure(s) it deems fit with respect to infringements of these Guidelines, including taking legal action for monetary damages and imposing other sanctions.

Klenk & Hoursch Corporate Communications
Klenk & Hoursch ist ein bekannter Dienstleister für Public Relations und daher dem Kunden gegenüber in gewisser Weise ein Vorbild – mit knappen, aber präzisen Richtlinien: http://www.klenkhoursch.de/?cat=174.

Social Media Guidelines

Wir begreifen das Social Web als große Chance und ebenso große Herausforderung für die Unternehmenskommunikation. Wir ermutigen daher unsere Mitarbeiter zu bloggen, zu twittern und aktive Teilnehmer in sozialen Netzwerken zu sein. Auch im Social Web streben wir nach der richtigen Hirn-Herz-Hand-Relation. Und: Es regiere der gesunde Menschenverstand! Darüber hinaus halten wir uns an folgende Regeln:

1. Transparent: Sei offen, spiele nicht mit verdeckten Karten und täusche keine falschen Tatsachen vor. Wenn Du willst, schreibe auch über Deinen Beruf, Deinen Arbeitgeber, über Kommunikation. Spreche oder schreibe jedoch nie über Kunden oder über Projekte

von Kunden ohne die ausdrückliche Genehmigung der Kunden oder der Geschäftsführung.

2. Anspruchsvoll: Kommunikation unter Freunden ist oft banal, auch im Internet. Das ist in Ordnung. Versuche aber immer dort, wo es um berufliche Themen geht, auf hohem Niveau zu kommunizieren. Sei umsichtig, gut informiert, nie arrogant oder besserwisserisch. Weniger ist mehr.

3. Bewusst: Achte auf Deine „Digital-ID". Ob Du willst oder nicht, Privates und Berufliches verschwimmen. Du bist im (Social) Web immer auch als Repräsentant von Klenk & Hoursch identifizierbar. Schreibe nichts, was ein Mitbewerber gegen Dich bzw. gegen die Agentur oder einen Kunden verwenden kann! Wenn Du Dir nicht ganz sicher bist – dann lasse es! Plaudern über vertrauliche Informationen, negatives Blogging bzw. Microblogging können unangenehme rechtliche Konsequenzen haben für Klenk & Hoursch oder Dich.

4. Smart: Es ist gut, eine Meinung zu haben, doch überlege gut, wie und wo Du Deine Meinung vertrittst. Es ist nicht smart, andere anzugreifen oder gar Schmähkritik zu üben. Respektiere die Meinungen anderer. Unterläuft Dir mal ein Fehler, gib es zu und korrigiere ihn so schnell wie möglich. Denke immer daran, dass Du ein Kommunikationsprofi bist.

5. Korrekt: Nicht alles, was Du „besitzt", ist Dein Eigentum! Beachte die Rechte anderer. Stelle keine Bilder oder andere Inhalte von anderen Personen ins Netz. Einfache Regel: Was nicht von Klenk & Hoursch erstellt und freigegeben wurde und was nicht von Dir stammt oder Dein Eigentum ist, gehört nicht ins Netz.

Kodak

Wegen ihrer besonderen grafischen Aufmachung hier nicht vollständig wiedergegeben sind die Guidelines des Foto- und Grafikanbieters Kodak. Sie können auf http://www.kodak.com/US/images/en/corp/aboutKodak/onlineToday/Kodak_SocialMediaTips_Aug14.pdf abgerufen werden.

Dennoch ein wesentlicher Ausschnitt (zum Thema Transparenz):

> "Even when you are talking as an individual, people may perceive you to be talking on behalf of Kodak. If you blog or discuss photography, printing or other topics related to a Kodak business, be upfront and explain that you work for Kodak; however, if you aren't an official company spokesperson, add a disclaimer to the effect: 'The opinions and positions expressed are my own and don't necessarily reflect those of Eastman Kodak Company.'"

Einfach, direkt und klar formuliert ...

Krones

Der Krones-Konzern mit Hauptsitz in Neutraubling, Deutschland, plant, entwickelt und fertigt Maschinen und komplette Anlagen für die Bereiche Prozess-, Abfüll- und Verpackungstechnik sowie Intralogistik. Mit weltweit über 10.000 Mitarbeitern wurde 2009 ein Umsatz von 1,865 Milliarden Euro erzielt. Auch als klassischer B-to-B-Anbieter ist Krones im Social Web aktiv.

Einen sehr ambitionierten Ansatz verfolgt Krones mit „Sie sind Krones – Tipps für den Umgang mit Social Media"
http://www.krones.com/downloads/social_media_d.pdf.
Ausgehend von einer Beschreibung „Social Media – was ist das?" (hier nicht wiedergegeben) wird zunächst allgemein von Kundennähe und Verantwortung gesprochen:

Kundennähe 2.0
Viele unserer Kunden – allen voran die „großen Player" – machen von den Möglichkeiten der sozialen Medien schon ganz selbstverständlich Gebrauch: beispielsweise, um ihre Produkte zu bewerben, um Informationen zu erhalten und um ihre geschäftlichen Kontakte zu pflegen. Und das Gleiche erwarten sie auch von ihren Lieferanten – allen voran vom Markt- und Technologieführer Krones. Deshalb dürfen wir bei den neuen „Mitmach-Medien" nichts verschlafen: weder die Chancen noch die Risiken.

Verantwortung 2.0
Über die sozialen Medien können wir uns und unsere Kunden schneller und gezielter informieren als je zuvor. Umgekehrt besteht aber auch die Gefahr, unbedacht Informationen zu verbreiten, die nicht für die Öffentlichkeit bestimmt sind. Deshalb gilt auch in den sozialen Medien: Der Schutz unserer Kunden sowie unseres eigenen Know-hows als Basis unserer Markt- und Technologieführerschaft hat unbedingten Vorrang. Denn neun von zehn Liefergeschäften in unserer Branche stehen unter strikter Geheimhaltung, damit neue Produkte, Technologien und Strategien nicht vorzeitig bei Wettbewerbern und Endkunden bekannt werden. Bitte nehmen Sie diese Verantwortung ernst. Sie schützen dadurch sich selbst, die Krones AG und unsere Kunden.

Krones 2.0
Die Persönlichkeit von Krones wird nicht vom Vorstand bestimmt – sie wird von den Mitarbeitern geschaffen. Denn Sie sind es, denen Krones sein Gesicht verdankt. Ein Gesicht, das unsere Kunden überall wiedererkennen, dem sie vertrauen und das sie schätzen. Das ist ein wertvoller Vorteil, der uns vor unseren Wettbewerbern auszeichnet.
Damit das auch weiterhin so bleibt, brauchen wir Ihre Hilfe: Wenn Sie Online-Netzwerke privat oder beruflich nutzen, dürfen Sie sich natürlich als Krones-Mitarbeiter „zu erkennen geben". Aber bitte beachten Sie dabei: Sprechen Sie nie für Krones und treten Sie auch nicht „als Krones" auf – es sei denn, Sie wurden im Rahmen Ihrer Tätigkeit dazu beauftragt.

[...]

Den Kern der Policy bilden:

„Elf Tipps für Ihr Online-Leben"

Wie verhalte ich mich in den sozialen Medien? Darf ich mich als Krones-Mitarbeiter zu erkennen geben? Und was passiert, wenn ich über meine Arbeit twittere?

Wer sich im Internet bewegt, kann schnell in kleine Fettnäpfchen und große Fallen treten. Damit Sie immer auf der sicheren Seite sind, haben wir die folgenden elf Tipps für Sie zusammengestellt.

1 Prinzipiell dürfen Sie soziale Medien gerne dienstlich nutzen. Hier gilt dieselbe Regel wie bei anderen Internet-Anwendungen auch: während der Arbeitszeit nur im ausdrücklichen Auftrag sowie im Sinne des Unternehmens und nicht für private Zwecke.

2 Seien Sie immer Sie selbst! Das Netz macht es einem scheinbar leicht, anonym oder inkognito aufzutreten. Doch je authentischer Sie sich geben, desto bereitwilliger wird man Ihnen zuhören.

3 Schützen Sie Ihre Privatsphäre. Denken Sie immer daran: Alles, was Sie im Internet veröffentlichen, machen Sie einer breiten Masse zugänglich. Wie diese dann mit Ihren Angaben verfährt, entzieht sich Ihrer Kontrolle. Statements, die Sie aus einer spontanen Laune heraus oder im Affekt kundtun, lassen sich noch Jahre später im Netz auffinden – sogar dann, wenn Sie sie sofort nach dem Veröffentlichen wieder löschen!

4 Bedenken Sie, dass das, was Sie im Netz tun, Auswirkungen auf Ihr reales Leben haben kann. Wägen Sie deshalb auch online die Chancen und Risiken Ihres Handelns immer sorgfältig ab.

5 Vergessen Sie nicht, dass Sie es auch online immer mit echten Menschen zu tun haben, die – wie Sie selbst auch – mit Respekt und Höflichkeit behandelt werden wollen. Möchten Sie online über Ihre berufliche Tätigkeit sprechen, so äußern Sie sich auch über Kollegen, Vorgesetzte und Wettbewerber der Krones AG immer respektvoll und fair.

6 Verletzen Sie nie die Urheberrechte anderer. Veröffentlichen Sie keine Fotos, Filme und andere Medien, die nicht von Ihnen selbst stammen oder deren Rechte Sie nicht besitzen. Dies gilt auch für Dokumente, die Eigentum von Krones sind, wie beispielsweise Fotos aus der media suite.

7 Bitte denken Sie daran, dass auch bei Veröffentlichungen im Internet die Stillschweigevereinbarungen Ihres Arbeitsvertrags gelten. Gehen Sie deshalb immer sorgsam mit unternehmensbezogenen Informationen um. Zudem stehen Betriebs- oder Geschäftsgeheimnisse ebenso wie Persönlichkeitsrechte unter besonderem gesetzlichen Schutz. Sollten Sie sich im

Einzelfall nicht sicher sein, ob und wie Sie eine bestimmte Information weitergeben dürfen, besprechen Sie sich bitte zuerst mit Ihrer Führungskraft.

8 Bitte kennzeichnen Sie private Äußerungen auch als solche. Als Mitarbeiter der Krones AG haben Sie das Recht, sich – innerhalb des vertraglich und gesetzlich vorgegebenen Rahmens – ehrlich über das Unternehmen zu äußern. Wenn Sie das tun, sollten Sie aber immer deutlich machen, dass Sie als Privatperson sprechen und Ihre persönliche Meinung vertreten.

9 Wenn Sie ein privates Blog betreiben und dort auch über Krones schreiben wollen, sichern Sie sich am besten mit folgendem Disclaimer ab: „Die Postings auf dieser Site entsprechen meiner persönlichen Meinung und repräsentieren nicht die Positionen, Strategien und Meinungen der Krones AG."

10 Veröffentlichungen im Namen der Krones AG müssen unbedingt vorher mit der zentralen Stelle bei Corporate Communications abgesprochen werden. Wenn es für Ihre Arbeit erforderlich ist, einen Krones-Account in einem sozialen Netzwerk einzurichten, stimmen Sie sich bitte mit Ihrem Vorgesetzen und Corporate Communications ab.

11 Zitieren und verweisen Sie möglichst nicht auf Geschäftspartner der Krones AG. Vor allem Aufnahmen, die von den Mitarbeitern, in den Räumlichkeiten oder auf Baustellen eines Kunden angefertigt wurden, dürfen ohne dessen schriftliche Einwilligung nicht veröffentlicht werden. Das Gleiche gilt selbstverständlich für alle Informationen über Kundenprojekte.

Abgerundet wird das Dokument durch Übersichten der gängigen Social Networks, Nutzerstatements zu Social Networks und einem kleinen Glossar.

Laub & Partner (PR-Beratung)

Die PR-Agentur Laub & Partner ermuntert im Rahmen ihrer 2010 veröffentlichten Social Media Guidelines die Mitarbeiter ausdrücklich zu Social-Media-Aktivitäten (http://www.slideshare.net/Laub_PR/laub-partner-social-media-guidelines2010).

Präambel
Das Engagement der Teammitglieder von Laub & Partner im Social Web ist ein wertvoller Beitrag zur Entwicklung unseres Portfolios und zur Positionierung der Agentur. Es gilt, diesen Wert zu erkennen, gemeinsam zu mehren, aber auch zu schützen.

Punkt 1
Wir unterstützen und fördern die berufliche bzw. beruflich konnotierte Social-Media-Kommunikation unserer Teammitglieder, solange sie nicht mit den Interessen der Agentur im Widerspruch stehen. Dazu gehören eigene Blog-Projekte oder andere Formen des Auf- und Ausbaus der persönlichen Webreputation zu bestimmten Fachthemen bzw. Kompetenzen. Die Geschäftsleitung ist vor dem Start eines solchen Projektes zu informieren.

Punkt 2
Die Nutzung von Social Media während der Arbeitszeit ist gestattet. Die Social-Media-Nutzung während der Arbeitszeit ist sogar erwünscht, wenn dies der Entwicklung der beruflichen Social-Media-Kompetenz dient (z. B. Auseinandersetzung mit neuen Tools), allerdings nur in dem Maße, wie es die laufenden Projekte zulassen. Alle Teammitglieder sind aufgefordert, eigenverantwortlich zu entscheiden, wann ihre Social-Media-Nutzung ausschließlich privaten Zwecken dient, und diese zeitlich zu beschränken.

Punkt 3
Alle Teammitglieder sind sich bei ihrer privaten Social-Media-Kommunikation darüber im Klaren, dass sie jederzeit als Mitarbeiter/in von Laub & Partner identifizierbar sind. Sie nutzen Social Media deshalb eigenverantwortlich auf eine Art und Weise, zu der sie jederzeit als Teammitglied von Laub & Partner stehen können, zum Beispiel wenn ein Geschäftspartner sie im Meeting darauf anspricht.

Punkt 4
Die Privatsphäre der Teammitglieder ist bei allen Social-Media-Aktivitäten – ob beruflich oder privat, ob während der Arbeitszeit oder außerhalb – in jedem Fall zu wahren. Wer sich namentlich über Teammitglieder äußern möchte oder Aussagen treffen will, durch die einzelne Teammitglieder eindeutig zu identifizieren sind, sollte dies vorab mit den jeweiligen Personen absprechen.

Punkt 5
Informationen über Interna aus der Agentur und aus Geschäftsbeziehungen – ob aktuelle, vergangene oder potenzielle künftige – sind unbedingt vertraulich zu behandeln. Vor jeder diesbezüglichen Äußerung im Social Web sollte kritisch hinterfragt werden, ob dadurch Interna preisgegeben werden, die Laub & Partner zum Nachteil gereichen oder die die Geschäftsbeziehungen belasten könnten.

Punkt 6
Die aktive Nutzung der Netzwerkplattform Xing zur Pflege beruflicher Kontakte ist ausdrücklich erlaubt und gewünscht. Die Geschäftsleitung begrüßt es und weiß es zu schätzen, wenn das persönliche Netzwerk auf Xing für Akquisitionszwecke sowie zur Kundenbindung oder zur Kontaktpflege mit Journalisten und anderen Multiplikatoren im Interesse von Laub & Partner genutzt wird. Wer – ab der Position Volontär/in aufwärts – sein Xing-Profil kontinuierlich pflegt und Angaben zum Arbeitgeber und im Bereich „Ich biete" nach bestimmten Kriterien ausfüllt, darf im L&P-E-Mail-Abbinder auf sein Xing-Profil verweisen.

Punkt 7
Social-Media-Beauftragte im Sinne von internen Ansprechpartner/innen für alle Fragen rund um das Thema Social-Media-Kommunikation sind Dörte Giebel und Daniel Seegers. Bei Unsicherheiten oder Anregungen kann sich jede/r vertrauensvoll an eine/n der beiden wenden.

MATERNA

Die MATERNA-Gruppe zählt nach Unternehmensangaben zu den führenden, unabhängigen Dienstleistern der Informations- und Kommunikationstechnologie in Europa. Das 1980 gegründete Unternehmen MATERNA beschäftigt mehr als 1.300 Mitarbeiter europaweit. Im Geschäftsjahr 2009 wurde ein Gruppenumsatz von 153 Millionen Euro erzielt.

Materna ist auf Twitter, Facebook, Xing, YouTube und LinkedIn präsent. Die Social Media Guidelines finden sich hier: http://www.materna.de/cae/servlet/contentblob/33244/publication-File/1815/Social%20Media%20Guidelines%20der%20MATERNA%20GmbH.pdf.

Social Media Guidelines der MATERNA GmbH

Soziale Medien bieten uns die Chance, mit Kunden, Interessenten, Partnern und Mitarbeitern direkt zu kommunizieren. In vielen Fällen nutzen unsere Mitarbeiter bereits täglich soziale Medien für geschäftliche sowie für private Zwecke. Im Zentrum sozialer Medien steht dabei der unmittelbare Dialog und Austausch. Unter sozialen Medien verstehen wir Medien mit nutzergeneriertem Inhalt, hierunter fallen z. B. Blogs, Mikroblogs, Wikis, Soziale Plattformen und Netzwerke sowie Foren.

Aktivitäten in sozialen Medien sind ein wichtiges Instrument unserer Online-Kommunikationsstrategie. Wir nutzen die sozialen Medien, um unsere Bekanntheit zu steigern, Inhalte mit Neuigkeits- und Mehrwert rund um MATERNA anzubieten und unseren Zielgruppen neue Kommunikationskanäle zur Verfügung zu stellen.

Wir wollen die Kommunikation in sozialen Medien ausdrücklich und gezielt fördern. Diese Social Media Guidelines sollen unseren Mitarbeitern helfen, erfolgreich in sozialen Netzen zu kommunizieren, und sollen definieren, wie und welche Inhalte Mitarbeiter im Namen von MATERNA in sozialen Medien kommunizieren sollen und dürfen.

Die einzelnen Richtlinien beziehen sich auf jegliche Nutzung von sozialen Medien unserer Mitarbeiter im Internet, die einen Zusammenhang zu MATERNA oder zur Tätigkeit bei MATERNA erkennen lässt.

1) Nutzung von sozialen Medien

Wir dürfen soziale Medien während unserer Arbeitszeit nur zu geschäftlichen Zwecken nutzen. Die Nutzung darf dabei unsere eigentliche Aufgabe nicht beeinträchtigen. Darüber hinaus ist uns die Verwendung unserer geschäftlichen E-Mail-Adresse zur Registrierung in sozialen Medien nur zum Zweck der geschäftlichen Nutzung erlaubt.

2) Eigenverantwortung und Sorgfalt

Wir sind für die von uns erstellten Inhalte in sozialen Medien selbst verantwortlich. Jeden Beitrag wägen wir sorgfältig ab und veröffentlichen ihn überlegt. Wir sind uns außerdem darüber bewusst, dass unsere Beiträge meist öffentlich und langlebig sind sowie von unserem Arbeitgeber MATERNA als auch von Kunden und anderen Geschäftspartnern gelesen werden können.

3) Arbeitsrechtliche Rahmenbedingungen
Wir halten uns an geltendes Recht und unsere arbeitsvertraglichen Pflichten und berücksichtigen bei allen Veröffentlichungen insbesondere Urheber-, Persönlichkeits- und Markenrechte wie auch die Datenschutzbestimmungen. Vertrauliche Informationen über MATERNA oder über Dritte dürfen wir nicht kommunizieren. Darüber hinaus zitieren oder referenzieren wir keine Kunden, Kundenprojekte oder Partner, wenn wir nicht ganz sicher sind, dass wir dazu die ausdrückliche Erlaubnis des Kunden bzw. des Partners haben.

4) Wertbeitrag und Kontinuität
Den Mehrwert und die Qualität unserer Beiträge für unsere Zielgruppe prüfen wir vor einer Veröffentlichung genau. Wenn wir uns in sozialen Medien engagieren, kommunizieren wir regelmäßig und reagieren auf Kommentare, Fragen und Kritik.

5) Transparenz
Wir treten bei unternehmensbezogenen Beiträgen immer unter unserem richtigen Namen auf, geben uns als Mitarbeiter von MATERNA zu erkennen und sorgen für eine Kontakt-/Rückmeldemöglichkeit.
Wir unterscheiden in unseren Beiträgen klar zwischen Fakten und unserer Meinung. Wir achten bei Nennungen des Firmennamens außerdem auf die richtige Schreibweise: „MATERNA GmbH" oder „MATERNA GmbH Information & Communications", im Fließtext auch nur „MATERNA" (jeweils in Großbuchstaben).

6) Unternehmensschädliche Beiträge
In sozialen Medien veröffentlichen wir keine geschäfts- oder rufschädigenden Beiträge, Drohungen oder Beleidigungen, falsche Tatsachenbehauptungen sowie Beiträge, die den Betriebsfrieden ernstlich gefährden. Probleme diskutieren und klären wir intern. Zu jeder Zeit respektieren wir unser Gegenüber und akzeptieren die Meinungsfreiheit.

7) Umgang mit Fehlern und Irrtümern
Von uns gemachte Fehler geben wir ohne Umwege zu und korrigieren diese umgehend und für alle sichtbar. Fehlerhafte Beiträge löschen wir nicht kommentarlos, sondern stellen diese richtig. Transparenz und Offenheit sind für eine vertrauensvolle Beziehung mit unseren Zielgruppen unerlässlich.

8) Umgang mit Kritik
Inhaltliche und höfliche Kritik nehmen wir immer ernst, antworten aber nicht im Affekt, sondern genau überlegt und spätestens am Vormittag des folgenden Arbeitstages. Wir antworten immer, wenn ein Kommentar uns zeigt, dass es dem Autor ernst ist – ob er mit uns diskutieren will, eine Anregung hat oder eines unserer Produkte kritisiert. Mindestens ein „Ich habe es gelesen und kümmere mich" ist notwendig. Bei Unsicherheit diskutieren wir mit der Abteilung Marketing und Kommunikation, ob sich eine Reaktion lohnt und ob sie sinnvoll ist.

Mayo Clinic

Unter dem Titel „Sharing Mayo Clinic" (http://sharing.mayoclinic.org/guidelines/for-mayo-clinic-employees/) veröffentlicht der weltbekannte Krankenhausbetreiber seine Social Media Guidelines

For Mayo Clinic Employees

The main thing Mayo employees need to remember about blogs and social networking sites is that the same basic policies apply in these spaces as in other areas of their lives. The purpose of these guidelines is to help employees understand how Mayo policies apply to these newer technologies for communication, so you can participate with confidence not only on this blog, but in other social media platforms.

1. Follow all applicable Mayo Clinic policies. For example, you must not share confidential or proprietary information about Mayo Clinic and you must maintain patient privacy. Among the policies most pertinent to this discussion are those concerning government affairs, mutual respect, political activity, Computer, E-mail & Internet Use, the Mayo Clinic Integrity Program, photography and video, release of patient information to media and patient confidentiality.
2. Write in the first person. Where your connection to Mayo Clinic is apparent, make it clear that you are speaking for yourself and not on behalf of Mayo Clinic. In those circumstances, you may want to include this disclaimer: "The views expressed on this [blog; website] are my own and do not reflect the views of my employer." Consider adding this language in an "About me" section of your blog or social networking profile.
3. If you communicate in the public internet about Mayo Clinic or Mayo Clinic-related matters, disclose your connection with Mayo Clinic and your role at Mayo. Use good judgment and strive for accuracy in your communications; errors and omissions reflect poorly on Mayo, and may result in liability for you or Mayo Clinic.
4. Use a personal email address (not your mayo.edu address) as your primary means of identification. Just as you would not use Mayo Clinic stationery for a letter to the editor with your personal views, do not use your Mayo Clinic e-mail address for personal views.
5. If your blog, posting or other online activities are inconsistent with, or would negatively impact Mayo Clinic's reputation or brand, you should not refer to Mayo Clinic, or identify your connection to Mayo Clinic.
6. Be respectful and professional to fellow employees, business partners, competitors and patients. Avoid using unprofessional online personas.
7. Ensure that your blogging and social networking activity does not interfere with your work commitments.
8. Ask the Department of Public Affairs (4-5005 in Rochester, 2-4222 in Arizona, 3-2299 in Florida) if you have any questions about what is appropriate to include in your blog or social networking profile. Remember that if you wouldn't want your manager or others at Mayo to see your comments, it is unwise to post them to the Internet.

Guidelines for Official Mayo Clinic Participation

- Some Mayo staff may be interested in engaging in internet conversations for work-related purposes, or may be asked by supervisors or leadership to participate, in support of Mayo Clinic's organizational objectives. Such engagement on behalf of Mayo Clinic, including establishment of official external sites representing Mayo Clinic or any Mayo organization, must be approved and coordinated through the Department of Public Affairs. Mayo Clinic's Social Media Team provides oversight and assistance to guide development of new social media platforms, sharing knowledge and instituting best practices for successful implementation.
- Use of external Web sites for work-related purposes (e.g. photo sharing through Flickr. com) must be first approved by Public Affairs in conjunction with the Office for Compliance.

Code of Ethics

As Mayo Clinic engages in conversations on the Internet, the following code of ethics applies, both in Mayo-sponsored sites and in comments on other sites.

- Mayo Clinic blog posts and comments will be accurate and factual.
- Mayo Clinic will acknowledge and correct mistakes promptly.
- When corrections are made, Mayo Clinic will preserve the original post, showing by strike-through what corrections have been made, to maintain integrity.
- Mayo Clinic will delete spam and/or comments that are off-topic.
- Mayo Clinic will reply to emails and comments when appropriate.
- Mayo Clinic will link directly to online references and original source materials.
- Mayo Clinic staff will disclose conflicts of interest and will not attempt to conceal their identity or that they work for Mayo Clinic.

Microsoft

Eine Vielzahl von Einzelregelungen hat der Softwareanbieter Microsoft über die Jahre erlassen – ausgehend von einer Regelung für Unternehmens-Blogs über Richtlinien für Twitter bis zu Hinweisen für besondere Plattformen. Interessant ist der Fokus darauf, Mitarbeiter in Sozialen Medien darauf zu verpflichten, selbst Personen zu identifizieren, die sich als Microsoft ausgeben. Ob die hier angegebenen Regelungen vollständig sind, konnte bis Redaktionsschluss nicht in Erfahrung gebracht werden. Auf Anfrage durch den Autor teilte Microsoft Deutschland mit, dass es selbstverständlich Regelungen für Social Media gebe, diese aber nicht öffentlich seien (was zumindest für die nachfolgend wiedergegebenen Regelungen und insbesondere die vom Bitkom veröffentlichte deutschsprachige „Microsoft Social Media Guideline" so nicht korrekt ist).

Blogging Policy

Erstmals 2005 wurde auf einer Konferenz die Microsoft Blogging Policy vorgestellt (zitiert nach http://kevin.lexblog.com/2005/01/articles/cool-stuff/microsofts-employee-blogging-policy/):

- Above all, be smart
- Respect existing confidentiality agreements
- Don't break news – don't disclose confidential information
- Be cautious with third-party information
- Respect prior employers
- Identify yourself
- Be cautious in how you offer support or advice
- Speak for yourself
- Think about reactions before you post

Channel 9 Doctrine
1. Channel 9 is all about the conversation. Channel 9 should inspire Microsoft and our customers to talk in an honest and human voice. Channel 9 is not a marketing tool, not a PR tool, not a lead generation tool.

2. Be a human being. Channel 9 is a place for us to be ourselves, to share who we are, and for us to learn who our customers are.

3. Learn by listening. When our customers speak, learn from them. Don't get defensive, don't argue for the sake of argument. Listen and take what benefits you to heart.

4. Be smart. Think before you speak, there are some conversations which have no benefit other than to reinforce stereotypes or create negative situations.

5. Marketing has no place on Channel 9. When we spend money on Channel 9 the goal is to surprise and delight, not to promote or preach.

6. Don't shock the system. Lasting change only happens in baby steps.

7. Know when to turn the mic off. There are some topics which will only result in problems when you discuss them. This has nothing to do with censorship, but with working within the reality of the system that exists in our world today. You will not change anything by taking on legal or financial issues, you will only shock the system, spook the passengers, and create a negative situation.

8. Don't be a jerk. Nobody likes mean people.

9. Commit to the conversation. Don't stop listening just because you are busy. Don't stop participating because you don't agree with someone. Relationships are not built in a day, be in it for the long haul and we will all reap the benefits as an industry.

Microsoft Twitter Regelung
(http://socialmediagovernance.com/MSFT_Social_Media_Policy.pdf)

TweetingGuidelines

As the name suggests, Micro-blogging is a form of blogging typified by a focus on short – or "micro" – posts and the formation of communities of "followers". Please refer to Microsoft's Blogging FAQ and best practices for general guidance on blogging at Microsoft. These micro-blogging guidelines are intended to complement the general guidance and address issues more specific to micro-blogging and third party micro-blogging services.
Since Twitter is currently the most popular micro-blogging service, specific questions about appropriate use of Twitter are also addressed below.

Does Microsoft permit employees to use third party micro-blogging services?
Microsoft does not maintain lists of recommended or restricted micro-blogging services, but encourages employees to use their judgment when choosing to use these services, to read theservice terms and conditions and adhere to them, and to post sensibly and responsibly in accordance with Microsoft policies and blogging guidelines. If you are unsure of the requirements of the terms and conditions for a specific microblogging service you should not use it.

Should I register an account that identifies me as a Microsoft employee?
Since the majority of micro-blogging sites are individual-rather than group-oriented, it can be difficult to indicate a professional affiliation. However, if you plan to tweet about any professional matters (such as about the business of Microsoft or other companies, products or services in the same business space as Microsoft), in addition to referencing your alias@ microsoft.com mail address, whenever possible use the service's profile or contact information to assert that you are a Microsoft employee and/or affiliated with a specific group/team at Microsoft.

Are there limits on the kind of micro-blogging account names I can create?
As stated in other places, make sure to work with your team and get appropriate approval before registering a new micro-blogging account for company business. If you intend to use a Microsoft product name or trademark in the account name, make sure to be a good steward for our company by using the full, appropriate name of the product, i. e. Silverlight, not Slvrlite.
This helps build consumer awareness in our names, and shows the same respect for our trademarks that we ask other companies to give us. Also, do not use other companies' product names or trademarks for an account name, i. e. Switch from Flash or Flashsucks. This potentially creates legal risk for Microsoft, and may cause PR problems for the company.

Should I register accounts on behalf of Microsoft teams/groups?
Generally, employees should not register micro-blogging accounts on behalf of Microsoft teams and groups unless they are clearly responsible for the team's or group's community

engagement activities and have checked to make sure an account for that team or group doesn't already exist.

If in doubt, don't. Also, as a best practice and to reflect the frequent career moves employees make at Microsoft, please choose an alias for the account that can be easily managed by your group if you move to a new role, such as silverlighttwitter@microsoft.com, rather than johnsmith@microsoft.com. Micro-blogging accounts that you register for company business, and any accounts you register that contain Microsoft product names and trademarks are considered Microsoft intellectual property, per the terms of your employment agreement with the company.

What should I do if I encounter an instance of impersonation or name-squatting?

If you find a service in which you feel Microsoft, one of its brands, products or teams is being impersonated or victimized by name squatting on the third party micro-blogging service, you should send detailed information on the service/account to your Trademark LCA representative and work with them to resolve the issue. Some micro-blogging services (e.g. Twitter) have specific notice and takedown processes for removing impersonators or squatters. To make sure we take a consistent approach as a company to impersonation and name-squatting issues, it's important to route all notice and takedown requests through LCA Trademarks. You can find your Trademark contact at//lcaweb/trademarks.

What content may I post? What content must I not post?

Please refer to Microsoft's Blogging FAQ for general guidance on blogging at Microsoft. In line with those guidelines, Microsoft encourages and trusts its employees to micro-blog sensibly and responsibly.

How should I tag content?

Micro-blogging sites use different mechanisms to help tag content. A primary goal for tagging is to coalesce related content and to help users find relevant content. You are encouraged to utilize any common tagging practices of the micro-blog services that you use. Please make sure that Microsoft trademarks are not abbreviated in hash tags or other mechanisms of tagging content – use the full names of Microsoft trademarks in all tagging.

Does Microsoft recommend URL shortening services?

Because micro-blogging services focus on short/micro messages, the inclusion of URLs in posts often causes the post to exceed a maximum length. To overcome this problem, URL shortening services (e.g. http://tinyurl.com) are used. Microsoft does not maintain lists of preferred or restricted URL shortening services. Some micro-blogging services may recommend/include a URL shortening service but, for those (e.g. Twitter) that do not, you may use the service that you prefer as long as you have read and can abide by the shortening service's terms and conditions and the use of the shortening service does not contravene the micro-blogging site's terms and conditions. If you are unsure of either service's terms and conditions, you should not use them.

May I create Twitter accounts that represent a Microsoft team or group?
Generally , you should not register a micro-blogging account on behalf of a Microsoft team or group unless you are clearly responsible for the team's or group's community engagement activities and have ensured that an account does not already exist. If in doubt, you should not create Twitter accounts for teams at Microsoft.

How do I advertise my Twitter account?
Twitter accounts may be advertised through other digital channels by providing a URL to your Twitter account (e.g. http://twitter.com/[[MyTwitterAccount]]). A common shorthand for the URL is "Twitter: @[MyTwitterAccount]". Twitter communities are formed by following others. People interested in your Twitter posts (the set is called a 'feed' or 'event stream') may follow you. Similarly, you may follow other people that interest you.

Blogging Guidelines –
Frequently Asked Questions About Blogging At Microsoft
These FAQs were created to answer some of the most common general questions about company policies relating to blogging.

– Does Microsoft have a specific policy governing employee blogs?
– Can I disclose confidential information when blogging?
– How do I handle personal information in my blog?
– Do I need to clear my posts before making them?
– Can I post about our competitors?
– Can I post about my prior employer?
– Should I disclose my Microsoft affiliation?
– Can I solicit feedback in my blog?
– Can I offer technical assistance in my blog?
– Can I post code in my blog?
– Do I own my blog content?
– Can I use photos in my blog?
– Can I make commitments on behalf of the company?
– How do I respond if I'm contacted by the press?
– Do I have to use a disclaimer on my blog?
– Do I have to blog on Microsoft sites?
– If I blog on a Microsoft site, what happens to my blog when I leave Microsoft?

Q. Does Microsoft have a specific policy governing employee blogs?
A. The company expects employees to exercise good judgment and "be smart" when blogging. The same principles and policies that apply to public interactions generally also apply to blogging, such as the:
– Confidential Information Policy,
– Competitive Intelligence Policy,
– Employee Handbook,

- Standards of Business Conduct,
- IT Guidelines and Policies,
- Anti-Harassment Policy,
- Sexually Explicit or Otherwise Offensive Material Policy, and
- Microsoft Corporation Employee Agreement that each employee
- signs upon hire.

You should familiarize yourself with these policies before you begin blogging. Finally, individual managers, teams, or divisions may develop their own specific policies about blogging, and blogs hosted on Microsoft servers may be subject to certain additional requirements. It is your responsibility to familiarize yourself with any such specific policies or requirements. You should also discuss your blogging plans with your manager before beginning.

Q. Do I need to clear my posts before making them?
A. As a general rule, Microsoft does not review, edit, censor, or, obviously, endorse individual posts. You should "be smart" and, as an employee of the company, you should not only think about how your blog reflects on you as an individual, but also about how your blog affects Microsoft as a whole. How would it look on Slashdot or on the front page of the New York Times? What would your manager or VP think? If you're posting about another team's product, what would they and their management think? Could a customer or partner make a wrong decision based on your posting? What would a competitor do with your posting? Using your public blog to gratuitously trash Microsoft, our products, partners or competitors reflects poorly on all of us.

Q. Can I disclose confidential information when blogging?
A. As with all public communications, you should not disclose Microsoft confidential information unless there is a compelling business purpose and you have at least Director-level approval, pursuant to the company's Confidential Information Policy. You should not disclose confidential information of a customer, partner, vendor or other third party without consulting your LCA contact. In general, do not post any information, code, inventions, or other material that may be confidential to Microsoft or its customers, partners or vendors. Don't post anything marked "Confidential," "Proprietary," or "Privileged" or material from any internal corporate emails, web pages or documents (including these FAQs). Be especially careful in talking about patents, open source software, antitrust law, or our legal strategies; or revealing anything related to Microsoft facilities, product release schedules, or other employees. Most importantly, to preserve Microsoft's rights to protect its innovations through patents, do not disclose or describe any new features, functionalities, or innovations that have not been publicly disclosed or released without first checking with your business unit management or your LCA patent contact.

Finally, don't break news without clearing it through your manager and your PR contact; breaking news not only risks destroying trade secret and patent protection, it could even be deemed to violate the company's disclosure obligations under the securities laws. If you have any doubts about whether something is confidential, check with your manager or your LCA contacts before you post.

Q. How do I handle personal information in my blog?
A. Your blog is a permanent record so treat your own and other's personal information with appropriate care. Make sure you have permission before including anyone else's personal information in your blog. If you are planning to use personal information attained from blogs, your use must be consistent with any restriction on such use contained in the terms or privacy statement of the blog in question, as well as with our own corporate privacy policy and standards. If you unsure of the requirements contact your Privacy Lead.

Q. Can I post about our competitors?
A. There is no company rule against discussing competitors, so long as you use good judgment and comply with the Competitive Intelligence Policy. In particular, do not solicit any information or materials that appear to be confidential or proprietary to a third party, and delete any comments that you suspect the commentator did not have the right to share. Be especially careful about criticizing competitors or any third parties or their products or service, and make sure that any criticism you feel compelled to offer is totally accurate and substantiated – critical blog posts about competitors and others generate ill will and can even lead to lawsuits, justified or not.

Q. Can I post about my prior employer?
A. If you must discuss a prior employer, do not disclose any of their trade secrets orother information you were required to keep secret.

Q. Should I disclose my Microsoft affiliation?
A. You may not hide or mislead others about your affiliation with Microsoft, and if asked, should respond honestly. If you think it will matter to the audience that you are a Microsoft employee, you should say that you are. If you are blogging on behalf of Microsoft, you should not give the impression that you are blogging on your own behalf. For more information, read the Competitive Intelligence Policy.

Q. Can I solicit feedback in my blog?
A. Blogs are a great resource to gather feedback on a product, a plan, or an idea. These are some guidelines to make sure that you gather and use feedback the right way to protect both Microsoft and those providing their opinions to you: Generally, you may solicit, use, and share your readers' opinions about the appearance, usability, quality, or desired feature sets or functionalities of Microsoft offerings, or about whether Microsoft should follow a particular course of action. Even this kind of feedback could increase the risk of others claiming patent infringement, however, if it leads to additions or other changes to a Microsoft product or service. Accordingly, if you are involved in product development and want community feedback, you should educate yourself on patent risks and your team's position on community feedback.
Do not solicit, review, use, or share source code for implementation in Microsoft products or services without at least Director-level approval and/or involving LCA.

Do not solicit, review, use, or share APIs, file formats, schema, or similar items from your readers without at least Director-level approval and/or involving LCA.

If your job responsibilities include soliciting specific or detailed community feedback on Microsoft products or services, work with your LCA contact to evaluate the attendant risks and/or to design a streamlined process for handling the feedback.

Our readers often have great ideas to share, and we are constantly looking at new ways to help them share ideas in a safe and effective way for the company. For product feedback, consider directing readers to the MSWish and Product Feedback Center web sites. For any business development proposals, including proposed partnerships or sales pitches, refer readers to the Opportunity Management Center.

Q. Can I offer technical assistance in my blog?

A. Customers and partners sometimes look to Microsoft bloggers for help with an existing or future product when they can't find the answer in one of our web resources.

It's great to send someone away happy with an answer if you can help, but follow these basic guidelines to make sure you are doing the best thing for all involved:

Make sure your information is accurate, up to date, and suitable for public disclosure (e.g., not confidential).

If you're not the expert, don't imply you are or make up the answer. Security in particular is a really complicated topic where wrong advice can be damaging for the recipient and Microsoft, so unless you are a true expert whose job is focused on security, don't try to go too deep into prescriptive guidance beyond telling people to use anti-virus software, run a firewall, and keep their software up to date. For more guidance on this topic, read the Microsoft Security & Privacy Messaging Guidelines.

Don't speak for other product teams.

Don't forget about other sources of technical support such as Product Support Services, Newsgroups, other blogs, user groups, and Microsoft and community run Web sites.

Q. Can I post code in my blog?

A. There isn't a one size fits all answer to this question. Whether you are posting code as part of your job at Microsoft or code related to Microsoft products on your own time, you need to comply with the release and approval procedures established by your business unit. The release and approval procedures vary depending on what you are posting, so before doing anything you should discuss what you want to do with your manager and involve your LCA contact.

Q. Do I own my blog content?

A. Under the Microsoft Corporation Employee Agreement you signed upon hire, Microsoft owns all copyrightable works prepared within the scope of your employment at Microsoft.

Whether a post is made within the scope of your employment depends on a number of factors, including the extent to which the post relates to your duties at Microsoft. Accordingly, if you blog in connection with the business of Microsoft, then, regardless of whether you blog on a non-Microsoft site and/or after work hours, don't sell, convey, or monetize rights in your postings (such as by selling advertising) without first consulting your manger and LCA contact. This also applies after you leave Microsoft – if you'd like to make use of blog postings made during your time here, please consult your manager and LCA contacts before you leave.

Q. Can I use photos in my blog?
A. As long as you have the right to use the photo (from the photographed individuals and the photographer), the photo does not contain any confidential information, and you comply with applicable corporate policies such as Sexually Explicit or Otherwise Offensive Material Policy, you can post photos on your blog. However, if you would like to use photos taken at Microsoft, make sure that you comply with all corporate security and PR policies regarding on-campus photography, and remember that no photos may be taken in labs or executive areas. Please consult your PR and/or security contact if you have any questions.

Q. Can I make commitments on behalf of the company?
A. Unless you are empowered to do so, don't try to speak on behalf of the company – be yourself and use your own voice. As you know, Microsoft is often the target of lawsuits, and opposing parties may seek to use statements taken from employee blogs against the company or as an admission by Microsoft in court. Many bloggers include a disclaimer saying that they are speaking for themselves, e.g., 'this blog contains my own views and does not necessarily reflect the view of employer.' In any case, avoid stating your or other's opinions as facts, drawing legal conclusions, or making exaggerated or broad generalizations about our products, competitors, or markets in which they compete. Similarly, when expressing an opinion or making a commitment,you should make it clear that you are speaking for yourself. For example, in offering opinions, lead with "IMO" or "IMHO."

Q. How do I respond if I'm contacted by the press?
A. If you think you may be dealing with the press, involve your PR lead immediately. For more information, see Talking to the Press in the Employee Handbook.

Q. Do I have to use a disclaimer on my blog?
A. Unless your business unit requires it, there is no hard and fast rule that requires disclaimers on your blog site or individual postings. Using an appropriate disclaimer can help you emphasize that your opinions are your own, not those of Microsoft generally. If you host your blog on a Microsoft blog site, you may want to reference that your blog is governed by the site terms of use. In addition, if you wish, you may choose to indicate on your blog that the contents are licensed under the Creative Commons Attribution-NonCommercial-NoDerivs license (note that this license is NOT Appropriate for software). Finally, if you feel that the

nature of your blog or an individual posting warrants a disclaimer, please consider using the disclaimer at http://mscommunity/Disclaimer.aspx.

Q. Do I have to blog on Microsoft sites?
A. If you are blogging in connection with the business of Microsoft, we encourage you to blog on blogs.msdn.com or blogs.technet.com, as appropriate. Having employees blog on these sites helps the company ensure that blog postings are archived, enables us to put any required legal language on the blog templates so you don't have to worry about it, and helps our customers and partners by creating a centralized resource for Microsoft blogs. Of course, if you have an existing blog hosted elsewhere when you join Microsoft, it may make sense to keep the same URL for your readers.

Q. If I blog on a Microsoft site, what happens to my blog when I leave Microsoft?
A. If you are leaving Microsoft, and you have a blog hosted on blogs.msdn.com or blogs. technet.com, you must notify the bloghelp@microsoft.com alias of your last day with the company. Generally, Microsoft will not delete your blog, but will freeze it so that no posts are made after you leave. This policy may not apply to blogs hosted on sites Microsoft makes generally available to the public, but you should cease holding yourself out as a Microsoft employee after you leave.

Q. I still don't have an answer to my specific question.
A. For additional guidance about blogging, visit http://community/blogs.aspx, query the Bloggers alias, talk with your manager, or reach out to your HR representative, PR lead, or LCA contact, as appropriate.

Microsoft Social Media Guide
Darüber hinaus verfügt Microsoft Deutschland über einen eigenen Social Media Guide (zitiert nach Bitkom „Leitfaden Social Media", 2010):

Microsoft Social Media Guide

Ich MUSS Social Media machen

Der anhaltende Hype rund um das Thema Social Media macht viele von uns nervös. Oft entsteht der Eindruck, jeder von uns sollte sofort einen Facebook-, Twitter- oder Flickr-Account für sein Thema oder sein Produkt starten – oder am besten gleich alle zusammen.
Es stimmt, das Social-Media-Kommunikation neue Möglichkeiten für erfolgreiche Kommunikation eröffnet. ABER bevor Ihr Euch für einen eigenen Social-Media-Kanal/eine Kampagne entscheidet, bitte denkt über die folgenden Fragen nach.

Ist Social Media überhaupt das passende Kommunikationsinstrument für mich und/oder mein Produkt?

Es gibt viele Gründe, warum man sich gegen Social-Media-Kommunikation entscheidet – und sie sind alle legitim. Ihr solltet Euch genau überlegen, ob Ihr Euch in diesem neuen Kommunikations-Setting wohlfühlt und ob Ihr genug Zeit und Ressourcen für Social-Media-Kommunikation habt. Denn ein vorschnell eröffneter Facebook-Kanal oder Twitter-Account schafft beim Publikum eine Erwartungshaltung, und wenn diese nicht eingehalten wird, wirkt das schlecht auf Microsoft und Eurer Produkt, vielleicht sogar auf Euch direkt.

Gibt es schon einen Kanal zu meinem Thema?
In den meisten Fällen wird es wahrscheinlich sogar schon mehrere Microsoft-eigene Social-Media-Kanäle zu Eurem Thema geben. Bitte prüft, ob Ihr mit Eurem Kanal einen wirklichen Mehrwert liefert im Vergleich zu den anderen. Sollte das nicht der Fall sein: Kontaktiert die Owner des bereits vorhandenen Kanals und bietet an, ihm/ihr mit Euren Inhalten zu helfen.

Biete ich einen wirklichen Mehrwert?
Social-Media-Kommunikation basiert auf dem Pull-Konzept, also darauf, dass Menschen freiwillig Fans oder Followers eines Kanals werden. Das tun sie aber nur, wenn ihnen dieser Kanal auch konstant einen Mehrwert bietet. Bevor Ihr also loslegt: Was ist Euer Mehrwert?

Social Media ist kostenlos
Es stimmt zwar, dass man für die meisten Social-Media-Plattformen und -Applikationen in den meisten Fällen keine Gebühren bezahlen muss. Allerdings darf man nicht außer Acht lassen, dass erfolgreiches Relationship-Building online wie offline ein konstantes Engagement bedeutet. Bei den Kosten für Social-Media-Kommunikation muss also die Personalressource Zeit einkalkuliert werden.
Ein weiterer Kostenfaktor kann durch Agenturengagement entstehen oder durch Inhalte, die Ihr speziell für Social-Media-Formate produziert.

Social Media ist einfach
Es gibt keine Patentlösung. Erfolgreiche Kommunikation muss gut überlegt und geplant sein, und das gilt auch und besonders für Social-Media-Kommunikation. Um eine gute Beziehung zu Eurer Zielgruppe aufzubauen, ist es wichtig, sich an die Gepflogenheiten und Regeln einer Community anzupassen.

Social Media geht schnell
Das trifft nicht auf zeitlich begrenzte Social-Media-Kampagnen und schon gar nicht auf permanente Social-Media-Kommunikation zu. Eine gute Social-Media-Kampagne braucht eine solide Planung, ein professionelles Seeding und nicht zuletzt eine konstante und somit sehr zeitintensive Betreuung während der Laufzeit.
Permanente Social-Media-Kommunikation muss hier noch einen Schritt weiter gehen – das

bedeutet konstantes Engagement. Wir wollen eine Beziehung zu unserer Zielgruppe aufbauen, ohne dabei fordernd und unsympathisch zu wirken.

Social Media mache ich nebenbei
Da Social Media kein „schnelles" Medium ist, hier Beziehungen aufgebaut werden sollen und der Ruf von Microsoft und Eurem Produkt nicht geschädigt werden soll, ist es wichtig, nicht einfach loszustürzen und im Alleingang einen Facebook-, Twitter- oder YouTube-Kanal zu starten, den Ihr neben Euren eigentlichen Aufgaben betreut. Informiert Euch im Vorfeld bei unseren internen Spezialisten (siehe Ansprechpartnerseite) oder konsultiert eine unserer Social-Media-Agenturen (siehe Ansprechpartnerseite Agenturen), um eine Einschätzung für ein realistisches Zeitinvestment zu bekommen.
Ein weiterer Punkt für erfolgreiche Social-Media-Kommunikation ist ein ordentliches Monitoring. Um in der Community angenommen zu werden und Vertrauen aufzubauen, ist es wichtig, aktiv am Geschehen teilzunehmen. Das bedeutet, dass Ihr Euch kontinuierlich darüber informieren müsst, was über Euch, Euer Produkt und Microsoft gesagt wird, und darauf reagiert – sei es durch Lernen aus kritischen Kommentaren oder dass Ihr Euch als Ansprechpartner zu Euren Themen anbietet.

Social Media funktioniert einfach
Nur weil Social Media momentan in aller Munde ist, heißt das nicht, dass jedes Format und jeder Inhalt wie von Zauberhand zum nächsten Viral-Hit wird. Wenn Ihr Zeit und Kreativität investiert, gute Inhalte habt und am Ball bleibt, wird Euer Kanal auch bekannt.

Social Media hat keinen ROI
Social-Media-Plattformen bieten im Allgemeinen sogar sehr gute Möglichkeiten zur Auswertung. Für diese Art der Kommunikation gelten die gleichen Metriken wie bisher: Exposure, Engagement und Conversion. Nur die Indikatoren für diese Kriterien haben sich geändert. Bitte seht Euch hierzu das Kapitel „Reporting" an.

Namics

Die Online-Agentur Namics versucht unter allen Umständen, „keine Guideline" zu entwerfen, de facto ist es natürlich dennoch eine (http://blog.namics.com/2010/09/social-media-keine-guidelines.html).

Social Media Starter – der keine Guideline ist

Namics pflegt einen offenen, ehrlichen und partnerschaftlichen Dialog sowie eine Lern- und Teilkultur. Intern zwischen Mitarbeitern wie auch außerhalb von Namics. Der vorliegende Social Media Starter soll dafür eine Hilfestellung bieten.

1. Zeige Identität
Beiträge und Kommentare erfolgen immer unter Angabe Deines Namens und, wenn ein

Zusammenhang mit Deiner Arbeit bei uns besteht, mit der Nennung von Namics als Arbeitgeber. Absender bist immer Du als Person.

2. Übernehme Verantwortung
Formuliere Inhalte in der Ich-Form und vertrete Deine persönliche Meinung. Verantwortung übernehmen heißt auch, Kritik gelten zu lassen, Fehler zuzugeben, ehrlich zu sein und keine gemachten Aussagen zu löschen (aber diese bei Bedarf zu kommentieren/zu ergänzen).

3. Nennung der Quellen
Lege Deine Quellen offen, verlinke diese aktiv und nenne den Absender immer auch im Kontext. Auch wenn es sich dabei um einen Konkurrenten handelt. Social Media lebt von Verlinkung und Vernetzung.

4. Wert für Leser schaffen
Inhalte sind für Leser geschrieben und sollen diese weiterbringen, inspirieren oder auch amüsieren. Stifte Mehrwert und verzichte auf Selbstdarstellung! Erfolgreich sind originäre Inhalte, persönliche Meinungen und Verweise auf „Perlen". Davon leben besonders unsere Blogs.

5. Suche den Dialog
Zeige in Deinen Blog-Beiträgen Interesse an Dialog und antworte auf Kommentare, Verlinkung und Nennungen zeitnah, höflich und konstruktiv. Sei aktiver Kommentator, wo über Dich oder eines Deiner Themen geschrieben wird.

6. Höflichkeit und Respekt
Sprich respektvoll über andere Marktteilnehmer und versuche nicht, deren Schwächen auszunutzen. Auch wenn jemand Kritik übt, lasse Dich nicht aus der Ruhe bringen und bleibe sachlich.

7. Vertraulichkeit und Gesetz
Halte Dich zu jeder Zeit an geltendes Recht. Dies insbesondere in Bezug auf Urheberrechte und Betriebsgeheimnisse. Information über Kundenarbeit, die nicht bereits öffentlich bekannt ist, bedarf immer der ausdrücklichen Zustimmung des Kunden. So auch die Tatsache, dass wir für einen Kunden arbeiten.

Ergänzende Gedanken und Tipps

Jeder wird von Außenstehenden immer auch für seinen Beruf und als Mitarbeiter einer Firma wahrgenommen. Veröffentliche nur, was Du auch einer flüchtigen Bekanntschaft erzählen würdest, und stell Dir vor, es steht morgen in der Zeitung.

Sei Dir bewusst, dass alles Publizierte auch nach Jahren noch auffindbar ist, von Freunden, Arbeitgebern, Kollegen, Partnern, Kunden, potenziellen Kunden, Bloggern und Journalisten gleichermaßen.

Bevor Du einen neuen Namics-Accounts anlegst, besprich Dich bitte vorerst mit MarKom. Wir möchten mit lebendigen Accounts am Markt auftreten.

Nutzt Du Slideshare? Biete für Handouts (von Deinem Referat zum Beispiel) zusätzlich auf einer Namics-Plattform einen Download als pdf ohne Login an.

Opera

Der norwegische Browser-Hersteller Opera – besonders bekannt für seine Browser für Mobiltelefone – fokussiert sich mit seiner unter http://my.opera.com/community/blogs/corp-policy/ einsehbaren „Opera Emloyee Blogging Policy" auf eine knappe prägnante Darstellung:

Opera Employee Blogging Policies

My Opera Community has opened an area in which users can maintain a blog (among other services). We encourage Opera employees to participate in this same community – whether you are obsessively writing about the browser, or about nothing but your favorite Norwegian (or sub-Saharan) wildflowers.

Sometimes Opera employees may want to write about something but worry that it is not for disclosure. This may lead to a missed opportunity to talk about something that is, in fact, public. They also may not realize that something is strategically sensitive and should not be written about. To shed some light on these issues, Opera employees may refer to the following guidelines:

Share your thoughts
Be open and use this service for discussing life at Opera, or talking about topics outside of work. This area is yours, use your personality and use your language, whether that's English, norsk, casual, refined, techy-jargon, or Pig-Latin.

Be active
Interact with other community members, both inside and outside Opera. We want to encourage other users to become active in the community too.

We're not your mama
No one is here to look over your shoulder, but please use common sense when it comes to the use of objectionable language, sensitive topics, etc. Also be sure to proof-read and use proper grammar/spelling.

Don't give away the farm
Remember your obligations to your NDA. If an item is questionable, in terms of secrecy (unreleased versions, release dates, project names, features under development, status of internal development, etc), it may be better to err on the side of caution as we are under

strict obligations of secrecy with our partners. If you have specific questions, feel free to bring them up with your manager.

Check your sources
Some sources may acquire inside knowledge that is not meant for publication. Just because you may see something on the Web does not mean it is meant to be public knowledge. As a general rule, an item that has appeared in a press release may be considered fair game.

Our friends are your friends
Remember to protect the privacy of Opera's partners and customers. If there's a new deal with Widget Co. that has not been mentioned in a press release, it is probably not public knowledge.

For the squeamish
Some may feel more comfortable posting a disclaimer claiming that the opinions posted are not those of Opera Software. This may help readers understand that your comments are from your perspective.

Above all
Remember to use common sense. If you need help in a situation, don't hesitate to ask your manager. Your blog is meant to be an open window, but remember there are legal obligations.

Oracle

Auch der Datenbankspezialist Oracle nutzt Social Media und gibt seinen Mitarbeitern eine entsprechende Regelung an die Hand (http://blogs.oracle.com/otn/entry/the_oracle_social_media_partic). Die Ähnlichkeiten zur SUN Policy (s. u.) sind in der Tat auffällig. Oracle profitiert hier vom Know-how der Übernahme von SUN.

Oracle Social Media Participation Policy

SOCIAL MEDIA PARTICIPATION AT ORACLE
As a company, we encourage communication among our employees, customers, partners, and others – and Web logs (blogs), social networks, discussion forums, wikis, video, and other social media – such as Twitter – can be a great way to stimulate conversation and discussion. They're also an invaluable tool for experienced Oracle users who want to share information and tips on the use of Oracle products.

The Oracle Social Media Participation Policy applies to:
– All blogs, wikis, forums, and social networks hosted or sponsored by Oracle
– Your personal blogs that contain postings about Oracle's business, products, employees, customers, partners, or competitors

- Your postings about Oracle's business, products, employees, customers, partners, or competitors on external blogs, wikis, discussion forums, or social networking sites such as Twitter
- Your participation in any video related to Oracle's business, products, employees, customers, partners, or competitors, whether you create a video to post or link to on your blog, you contribute content for a video, or you appear in a video created either by another Oracle employee or by a third party.

Even if your social media activities take place completely outside of work, as your personal activities should, what you say can have an influence on your ability to conduct your job responsibilities, your teammates' abilities to do their jobs, and Oracle's business interests.

REQUIREMENTS

This section describes the requirements that are most relevant to Oracle employees participating in social media of various kinds (Oracle hosted and external). It is extremely important that you follow these requirements. Failure to do so may result in disciplinary action, up to and including termination of your employment with Oracle.

Follow the Code
The Oracle Code of Ethics and Business Conduct and Oracle's corporate policies – including the Acceptable Use Policy, Information Protection Policy, and Copyright Compliance Policy – apply to your online conduct (blogging or other online activities) just as much as they apply to your offline behavior. Make sure you're familiar with them.

Protect Confidential Information
You may not use your blog or other social media to disclose Oracle's confidential information. This includes nonpublic financial information such as future revenue, earnings, and other financial forecasts, and anything related to Oracle strategy, products, policy, management, operating units, and potential acquisitions, that has not been made public.

Protecting the confidential information of our employees, customers, partners, and suppliers is also important. Do not mention them, including Oracle executives, in social media without their permission, and make sure you don't disclose items such as sensitive personal information of others or details related to Oracle's business with its customers. Third party social media services use servers that are outside of Oracle's control and may pose a security risk. Don't use these services to conduct internal Oracle business.

In addition, you may not publish (nor should you possess) our competitors' proprietary or confidential information. You may make observations about competitors' products and activities if your observations are accurate and based on publicly available information. Take care not to disparage or denigrate competitors.

Don't Comment on M&A Activity

You must not comment publicly on Oracle's M&A activity, including potential and pending acquisitions. This applies to potential acquisitions regardless of their status – in diligence, announced but not closed, etc. Any commentary on what a transaction or potential transaction may mean to Oracle, positive, negative or neutral can be problematic.

Don't Discuss Future Offerings

As a general rule, don't discuss product upgrades or future product releases. Because of potential revenue recognition issues, it is especially important that we do not give the impression to customers or potential customers that a given product upgrade will include specific features that will be incorporated into the product within a specific time frame. See Revenue Recognition Guidelines. Any exceptions must be approved by senior management, Legal, and Revenue Recognition.

Refrain from Objectionable or Inflammatory Posts

Do not post anything that is false, misleading, obscene, defamatory, profane, discriminatory, libelous, threatening, harassing, abusive, hateful, or embarrassing to another person or entity. Make sure to respect others' privacy. Third party Web sites and blogs that you link to must meet our standards of propriety. Be aware that false or defamatory statements or the publication of an individual's private details could result in legal liability for Oracle and you.

Don't Speak for Oracle

Remember that you are not an official spokesperson for Oracle. Make it clear that your opinions are your own and do not necessarily reflect the views of the corporation. See Policy Regarding Communications with Press and Analysts.

For this reason, Oracle employees with personal blogs that discuss Oracle's business, products, employees, customers, partners, or competitors should include the following disclaimer in a visually prominent place on their blog:
"The views expressed on this [blog; Web site] are my own and do not necessarily reflect the views of Oracle."

Similarly, if you appear in a video, you should preface your comments by making it clear that you are not an Oracle spokesperson and your opinion doesn't necessarily reflect Oracle's.

Don't Post Anonymously

While you are not an official spokesperson, your status as an Oracle employee may still be relevant to the subject matter. You should identify yourself as an employee if failing to do so could be misleading to readers or viewers. Employees should not engage in covert advocacy for Oracle. Whenever you are blogging about Oracle-related topics or providing feedback relevant to Oracle to other blogs or forums, identify yourself as an Oracle employee.

Respect Copyrights
You must recognize and respect others' intellectual property rights, including copyrights. While certain limited use of third-party materials (for example, use of a short quotation that you are providing comment on) may not always require approval from the copyright owner, it is still advisable to get the owner's permission whenever you use third-party materials. Never use more than a short excerpt from someone else's work, and make sure to credit and, if possible, link to the original source.

Use Video Responsibly
Remember that you may be viewed as endorsing any Web video (whether hosted by YouTube or elsewhere) or other content you link to from your blog or posting, whether created by you, by other Oracle employees, or by third parties, and the Social Media Participation Policy applies to this content. Also, recognize that video is an area in which you need to be particularly sensitive to others' copyright rights. You generally cannot include third party content such as film clips or songs in your video without obtaining the owner's permission.

Stick to Oracle Topics on Oracle-Sponsored Blogs
Blogs that are hosted or run by Oracle should focus on topics that are related to Oracle's business. Take care to avoid subject areas that are likely to be controversial, such as politics and religion.

Don't Misuse Oracle Resources
Personal social media activities must not interfere with your work or productivity at Oracle. Don't use company resources to set-up your own blogging environment, even if you are blogging about matters related to Oracle. Oracle resources, including servers, may be used solely in connection with formally authorized blogging environments that have been established following consultation with Global IT, GIS, Legal, and Oracle Brand and Creative.

Otto Group
Die Otto Group hat es über die Jahrzehnte immer wieder geschafft, sich selbst als Versandhändler neu zu erfinden, und bereits frühzeitig auf Social Media gesetzt – unter anderem sehr erfolgreich auf Facebook.

Nur knapp zehn Punkte umfasst die Social Media Policy der Otto Group (zitiert nach: http://pr-blogger.de/2010/01/25/social-media-policy-2-otto-group/), deren Besonderheit die ausdrückliche Erlaubnis ist, Kritik zu üben:

1. Gehen Sie bei jeder Veröffentlichung im Internet sorgsam mit unternehmensbezogenen Informationen um. Als Mitarbeiter/in von OTTO oder der Otto Group haben Sie sich arbeitsvertraglich verpflichtet, Stillschweigen über Geschäfts- und Betriebsgeheimnisse zu wahren. Sollten Sie Zweifel haben, wenden Sie sich an Ihre Führungskraft.

2. Bitte denken Sie daran, dass Vorträge und Veröffentlichungen der vorherigen schriftlichen Einwilligung des Unternehmens bedürfen, wenn die Interessen von OTTO oder der Otto Group berührt werden. Stimmen Sie sich mit Ihrem Bereichsleiter und dem Direktionsbereich Unternehmenskommunikation ab. Geben Sie sich bei einem Vortrag oder einer Veröffentlichung mit Namen und Funktion zu erkennen.

3. Private Online-Veröffentlichungen auf Social Sites, in Communities, Foren, Blogs, Wikis und andere Formen der Online Kommunikation sollten Sie stets als privat kennzeichnen. Für diese Äußerungen sind Sie persönlich verantwortlich. Seien Sie sich bewusst, dass Ihre Äußerungen im Web öffentlich sind und für einen langen Zeitraum bleiben. Schützen Sie Ihre Privatsphäre.

4. Als Mitarbeiter/in haben Sie das Recht, sich privat und auch öffentlich über das Unternehmen zu äußern – positiv wie negativ. Wenn Sie dies tun, sollten Sie in Ihrem eigenen Interesse und aus Respekt gegenüber der Community möglichst deutlich machen, dass Sie nur aus Ihrer persönlichen Sicht schreiben.

5. Wenn Sie einen eigenen Blog betreiben und die Inhalte mit dem Unternehmen zu tun haben, nutzen Sie bitte einen Disclaimer wie: „Die Postings auf dieser Site sind meine persönliche Meinung und repräsentieren nicht die Positionen, Strategien oder Meinung von OTTO oder der Otto Group."

6. Denken Sie daran, Urheberrechte anderer – auch die von OTTO oder Otto Group – nicht zu verletzen.

7. Respektieren Sie die Netz-Community. Verzichten Sie auf obszöne Äußerungen, persönliche Beleidigungen, Verunglimpfungen wegen Rasse, Religion, Geschlecht oder Herkunft. Respektieren Sie die Privatsphäre anderer.

8. Zitieren oder verweisen Sie möglichst nicht auf Geschäftspartner.

9. Erfahrungen zeigen: Im Netz sollten Sie auf Streit und Besserwisserei verzichten. Wenn Sie einen Fehler machen, korrigieren Sie diesen schnellstmöglich. Und wenn Sie frühere Postings ändern, dann kennzeichnen Sie diese nachträglichen Änderungen.

10. Ob auf Ihrer Website, einer Social Site, in Blogs, Foren oder in Twitter: Seien Sie stets authentisch!

Plaxo

Plaxo ist ein Anbieter von Software- und Dienstleistungen rund um die Adressverwaltung. Plaxo's Communication (Blogging) Policy (http://plaxoed.wordpress.com/2005/03/29/plaxos-communication-policy/) wurde bereits im März 2005 veröffentlicht.

Since joining Plaxo, I've been on a team that's working to define our policy regarding employees that want to participate in public communication. We wanted to include blogging, message boards, e-mail groups and any other media by which people are able to share ideas nowadays. Here's what we came up with; have a gander at it and feel free to give feedback through the comments or e-mail me: mark @t plaxo.com.

Plaxo Public Internet Communication Policy

The following policy applies to all employees and contractors of Plaxo, and covers all publicly accessible communications via the Internet relating to Plaxo. This includes, but is not limited to: blogs, discussion forums, newsgroups, and e-mail distribution lists.

OVERVIEW

This company depends upon not only the strong formal competencies of its workers (programming abilities, writing skills, etc.), but their "soft skills" as well. Specifically, the fabric of this company is sustained by a sense of camaraderie and trust.

While we encourage open communication both internally and externally in all forms, we expect and insist that such communication does not substantively demean our environment. This means that constructive criticism – both privately and publicly – is welcome, but harsh or continuous disparagement is frowned upon.

Externally communicating about aspects of the company that are part of your non-disclosure agreement (partnership deals, earnings, upcoming unannounced features, etc.) is ALWAYS forbidden, however, and grounds for immediate termination and legal action.

In a nutshell, be prudent. Ask yourself: "Would this public expression regarding Plaxo impair my ability to work with my colleagues on a friendly basis? Would it give a leg up to our competition? Would it make our current or upcoming partners uncomfortable?" If you could answer yes to any of those questions, please avoid this communication.

Additionally, you should first express with your management and co-workers any Plaxo concerns you may have. Voicing concerns about Plaxo publicly without first communicating such concerns to your management and co-workers is counterproductive and inadvisable.

SPECIFIC POLICIES

1. Your public communications concerning Plaxo must not violate any guidelines set forth in your employee handbook, whether or not you specifically mention your employee or contractor status.

2. You may participate in Plaxo-related public communications on company time. However, if doing so interferes with any of your work duties and/or responsibilities, Plaxo reserves the right to disallow such participation.

3. You must include the following disclaimer on published public communications if you identify yourself as a Plaxo employee or if you regularly or substantively discuss Plaxo publicly: "The opinions expressed here are the personal opinions of [your name]. Content published here is not read or approved by Plaxo before it is posted and does not necessarily represent the views and opinions of Plaxo."

4. You may not communicate any material that violates the privacy or publicity rights of another.

5. You may not attack personally fellow employees, authors, customers, vendors, or shareholders. You may respectfully disagree with company actions, policies, or management.

6. You may not disclose any sensitive, proprietary, confidential, or financial information about the company. This includes revenues, profits, forecasts, and other financial information, any information related to specific authors, brands, products, product lines, customers, operating units, etc. You may not disclose any information about any specific customer. Further detail is provided in the "Security and Confidentiality" section of your employee handbook.

7. You may not post any material that is obscene, defamatory, profane, libelous, threatening, harassing, abusive, hateful or embarrassing to another person or any other person or entity. This includes, but is not limited to, comments regarding Plaxo, Plaxo employees, Plaxo's partners and Plaxo's competitors.

Failure to follow these policies may result in disciplinary action, up to and including discharge. Only a written document signed by the President of Plaxo can approve an exception of any of the above policies.

Additionally, here are some guidelines you may wish to follow for your own protection. This is not a comprehensive list and Plaxo will not indemnify you from legal action if you follow these guidelines.

1. If you think you will get in trouble directly or indirectly because of any communication you are about to make, please discuss it with your manager first.

2. Remember that you are not anonymous. Even if you write anonymously or under a pseudonym, your identity can still be revealed. You should communicate as if you are doing so under your own name. Indeed, it is recommended that you do communicate using your real name.

3. You will probably be read or heard by people who know you. Post as if everyone you know reads or hears every word.

4. You are personally legally responsible for any content you publish. Be aware of applicable laws regarding publishing your content or regarding the content itself before you post. This includes adhering to applicable copyright laws.

Razorfish

Wie die bereits genannte Namics ist Razorfish ein Beispiel für eine Online-Agentur. Die Richtlinien finden sich auf der Firmen-Website: (http://www.razorfish.com/img/content/Razorfish-SIMguideWebJuly2009.pdf)

Razorfish Employee Social Influence Marketing Guidelines

If you are not using Social Influence Marketing in your job, please get started. Razorfish encourages employees to adopt Social Influence Marketing – whether you're on Twitter, running your own work blog, posting comments on someone else's blog, uploading presentations on community sites like SlideShare, or otherwise participating in the world of social media.
When you live the social values, Razorfish exercises leadership and becomes a more experienced counselor for our clients.
The following guidelines are intended to help you live the social values and represent Razorfish professionally. There is no attempt here to stifle your social voice. Rather, the intent is just the opposite – to encourage you to embrace the social media world by providing you some guidelines. Please read these guidelines closely and contact David Deal if you have any questions or suggestions for improving these.

Do these guidelines apply to me?
These guidelines have been developed for employees and contractors who:
– Maintain blogs – personal or professional – that mention Razorfish or our client work.
– Post content about Razorfish and our client work on social properties including, but not limited to: Twitter, YouTube, Facebook, MySpace, SlideShare, Flickr, any public blog.
Employees and contractors are personally responsible for what we write on blogs including Twitter. Irresponsible blogging can risk legal action against Razorfish. However, thoughtful commentary makes you and your colleagues shine.

The dos and don'ts

Be professional
- You represent Razorfish at all times. Review the Razorfish Employee Handbook. The rules for employee conduct apply to you in the social world, too.
- Adhere to Razorfish financial disclosure policies.
- Don't cite clients or talk about specific client projects without first getting permission from the appropriate Razorfish client partner or account director. Even acknowledging a client relationship on Twitter can violate a client privacy agreement.
- Communications inside Razorfish, including emails among employees, are proprietary to Razorfish. (The same holds true for emails among Razorfish employees and our clients and partners.) Sharing internal communications outside Razorfish may result in disciplinary action. A general rule of them: if you are interested in posting or quoting from an email publicly, please check with the sender first.
- Respect copyright. Do not post any images or other content from another source unless you are sure it is in the public domain or that the owner has granted permission. Check website terms of service to see if the site has rules about when you may reproduce content.
- Respect the law – including laws and regulations in the country, state, and local jurisdictions where business is conducted.
- Do not post material that is harassing, obscene, defamatory, libelous, threatening, hateful, or embarrassing to any person or entity. Do not post words, jokes, or comments based on an individual's gender, sexual orientation, race, ethnicity, age, or religion.
- Posting pornography is forbidden. You know it when you see it.
- If you are just uncertain about whether it's OK to post something, first talk with your manager.
- Before you post a comment or voice an opinion, ask yourself: would I be OK having a client see what I write? Am I writing something a competitor could use against me?
- It's great to have an opinion. But it's just not cool to attack others with unprofessional remarks. When you disagree with someone, exercise grace. Before you post something, ask yourself: how would I feel if this post were about me?
- Strive for balance. Set aside time to participate in the social world. Don't neglect the social values, but also be practical: we have demands of our clients to meet, too.

Be truthful, open, and accountable
- Never plagiarize
- Be truthful
- Be authentic. Too busy to blog or tweet? Please don't ask someone else to ghostwrite your content. It's better not to write at all then to be inauthentic.
- Correct mistakes promptly
- Cite and link to all sources when you can
- Allow comments on your public content, whether a presentation on SlideShare or a Twitter post.
- Exercise full disclosure. When you mention Razorfish, identify Razorfish as your employer. Do the same with client work you mention. Reveal your personal affiliations and conflicts of interests.

Special considerations for Twitter

Twitter has exploded as a means of self-expression and sharing Razorfish content. It's easy to post content on Twitter. And fun. Razorfish encourages employees to be on Twitter. As you tweet, do remember that the guidelines mentioned in this document apply to you. Moreover, it's good to bear in mind these considerations:

General guidelines
– Twitter is a public micro-blog. Unless you make your account private, everything you write on Twitter can be seen by journalists, bloggers, competitors, clients, and your cow-orkers. If you are in doubt about whether content is appropriate for public viewing, try the private Razorfish Yammer network or the private direct message function on Twitter as an alternative to a public tweet. (Just sign up using your Razorfish email to join the network.)
– Twitter is all about sending short bursts of information. Within 60 seconds you can tweet about your personal life and your client work all in one Twitter stream. If you're going to be mixing your professional and personal life for everyone to see on Twitter, do exercise discretion. Again, a good rule of thumb: if I'm mentioning something about Razorfish on Twitter, would I be comfortable with a client seeing what I wrote? Would I be comfortable having The Wall Street Journal reproduce my tweet and attribute it to me?
– Exercise common sense. Someone want to follow you on Twitter? At least find out who they are before following them back. Twitter is flooded with spammers looking for followers to build their presence.
– Be especially mindful of checking with client partners before you tweet about work. Did you know that even congratulating a teammate for great client work can violate a client privacy policy if you name the client or cite the URL for a website we've designed?

Before you open a team Twitter account
If you are creating a group account under the Razorfish brand, please note:
– Before you open a new Razorfish-branded account, make sure you have a strategy and a purpose that justifies a separate corporate Twitter account. (The @SearchTrends account is an example of doing it right).
– Please complete the Twitter biography field. Identify who you are. Cite top contributors. For example: @Razorfish lists this: "Global agency; this account managed mostly by @davidjdeal, @eunmac, @shivsingh, & @heathergately."
– Please contact David Deal in before you go live so that the Razorfish corporate account (@Razorfish) can follow you (and vice versa). Razorfish Employee Social Influence Marketing Guidelines Page 4
– When you tweet under a corporate account, it's best to sign your tweets when you can. For example, a recent post on @Razorfish: "Social media score proposed by @Razorfish; #fluent coverage from @ClickZ http://bit.ly/cBuU9 ~@davidjdeal"

Special Considerations for Razorfish Bloggers

All of the guidelines mentioned in this document apply to bloggers. In addition, please be mindful of these considerations:

- Include a statement identifying that these are your own thoughts and not necessarily representative of the company. ("The blog reflects the views of the individual author and not necessarily the views of Razorfish" will suffice.)
- Be personal. Write as "I." Let people know who you are and your background.
- Be clear. If you blog, state the purpose of your blog upfront.
- Be relevant. Are you contributing to a blog about technology? Keep your comments focused on the topic.
- Be interesting. Have an opinion.
- Be credible. Write about what you know.
- Be responsive. Has someone posted a question for you? Follow up.
- Do not restrict access to your blog by specific individuals or groups.
- Do not self censor by removing posts or comments once they are published unless they are inappropriate under these guidelines (e.g., comments that reveal confidential information).
- Maintain your blog. Don't blog just for the sake of blogging, but try to post at least once every few weeks. Over the long run, if you find yourself not posting, consider whether you should continue blogging (or become a contributor to a group blog).

Agency monitoring
Razorfish may monitor agency-sponsored blogs and reserves the right to remove an agency-sponsored blog at any time. If you choose to have a Razorfish blog created as part of your employment, as per your employment agreement, the blog is owned by Razorfish. In the event that an employee does not comply with the guidelines, a number of actions may be taken, including counseling by management, reprimand, and termination with cause.

Privacy policy
If your blog is hosted by Razorfish, it must link to a privacy policy. Please review the Razorfish privacy policy. If you operate a blog that is in compliance with the Razorfish privacy policy, please provide a link to Razorfish Employee Social Influence Marketing Guidelines Page 5 the Razorfish privacy policy on every page of your blog. Your Razorfish blog template may be set up so that you automatically link to the Razorfish privacy policy. If your blog is not in compliance with the Razorfish privacy policy, please contact the privacy team for assistance with your privacy policy before publishing your blog.

Additional requirements
Finally, individual managers or teams may develop their additional requirements related to blogging, and blogs hosted on Razorfish servers may be subject to certain additional requirements. It is your responsibility to familiarize yourself with any such specific policies or requirements. You should also discuss your blogging plans with your manager before you start.

Examples of where the guidelines apply
- Joe, a designer, operates his own personal blog regarding his insights into user experience design. He sometimes cites his work for Razorfish to illustrate his ideas.
- Alex, an account director, uses his Twitter account to announce that Razorfish has helped a client launch a new website.
- Nancy, an employee, creates a Facebook user group for Razorfish employees to discuss their work experiences. She occasionally posts information about her client experiences on her own Facebook profile.
- Eric, a discipline lead, wants to launch a blog for the Creative discipline. Many employees will be invited to contribute.
- Roberta, a contractor hired to help a website development team, writes about her new assignment on her personal blog.

Examples of where the guidelines do not apply
- Frank, a creative lead, maintains his own blog about his passions for creativity and writing. He does not mention his work for Razorfish.
- Jackie, an employee, lists herself as a Razorfish employee on her MySpace profile for informational purposes but does not discuss Razorfish or her client work at all.
- Several Razorfish employees form their own MySpace group to discuss their passion for the films of Robert De Niro, but they do not discuss work.

Reuters

Die international bekannte Nachrichtenagentur Reuters hat 2010 Regelungen zum Internet und zu Social Media in seinem hauseigenen Handbuch in einem gesonderten Kapitel eingefügt. Das Handbuch ist im Volltext verfügbar (der hier wiedergegebene Text stammt von http://handbook.reuters.com/index.php/Reporting_from_the_internet – Auszug):

Using social media

We want to encourage you to use social media approaches in your journalism but we also need to make sure that you are fully aware of the risks – especially those that threaten our hard-earned reputation for independence and freedom from bias or our brand. The recommendations below offer general guidance with more detailed suggestions for managing your presence on the most popular social networks. This is a fast-changing world and you will need to exercise judgment in many areas. In framing this advice we've borne in mind the following principles and encourage you to think about them whenever using social media.

Basic Principles

The Trust Principles compel us to explore all new techniques for delivering news and information to our customers: our recommendations are designed to support rather than inhibit your exploration of these important new approaches.

One of the distinguishing features of Reuters is the trust invested in the judgment of its journalists – we will continue to look to you to use your common sense in dealing with these new challenges

Accuracy, freedom from bias and integrity are fundamental to the reputation of Reuters and your ability to do your job effectively. The advent of social media changes none of this and you should do nothing that would damage our reputation for impartiality and independence. We reserve the right to change your beat or responsibilities if there are problems in this area. In the case of serious breaches, we may use our established disciplinary procedures.

The advent of social media does not change your relationship with the company that employs you – do not use social media to embarrass or disparage Thomson Reuters. Our company's brands are important; so, too, is your personal brand. Think carefully about how what you do reflects upon you as a professional and upon us as an employer of professionals.

The distinction between the private and the professional has largely broken down online and you should assume that your professional and personal social media activity will be treated as one no matter how hard you try to keep them separate. You should also be aware that even if you make use of privacy settings, anything you post on a social media site may be made public.

While it is not practical to always apply the 'second pair of eyes rule' for journalists using social media, especially Twitter, in a professional capacity, you should consider that a 'virtual second pair of eyes rule' applies under which your manager and/or senior editors will retrospectively review your professional output.

Remember, too, that your sources, colleagues, peers, competitors and even future employers also can and will look at your output.

If you have your tweets aggregated onto reuters.com or another company property or have your blog hosted by us, we are your publisher and in some jurisdictions may even have a legal responsibility for what you have written. This makes it absolutely imperative that you remember basic rules about fairness, taste and libel. Even beyond the legal question, readers may well wonder if a mean-spirited or nasty comment is truly yours alone or if it somehow represents the view of the institution if it appears on a corporate property.

We're in a competitive business and while the spirit of social media is collaborative we need to take care not to undermine the commercial basis of our company.

Recommendations

Think before you post
One of the secrets to social media's success is how easy it has become to participate. But that also makes it easy to respond or repeat before you have thought through the consequences. Whether we think it is fair or not, other media will use your social media output as Reuters comment on topical stories. And we will play into the hands of our critics unless we take care
– Resist the temptation to respond in anger to those you regard as mistaken or ill-tempered
– Think about how you'd feel if your content was cited on the front page of a leading newspaper or website or blog as Reuters comment on an issue
– Don't suspend your critical faculties. It's simple to share a link on Twitter, Facebook and other networks but as a Reuters journalist if you repeat something that turns out to be a hoax, or suggests you support a particular line of argument, then you risk undermining your own credibility and that of Reuters News

Avoid raising questions about your freedom from bias
Your Facebook profile, Twitter stream or personal blog give clues to your political and other affiliations and you should take care about what you reveal. A determined critic can soon build up a picture of your preferences by analysing your links, those that you follow, your 'friends', blogroll and endless other indicators. We all leave an 'online footprint' whenever we use the Web and you need to think about whether your footprint might create perceptions of a bias toward or against a particular group.
– Think about the groups that you join – it may be safest not to join a group or to follow participants on just one side of a debate
– Think about using 'badges' expressing solidarity with some cause
– Think about whether it would be best to leave your political affiliation out of your Facebook profile
– Think about whether you link only or mainly to voices on one side of a debate
– Think about making use of the privacy settings on social networks and basic ways in which you can conceal your use of the Web like clearing your cache regularly

Be transparent
We're in the transparency business and we encourage you to be open about who you are.
– On your personal blog or social networking profile make it clear that you are a Reuters journalist and that any opinions you express are your own.
– When you post comments do so under your real name

If you use social networks for both professional and private activity then use separate accounts

Many of you are using social networks like Facebook or Twitter both as part of your news-gathering and as part of your personal social networking. In the online world private and professional are increasingly intertwined but we do expect you to maintain a professional face at all times in your work for us and this extends to your use of social media. Put simply, we're expecting you to apply standards to your professional use of social media that will probably differ to those you would use for your personal activity. For this reason we recommend that you set up separate profiles for your professional and private activity. This is not to say that we recommend that you strip out all personal content from your professional streams, but that you should think carefully about what personal content would be appropriate.

- Use a separate professional account for your newsgathering and professional community-building activity
- Social networking encourages you to share personal details but don't overload your professional network with personal content

Seek the permission of your manager before setting up a professional presence on a social networking site

- Effective use of social media requires a commitment of time and you should clear this with your manager before you get involved.
- Effective use of social media may also require you to share a lot of content and you need to be clear that this does not conflict with our commercial objectives. Again, your manager should be consulted on this
- Be aware that you may reveal your sources to competitors by using "following" or "friending" functionality on social networks

Twitter policy

What is Twitter?
Twitter is a "micro-blogging" system that lets users send out short 140-character posts to the Internet.

Can I use Twitter as a source?
Twitter may be used sometimes to post information and images of interest to our clients that are not available elsewhere. We will sometimes need to retransmit such material, or refer to it in text stories. Before using such content, please refer to "Picking up from Twitter and social media" in the section The Essentials of Reuters sourcing.

When should I 'tweet'?
There are several ways in which Reuters News journalists are using Twitter to micro-blog as part of their professional duties:

- Specialist journalists use Twitter to share articles and build up a following (see twitter.com/reutersBenHir and twitter.com/bobbymacReports)
- Online Editorial staff and bloggers use Twitter to distribute news and solicit reader comment (see twitter.com/mediafile, twitter.com/Reuters_FluNews and twitter.com/reuters_co_uk)
- Reuters journalists are using Twitter during live events such as Davos and to solicit questions for newsmaker interviews

1. If you wish to use Twitter as part of your professional role you should seek the permission of your line manager.

2. If you are using Twitter professionally you should use the word 'Reuters' in the name of your stream or somewhere else on the page.

3. The Trust Principles apply to Twitter – you should do nothing that compromises them.

4. Micro-blogging and use of social media tend to blur the distinction between professional and personal lives: when using Twitter or social media in a professional capacity you should aim to be personable but not to include irrelevant material about your personal life.

Does the 'second pair of eyes rule' apply to Twitter?
The short-form nature of Twitter means it is fast and well-suited to certain tasks including the live-blogging of events. It will not always be possible or even desirable to find someone to double-check your content.

Where practical you should ask someone to check content of Twitter posts. If there is no one to check then you should satisfy yourself that your posts conform to the Trust Principles. Be aware, however, that Reuters Twitter streams will and must be reviewed by an editor – not necessarily in real time or before publication, but eventually and regularly.

What guidelines apply to my personal Twitter use?
The same rules apply as for personal blogging – you should make it clear that you a) work for Reuters News; b) any views expressed do not represent those of your employer; and c) you say nothing that would damage the reputation of Reuters News or TR.

Can I break news via Twitter?
As with blogging within Reuters News, you should make sure that if you have hard news content that it is broken first via the wire. Don't scoop the wire. NB this does not apply if you are 'retweeting' (re-publishing) someone else's scoop.

Corrections
If a correction is required, a new tweet that begins "CORRECTION:..." should be published.

Blogging

Blogging is an informal approach to content creation that has evolved in response to Web users' need for a simple publishing tool giving maximum engagement with readers. Blogging is by nature a flexible format and there are few rules governing its use. Reuters journalists blog to trigger discussions on topical issues, point to the most interesting material on a subject elsewhere on the Web, take readers behind the scenes of our newsgathering, solicit questions for interviews, and to add colour, anecdote and angles that don't make it into our other story types. In addition, blogging is the easiest way we have of handling multimedia story-telling and some Reuters journalists produce video blogs, also known as 'vlogs'.

A Reuters blogger should:
– Be interesting.
– Be conversational: raise questions, invite contributions, discuss what's happening on other blogs, leave some loose ends, and respond to comments made by readers.
– Link to external sites with relevant information
– Monitor other bloggers in the same space and attempt to build reciprocal links with them.
– Tag posts so that they are easy for search engines to find.
– Inject some personality into their posts and include observation and anecdote.
– Make use of multimedia whenever possible and think about a post's layout.
– Credit the original source of all content embedded in posts.
– Make sure posts are seen by a second pair of eyes before publication.
– Ask desks to place a link to their blog/post on relevant stories.

A Reuters blogger should not:
– Be opinionated. You are free to make observations, ask questions and make an argument, but blogging in Reuters is not a license to vent personal views. You are still bound by the Trust Principles.
– Respond in anger to comments that appear on posts.
– End each post with the line, 'tell us what you think'. If you have a specific question for readers then ask it, otherwise let the comments box do the work for you.
– Knowingly link to material that infringes copyright.
– Have the colour and personality subbed out of their posts
– Take an idea or insight from another blogger or site without acknowledgement.

Reuters use of blogging is constantly evolving and up-to-date guidance on how blogs are being used is available on the blogging wiki at http://wiki.ime.reuters.com/index.php/Blogging

To correct a blog, see blogs under Corrections, Refiles, Kills, Repeats and Embargoes

RightNow.
Das US-Unternehmen bietet Lösungen für die Kundeninteraktionen von Unternehmen über Internet und Social Web an – vom E-Mail-Response-Management bis hin zum Aufbau von Online-Commuties.
Die Vorgaben für die eigenen Mitarbeiter sind in der Social Web Employee Policy (http://www.rightnow.com/privacy-social.php) zusammengefasst.

All of us at RightNow are working to rid the world of bad experiences. Contributing to online communities by blogging, wiki posting, participating in forums, etc., is a good way to extend our mission. We believe participation in online discourse through the social web can empower us as global professionals, innovators and citizens. Therefore, it is in RightNow's interest, and in each employee's own interest, to be aware of and participate in this sphere of information, interaction and idea exchange.

These are the official guidelines for social computing at RightNow. If you're an employee or contractor creating or contributing to blogs, wikis, social networks, virtual worlds, or any other kind of social media – these guidelines are for you. We require all who participate in social media on behalf of RightNow to be trained, to understand and to follow these guidelines. Failure to do so could put your future participation and employment at risk. RightNow has an open participation policy for all employees. The choice to participate in social media is yours. If you decide to participate, you are making a commitment to following these guidelines.

This Contact Policy Covers The Following:
Rules For Engagement
Your Responsibility
Be Transparent, But Don't Tell Secrets
Protect RightNow's Clients, Business Partners And Suppliers
Respect Your Audience And Your Coworkers
Write What You Know
Be Transparent
Be Interesting, And Be Honest
Are You Adding Value?
Be A Leader
Use Your Best Judgment
Don't Forget Your Day Job

Rules For Engagement
Emerging platforms for online collaboration are fundamentally changing the way we work, offering new ways to engage with customers, colleagues, and the world at large. It's a new model for interaction and we believe social computing can help you to build stronger, more successful business relationships. And it's a way for you to take part in global conversations related to the work we are doing at RightNow and the things we care about.

RightNow fully respects the legal rights of our employees in all countries in which we operate. In general, what you do on your own time is your affair. However, activities in or outside of work that affect your job performance, the performance of others, or RightNow's business interests are a proper focus for company policy. If you participate in social media, please follow these guiding principles:

Stick to your area of expertise and provide unique, individual perspectives on what's going on at RightNow and in the world.

Post meaningful, respectful comments – in other words, no SPAM and no remarks that are off-topic or offensive.

Always pause and think before posting. That said, reply to comments in a timely manner, when a response is appropriate.

Respect proprietary information, content, and confidentiality.

When disagreeing with others' opinions, keep it appropriate and polite.

Know and follow the RightNow Code of Ethics, Privacy Policy and Employee Forum Guidelines.

Your Responsibility

What you write is ultimately your responsibility and requires judgment. Participation in the social web on behalf of RightNow is not a right but an opportunity, so please treat it seriously and with respect. Anything you post is accessible to anyone with a web browser. It's OK to talk about your work and have a dialog with the community, but it's not OK to publish confidential or proprietary information. Please also follow the terms and conditions for any third-party sites.

RightNow has established accounts on several social websites. These sites include, but are not limited to, YouTube, LinkedIn, Twitter, Facebook, Slideshare.net and Flickr. The management of these accounts, and the creation of new corporate accounts across the social web, is the responsibility of RightNow's Social Web Committee. While you are encouraged to create your own individual accounts, please do not create RightNow-branded accounts which could be interpreted as representing the company.

Failure to abide by these guidelines and the RightNow's Code of Ethics could put your participation and employment at RightNow at risk. If you want to participate on behalf of RightNow, contact social@rightnow.com for more information and to learn about training opportunities.

Be Transparent, But Don't Tell Secrets

As a publicly traded company, there are all sorts of laws about what we can and can't say business-wise. Talking about revenue, future product release dates, pricing decisions, roadmaps, unannounced financial results, our share price or similar matters is apt to get you, the company, or both, into serious legal trouble. Stay away from financial topics and predictions of future performance.

Make sure your efforts to be transparent don't violate RightNow's privacy, confidentiality, and legal guidelines for external commercial speech. All statements must be true and not misleading, and all claims must be substantiated and approved. Please never comment on any of the following:

Anything related to legal matters
Financials
Litigation
Anything about competitors and their capabilities

Product roadmap
Also be smart about protecting yourself, your privacy, and RightNow's confidential informa-tion. What you publish is widely accessible and will be around for a long time, so consider the content carefully.

Protect RightNow's Clients, Business Partners And Suppliers
Clients, partners or suppliers should not be cited or obviously referenced without their approval. Externally, never identify a client, partner or supplier by name without permission and never discuss confidential details of a client engagement.

Respect Your Audience And Your Coworkers
Remember that RightNow is a global organization whose employees and clients reflect a diverse set of customs, values and points of view. Don't be afraid to be yourself, but do so respectfully. This includes not only the obvious (no ethnic slurs, personal insults, obscenity, etc.) but also proper consideration of privacy and of topics that may be considered objection-able or inflammatory – such as politics and religion. If your blog is hosted on a RightNow-owned or "sponsored" property (i. e. RightNowNews Twitter account), avoid these topics and focus on subjects that are business-related. If your blog is self-hosted, use your best judgment and be sure to make it clear that the views and opinions expressed are yours alone and do not represent the official views of RightNow.

Further, blogs, wikis, virtual worlds, social networks, or other tools hosted outside of RightNow's protected Intranet environment should not be used for internal communications among fellow employees. It is fine for RightNow employees to disagree, but please don't use your external blog or other online social media to air your differences.

Write What You Know
Write in the first person and make sure you write and post about your areas of expertise, especially as related to RightNow and our technology. If you are writing about a topic that RightNow is involved with but you are not the subject matter expert, you should make this clear to your readers. Please respect brand, trademark, copyright, fair use, trade secrets (including our processes and methodologies), confidentiality, and financial disclosure laws.

You should never quote more than short excerpts of someone else's work. And it is good general blogging practice to link to others' work or mention an individual's contribution in a re-tweet.

Be Transparent
If you are blogging about your work, please use your real name and identify that you work for RightNow, clearly stating your role with the company. If you have a vested interest in something you are discussing, be the first to point it out.

RightNow trusts and expects that employees exercise personal responsibility whenever they participate in social media. This includes not violating the trust of those with whom you are engaging. RightNow employees should not use social media for covert marketing or public relations. If and when members of RightNow's Marketing, Sales, Support or other external facing functions are engaged in advocacy for the company through social media, they should identify themselves as employees of RightNow.

For individuals who are not participating in social media as part of an official function of their job, make it clear that what you say does not necessarily represent the views and opinions of RightNow.

At a minimum in your own blog, you should include the following standard disclaimer: "The postings on this site are my own and don't necessarily represent RightNow's positions, strategies or opinions."

As disclaimers may be impractical at times within a post (i.e. 140-character limitation on Twitter), include the fact that you work for RightNow in your online profiles.

Be Interesting, And Be Honest

As a business and as a corporate citizen, RightNow is making important contributions to the world, to the future of technology, and to public dialogue on a broad range of issues. Our business activities are increasingly focused on high-value innovation. Let's share with the world the exciting things we're learning and doing – and open up the channels to learn from others.

Expose your personality; almost all of the successful online voices write about themselves, about families or movies or books or games; or they post pictures. People like to know what kind of a person is writing what they're reading. Once again, balance is called for; a social media site is a public place and you should avoid embarrassing the company and community members.

The lines between public and private, personal and professional are blurred in online social networks. By virtue of identifying yourself as a RightNow employee within a social network, you are now connected to your colleagues, managers and even RightNow customers. You should ensure that content associated with you is consistent with your work at RightNow.

Are You Adding Value?

There are millions of words out there. The best way to get yours read is to write things that people will value. Social communication from RightNow should help our customers, partners, and co-workers. It should be thought-provoking and build a sense of community. If it helps people improve knowledge or skills, build their businesses, do their jobs, solve problems, or understand RightNow better – then it's adding value.

Be A Leader
There can be a fine line between healthy debate and incendiary reaction. Do not denigrate our competitors or RightNow. Nor do you need to respond to every criticism or barb. Try to frame what you write to invite differing points of view without inflaming others. Some topics – like politics or religion – slide more easily into sensitive territory. So be careful and considerate. Once the words are out there, you can't really get them back. And once an inflammatory discussion gets going, it's hard to stop.
If you make a mistake, admit it. Be upfront and be quick with your correction. If you're posting to a blog, you may choose to modify an earlier post – just make it clear that you have done so.

Use Your Best Judgment
Remember that there are always consequences to what you publish. If you're about to publish something that makes you even the slightest bit uncomfortable, review the suggestions above and think about why that is. If you're still unsure, and it is related to RightNow business, feel free to discuss it with your manager. Ultimately, however, you have sole responsibility for what you post to your blog or publish in any form of online social media.

Don't Forget Your Day Job
You should make sure that your online activities do not interfere with your job or work commitments.
RightNow would like to thank progressive companies such as Intel, Sun Microsystems and IBM for their work and influence in the development of internal social media policies and guidelines.

Roche
Das weltweit tätige, in Basel (Schweiz) ansässige Pharmaunternehmen Roche hat seine Social Media Principles unter http://www.roche.com/social_media_guidelines.pdf veröffentlicht. Roche differenziert darin – vorbildlich nicht nur für die Branche – in Regeln für „Personal online activities" und „Professional online activities" und stellt jeweils eine Kurzfassung zur Verfügung.

Social media like blogs, wikis, social networks (e.g. Facebook, YouTube, LinkedIn etc.), team spaces or personalised web sites are changing the way we are communicating, interacting, and doing business – with patients, customers and other stakeholders outside Roche, but also within the Roche network.

Despite new social media tools and platforms emerging and changing all the time, its basic aspect remains constant and is similar to traditional ways of communication: to engage in dialogue, provide and exchange information, and build understanding. Social media's high speed, level of interactivity and global access to any information you publish merits particular consideration to the appropriate uses for these applications.

Roche recognizes the ubiquity and benefits of social media and welcomes its use – however, we also acknowledge that certain risks are associated with these new channels. We have therefore developed this guideline to help you use these new platforms in a responsible way. Given the fast changes and continuous new developments in this area, we will review the guidance regularly and update if new aspects arise.

The best advice is to approach online worlds in the same way we do the physical one – by using sound judgment and common sense, by adhering to the Company's values, and by following the Roche Code of Conduct and all other policies.

In case of questions please contact our communications teams or the Roche Social Media Advisory Board.

Basel, August 2010

Ground rules for participating in online communications

There is a big difference in speaking "on behalf of Roche" (as an official spokesperson) or speaking "about" Roche, our products or business partners. It is important that you always remember who you are or who you are representing and what your role is in the social media community.
Just as with traditional media, we have an opportunity – and a responsibility – to effectively manage the company's reputation online and to selectively engage and participate in the thousands of online conversations that mention us every day.

Do take time – despite the speed and urgency of the new opportunities and challenges – to think through and plan for your engagement in the social media field. Always remember that engaging in social media is not a one-off activity. What is the long-term concept: who do you want to engage with, for what aim and result, what are opportunities and risks?
Once you enter the dialogue, you will have to live up to the expectations of others regarding appropriate and knowledgeable responses, as well as commit to follow-up over a longer period of time. Define a clear plan and responsibilities as with any other communication project.
Hence, our core values – integrity, passion and courage – together with the rules outlined in the Roche Group Code of Conduct and the Communication Policy, provide the framework in which every colleague can use new media tools, while also minimizing the risks for the company and individuals.

Roche Social Media Principles in short:

7 Rules for PERSONAL online activities Speaking "about" Roche
– Be conscious about mixing your personal and business lives.
– You are responsible for your actions.

– Follow the Roche Group Code of Conduct.
– Mind the global audience.
– Be careful if talking about Roche. Only share publicly available information.
– Be transparent about your affiliation with Roche and that opinions raised are your own.
– Be a "scout" for sentiment and critical issues.

7 Rules for PROFESSIONAL online activities Speaking "on behalf of" Roche
– Follow the Roche Group Code of Conduct and Communications Policy.
– Follow approval processes for publications and communication.
– Mind Copyrights and give credit to the owners.
– Use special care if talking about Roche products or financial data.
– Identify yourself as a representative of Roche.
– Monitor your relevant social media channels.
– Know and follow our Record Management Practices.

7 Rules for personal online activities

Speaking "about" Roche
These principles apply to those personal online activities where you might refer to Roche or one of our products or businesses:

1. Be conscious about mixing your personal and business lives. There is no separation for others between your personal and your business profiles within social media. You must be aware of that. Roche respects the free speech rights of all our employees, but you must remember that patients, customers and competitors as well as colleagues may have access to the online content you post. Keep this in mind when publishing information online and know that information originally intended just for a small group can be forwarded on.

2. You are responsible for your actions. You are "speaking" publicly and your contribution may stay searchable and retrievable for a long time to a broad audience – both internally and externally. Anything that brings damage to our business or reputation will ultimately be your responsibility. This does not mean that you should refrain from any activity, but that you should use common sense and take at least the same caution with social media as with all other forms of communication.

3. Follow the Roche Group Code of Conduct. When "speaking", be compliant with the Roche Group Code of Conduct, as well as all other Roche Positions, Policies & Guidelines (i. e. Protection of Privacy, Rules on Insider Trading, etc.). Be respectful of all individuals, races, religions and cultures; how you conduct yourself in the online social media space not only reflects on you – it can fall back on Roche and all our employees.

4. Mind the global audience. Even if you are posting on a "local" platform, the information may be accessed globally. This is particularly important in our regulated business.

While your message may be accurate in some parts of the world, it could be inaccurate or violate regulations in others. Be mindful that different cultures have different values, and statements that are deemed acceptable or even funny in one culture may be considered offensive in others. Keep that "world view" in mind when you are participating in online conversations.

5. Be careful if talking about Roche. Only share publicly available information. You are not allowed to talk about the revenue, future plans, or the share price of Roche as this may have serious legal repercussions for you and the company. Engage only in discussions where you are comfortable and knowledgeable about the topic. Make sure to share only information that is publically available.
If you are unsure if information is publically available or is otherwise inappropriate to post, contact your Communications Department before posting any such information.

6. Be transparent about your affiliation with Roche. If you are commenting on any of Roche's or our competitors' products or initiatives in a public forum or on a website or personal blog, make sure to fully disclose your affiliation with Roche and that your opinions are personal and not attributable to Roche. (Example: "I work for Roche. All opinions expressed are my own and do not necessarily represent the position of my employer")

7. Be a "scout" for sentiment and critical issues. Even if you are not an official online spokesperson, you are one of our most vital assets for monitoring the social media landscape. If you come across positive or negative remarks about Roche or its products online that you believe are important, consider sharing them by forwarding them to your local communications department. This is most important in the case of so-called "Adverse Events": When you come across information where somebody mentions side-effects after having taken one of our drugs in a credible and identifiable way, you have to immediately forward such information to the global Drug Safety Team for further action.

7 Rules for professional online activities

Speaking "on behalf of" Roche
The following principles outline what to consider when representing Roche as an official online spokesperson:

1. Follow the Roche Group Code of Conduct and Communication Policy. In the core of all communication engagements is our commitment to transparency, balanced information and equal treatment of all parties. All interaction should be in the spirit of our corporate values and principles, tailored to each respective audience.

2. Approval processes for publications and communication. All of Roche's communications have to be correct and clear, and remain in line with our general standards for information. Principally, the same approval processes as with any other official communication and pub-

lications of Roche apply. Given the interactivity and speed of the new medium, however, it is not realistic to have each response undergo full approval by communications, legal and regulatory. Therefore, you should establish with your usual approval partners a common agreement on a bandwidth of topics and instances that may not require the normal process. Use your professional judgement as a communication expert, and if in you have any doubt about a specific message, seek advice from a senior communicator or the Social Media Advisory Board prior to posting.

3. Mind copyrights and give credit to the owners. Always make sure to give credit to the original authors of any content that you are publishing (text, images, trademarks, video etc.) from a 3rd party, and that Roche has the copyright or written approval for using said material.

4. Use special care if talking about Roche products or financial data. Communication about the revenue, future plans, or the share price of Roche as well as statements about our products ("promotional information") is reserved to experts in the field who have been trained to do so. If you need to provide information in one of these areas, stick to available Q&A or refer to content that is available in the public domain (e.g. on a Roche website). All such information has to be approved by legal and corporate communication before being posted. This is also applicable to contributions in forums or on knowledge data bases like Wikipedia.

5. Identify yourself as a representative of Roche. If you are communicating on behalf of Roche it should go without saying that you must always provide your full name and function in which you are communicating. Make clear what your role is in the respective social media environment and refer to these guidelines or a specific set of rules when needed (e.g. on a proprietary Roche channel).

6. Monitor your relevant social media channels. Make sure that you know what is being discussed, so that you can respond when issues arise. Have rules in place to deal with potential Adverse Event reports or potentially inappropriate or illegal content appearing in your sphere of responsibility. Also, be mindful of any obligations to preserve data that may be subject to a legal hold.

7. Know and follow record management practices. Roche has regulatory and legal obligations to retain certain information as records. You must therefore ensure that all relevant information which will be interpreted as a Roche position is captured and will be retained in a trustworthy and admissible manner in line with the Roche Records Management Directive. Keep records of our interactions in the online social media space. Because online conversations are often fleeting and immediate, it is important for you to keep track of them when you're officially representing Roche. Remember that online Company statements can be held to the same legal standards as traditional media communications.

Rotes Kreuz (Österreich)

Das Österreichische Rote Kreuz wählt einen kooperativen Ansatz zur Erstellung seiner Social-Media-Richtlinien.

Ausgehend vom Mission Statement:

„Unser Auftrag ist, das Leben von Menschen in Not und Sozial Schwachen durch die Kraft der Menschlichkeit zu verbessern"

und den Grundsätzen der Organisation:

„Menschlichkeit: Die Internationale Rotkreuz- und Rothalbmond-Bewegung, entstanden aus dem Willen, den Verwundeten der Schlachtfelder unterschiedslos Hilfe zu leisten, bemüht sich in ihrer internationalen und nationalen Tätigkeit, menschliches Leiden überall und jederzeit zu verhüten und zu lindern. Sie ist bestrebt, Leben und Gesundheit zu schützen und der Würde des Menschen Achtung zu verschaffen. Sie fördert gegenseitiges Verständnis, Freundschaft, Zusammenarbeit und einen dauerhaften Frieden unter allen Völkern.

Unparteilichkeit: Die Rotkreuz- und Rothalbmond-Bewegung unterscheidet nicht nach Nationalität, Rasse, Religion, sozialer Stellung oder politischer Überzeugung. Sie ist einzig bemüht, den Menschen nach dem Maß ihrer Not zu helfen und dabei den dringendsten Fällen den Vorrang zu geben.

Neutralität: Um sich das Vertrauen aller zu bewahren, enthält sich die Rotkreuz- und Rothalbmond-Bewegung der Teilnahme an Feindseligkeiten wie auch, zu jeder Zeit, an politischen, rassischen, religiösen oder ideologischen Auseinandersetzungen.

Unabhängigkeit: Die Rotkreuz- und Rothalbmond-Bewegung ist unabhängig. Wenn auch die nationalen Gesellschaften den Behörden bei ihrer humanitären Tätigkeit als Hilfsgesellschaften zur Seite stehen und den jeweiligen Landesgesetzen unterworfen sind, müssen sie dennoch eine Eigenständigkeit bewahren, die ihnen gestattet, jederzeit nach den Grundsätzen der Rotkreuz- und Rothalbmond-Bewegung zu handeln.

Freiwilligkeit: Die Rotkreuz- und Rothalbmond-Bewegung verkörpert freiwillige und uneigennützige Hilfe ohne jedes Gewinnstreben.

Einheit: In jedem Land kann es nur eine einzige nationale Rotkreuz- oder Rothalbmondgesellschaft geben. Sie muss allen offenstehen und ihre humanitäre Tätigkeit im ganzen Gebiet ausüben.

Universalität: Die Rotkreuz- und Rothalbmond-Bewegung ist weltumfassend. In ihr haben alle nationalen Gesellschaften gleiche Rechte und die Pflicht, einander zu helfen."

erfolgt die Herleitung einer Social Media Policy in einem eigenen Wiki:
http://blog.roteskreuz.at/wiki/index.php/Social_Media_Policy

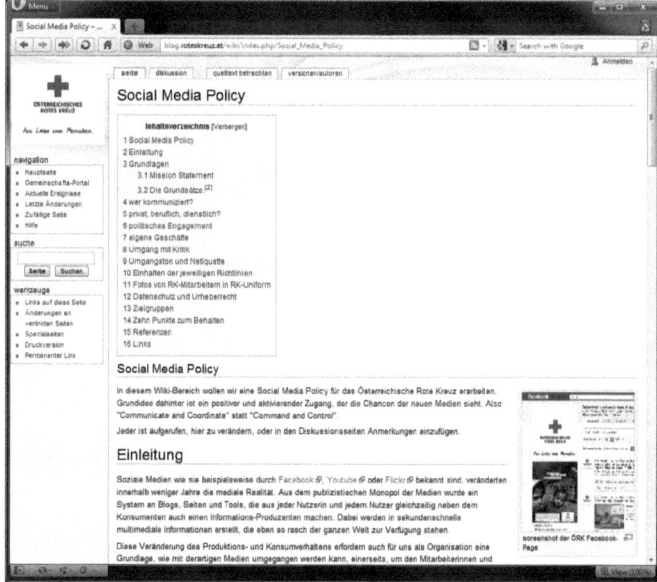

Wiki Rotes Kreuz Österreich

Wesentliches wird am Schluss unter dem einleuchtenden Titel „10 Punkte zum Behalten"
zusammengefasst:

1. Eigenverantwortung: Jeder Mitarbeiter, jede Mitarbeiterin ist selbst für den Inhalt verantwortlich, den er/sie im Netz verbreitet. Diese digitalen Hinterlassenschaften bleiben noch für
Jahre sichtbar und bleiben auch den Autoren zugeordnet. Höflichkeit und Respekt sind daher
soziale Grundlagen dieser Kommunikation.

2. Offenheit: Nennt euren richtigen Namen, identifiziert euch als Rotkreuz-Mitarbeiter,
beschreibt auch eure Funktion beim Roten Kreuz. Macht klar und deutlich, dass es sich um
eure persönliche Meinung handelt. Wenn ihr zitiert, dann beruft euch auf Fakten, die beispielsweise auf www.roteskreuz.at zu finden sind, und verlinkt auch dorthin.

3. Vertraulichkeit: Geheimes bleibt geheim. Respektiert vertrauliche Informationen, die ihr
beispielsweise von PatientInnen, aus der Organisation oder von euren Kollegen habt. Vertraulich heißt in jedem Fall, dass diese Informationen nicht publiziert werden.

4. Ruhe bewahren: Zorn, Ärger oder Frust sind keine guten Motivationen, um Beiträge zu
erstellen.

5. Respekt: Zum korrekten Auftritt gehört auch der Respekt für Konkurrenten, für PatientInnen oder für andere Organisationen. Daher bitte keine negativen Beiträge zu anderen Organisationen oder über Berufsgruppen, Nationalitäten, ...

6. Urheberrecht: Das Copyright ist zu akzeptieren. Wenn ihr zitiert, dann gebt an, wen ihr von wo zitiert. Bilder sind oftmals rechtlich geschützt – daher immer vor der Publikation abklären, ob die Verwendung möglich ist.

7. Sicherheit: In sozialen Plattformen kann man verschiedene Sicherheitseinstellungen wählen. Überprüft, ob eure Sicherheitseinstellungen korrekt sind, damit ihr einstellen könnt, wer eure Postings lesen kann und wer nicht.

8. Spam ist in jedem Fall zu unterlassen.

9. Interne Kritik ist erlaubt und erwünscht, muss aber intern bleiben.

10. Vor dem Senden oder Posten ist es immer gut, das Posting, den Status, ... noch einmal zu lesen und auch zu checken, ob man möglicherweise missverstanden werden könnte.

SAP
Der Softwareanbieter SAP veröffentlicht – wie viele internationale Unternehmen – seine Guidelines ebenfalls nur in englischer Sprache:
http://www.scribd.com/doc/17249115/SAP-Social-Media-Participation-Guidelines-2009 bzw.
http://www.sapweb20.com/blog/blog/page/4/

SAP Global Communications, SAP Global Marketing
June 2009

This document reflects the current guidelines as determined by SAP Global Communications, SAP Global Marketing and SAP Legal in collaboration with employees. This document is subject to modifications and amendments from time to time as required.

SOCIAL MEDIA PARTICIPATION GUIDELINES

The following guidelines describe private, individual participation in social media channels such as Facebook, Twitter, personal blogs, forums, YouTube, Flickr etc. for SAP employees. If your job requires you to be an SAP evangelist in social media channels and you have questions, or you want to establish social media channels on behalf of SAP or an SAP group, contact the SAP Social Media Group by sending a mail to [redacted]. For any other questions about social media at SAP, please visit the SAP-internal SAP 2.0 Community.

These guidelines are intended to assist you in your use of social media tools as an individual.

Please be aware that nothing in the use of these tools changes your responsibilities and obligations as an employee of SAP. SAP and its employees are required to act ethically, and it is every employee's obligation to review and understand SAP's Code of Business Conduct, our communications policy, and their confidentiality obligations in other policies, such as the Security Policy.

Social media channels such as (micro) blogging, video and photo sharing, forums, virtual worlds, opinion markets and collaboration environments represent an opportunity to facilitate conversation with all of our constituents regarding the enterprise software industry and our place in it. SAP provides these social media guidelines to help employees participate within social media channels safely, and with minimum personal liability.

The SAP employee community collaborated in writing these guidelines. Specifically, a draft set of guidelines was posted on an internal SAP Wiki and SAP employees from divisions throughout the organization were invited to make comments and suggestions aimed at developing an appropriate set of guidelines.

These guidelines reflect the principles that SAP employees should follow when engaging in online communication. They are intended to provide you with an understanding of both the proper and improper uses of social computing in an effort to make your conversations and interactions as rich as possible. At all times, SAP employees must obey their local laws and adhere to local legal and ethical regulations. Nevertheless, as online communication is global in nature, other laws and regulations may also be applicable to your communication.

Please note that any direct communication to analysts, the financial market and/or members of the media must be conducted only through SAP Global Communications. The following set of guidelines only pertains to your personal statements in any online media. Please be aware that, although SAP is providing you with these guidelines, the overall and final legal responsibility for any statement made by you will reside with you personally. Therefore, you should exercise caution and thoughtfulness to statements you make online.

Setting up personal spaces in social media channels – You are free to set up any blog, space or other area within the given framework of the terms provided by the host of such spaces (e.g. Facebook, LinkedIn, Twitter etc). Please contact the SAP Social Media Group whenever you intend to use "SAP" as any part of the name or URL to avoid confusion with official SAP communication. Any personal space should have a clear disclaimer that it is not an official space of SAP. The following template may be used for this purpose:

"This [Choose. Blog, Space …] is the personal [Blog, Space …] of [Name] and only contains my personal views, thoughts and opinions. It is not endorsed by SAP nor does it constitute any official communication of SAP."

Managers and executives take note: This standard disclaimer does not by itself exempt

SAP managers and executives from a special responsibility when blogging or otherwise communicating online. By virtue of their position, managers and executives must consider whether personal thoughts they publish may be misunderstood as expressing SAP positions, and a manager should assume that his or her team will read what is written. A public blog is not the appropriate medium for many types of communications, including, but not limited to: communicating SAP policies to SAP employees; negotiating with third parties; making disparaging remarks about any third party; or other communications, etc.

Write in the first person – When you contribute commentary about SAP or SAP-related matters to an external audience, it is vital that you make it clear that you are speaking only for yourself (i. e. use the first-person singular, such as "I believe …" and not "We at SAP believe …"). There are different ways to do this. A simple and accepted approach is to include a disclaimer at the very beginning of your blog. If the blog is lengthy or long-standing, you should consider repeating the disclaimer inside the message. The disclaimer should state at a minimum that your point of view is personal, and it is not an official SAP point of view. Make it simple. Make it clear.

Identify yourself – The value of social computing is diminished when people hide behind a pseudonym or an anonymous post. Trust is hard enough to establish and maintain over the Internet, and if you do not identify yourself, then do not be surprised if your well-considered contributions are brushed aside. Therefore, please identify yourself to provide additional authenticity to your online contributions.

Be Honest – Tell the truth and if you find you have made a mistake, issue a clarification or a withdrawal or whatever may suit the circumstance and make it abundantly clear that you have done so. Social computing is a tolerant neighborhood – mistakes and errors will not make you a social outcast if you take responsibility. Rather than editing your content once it has been published, find ways to make your corrections transparent.

Be Respectful – simply carry the professionalism norms and standards of any SAP office onto the social computing platforms.

Separate Opinions from Facts – and make sure your audience can see the difference.

Add Value – be informative and interesting. Contribute your thoughts, experiences, observations, and opinions regarding issues you know and care about, but make sure to check your facts and figures – if you don't, someone else probably will.

Be Engaged and Be Informed – Read the contributions of others. Know what the current conversations are and what people are saying in order to see if, and how, you may be able to contribute a new perspective. Participation is the fuel of social computing. And remember …

Aim for Quality, not Quantity – Offer your contribution with context whenever you can.

Provide links to other blogs, media articles or whatever sources you think are necessary. Make your content rich and interesting for others to read. Consider attaching documents when necessary (but not SAP internal documents, confidential or not, of course!). And in every case, keep the language simple and flowing. If you start a blog, encourage feedback and conversation – make sure your readers can add feedback to your blog and respond in a timely manner. A two-way communication exchange allows for a more meaningful conversation.

Don't Pick Fights – When you see misrepresentations or patently false statements about SAP by bloggers, the media, analysts or anyone else for that matter, you may certainly address these misrepresentations, even by joining someone else's conversation. But stick to the facts and make sure the facts you rely on are publicly available.

Protect Your Privacy – Never disclose personal information.

Remember that you are still an SAP employee – do not make false, misleading or detrimental statements about SAP or SAP products. Consider that, although you are writing a personal blog, your statements will be considered an indication of the internal proceedings in SAP and how the company and our products are seen internally.

How to Handle Media Inquiries – Your contributions to social computing and the online conversations around SAP products, solutions, and practices will help advance dialogue, maybe solve some problems, create awareness and possibly attract attention of all kinds, including the media. If a member of the media contacts you, simply notify the Media Relations team in Global Communications via press@sap.com. They will determine the best way to handle the inquiry.

Legal Considerations – Yes, you have legal responsibilities and they need to be considered. You must respect copyrights and other intellectual property, fair use and financial disclosure laws, and SAP deals in general. Remember the following – do NOT talk about: perceived product defects or deficits; revenue projections; future product launch details; acquisition targets yet to be defined, or disclose corporate topics, product roadmaps, customer wins, our relationship to customers or partners or any other material SAP internal information. Do not post materials from SAP partners or customers in your communication (whether marked as confidential or not) or otherwise make information public that you have received through interaction with customers or partners. Use your common sense, and when in doubt contact the SAP Social Media Group.

Social Computing and Your Primary Role – Active contribution to social computing in its many forms can be time-consuming, so it is important that this does not interfere with your role at SAP. If you find that your social computing activity interferes with your role at SAP, please speak with your manager to determine if your personal contributions can become official SAP communications in alignment with SAP Global Communications as part of your job. If your manager and SAP Global Communication determines that it is not possible to incorporate your social computing activity into your role at SAP, you should reduce your involvement in social computing and consider posting a statement that explains why you are reducing your online activity.

Scout24

Die Scout24-Gruppe ist Betreiber verschiedener Online-Marktplätze samt zugehöriger Blogs beziehungsweise Communities in 18 Ländern. Zu friendscout24.de gibt es etwa http:/www.doctors-of-love.de als Beziehungsratgeber mit einer Art virtuellem „Dr. Sommer".

Die Policy findet sich unter http://www.scout24.com/Newsroom.aspx (und Folgeseite).

Präambel: Scout24-Mitarbeiter sind leidenschaftliche Social-Web-Nutzer. Unsere Guidelines zeigen unser Selbstverständnis im Social Web: Sie dienen zur Orientierung der Mitarbeiter und geben Interessierten gleichzeitig die Möglichkeit, sich einen Eindruck davon zu verschaffen, wie sich die Scout24-Mitarbeiter im Social Web bewegen.

Scout24 Social Web-Guideline

Wir begreifen das Social Web als Chance, die es uns erlaubt, engere und persönlichere Beziehungen mit Kunden, Kollegen und dem Rest der Welt aufzubauen und zu pflegen. Als Teil des Internets verstehen wir, die Scout24-Gruppe, uns auch als ein Teil des Social Webs. Unsere Social Web Guidelines stellen die Grundlage für das Verhalten von Scout24 und unseren Mitarbeitern in der Social-Web-Sphäre dar. Sie dienen als Orientierung für unsere Mitarbeiter und geben gleichzeitig interessierten Personen die Möglichkeit, sich einen Eindruck davon zu verschaffen, wie wir das Social Web verstehen und wie wir uns dort verhalten.

Transparenz & Identität:
Sei offen, nutze Deinen echten Namen und gebe an, dass Du für Scout24 arbeitest. Wenn Du ein eigennütziges Interesse an einem Thema hast, erwähne dies selbst, bevor es jemand anderes tut. Gestalte Deine digitale Identität bewusst und gehe mit Deiner Reputation sensibel um – denn als Scout24-Mitarbeiter ist Deine Reputation eng mit der von Scout24 verbunden. Sei Dir bewusst, dass jeder veröffentlichte Inhalt für immer im Netz zu finden sein wird! Stelle daher sicher, dass Deine Privatsphäre im Netz geschützt ist. Nutze die Privacy-Setting-Möglichkeiten in Social Networks und poste keine Inhalte, von denen Du nicht möchtest, dass sie später auf der Seite 1 einer Tageszeitung zu sehen sind.

Ehrlichkeit:
Bleibe stets bei der Wahrheit, verdrehe keine Tatsachen und verbreite keine Lügen. Dies gilt auch und insbesondere gegenüber Wettbewerbern und Kunden! Ehrlichkeit schafft Vertrauen. Das ist die Basis für langfristigen Erfolg.

Respekt:
Äußere Dich immer respektvoll, wenn Du etwas schreibst. Werde nicht ausfallend und verbreite keinen Spam! Sei stets höflich und konstruktiv! Du musst nicht auf jede Kritik und spitze Bemerkung eingehen. Stößt Du aber auf einen sachlichen, negativen Kommentar zu Scout24, gib Hilfestellung oder informiere einen Kollegen/Abteilung, der/die Dir weiterhelfen kann. Werde auch bei hitzigen Diskussionen nicht ausfallend!

Vertrauenswürdigkeit:
Als Mitarbeiter von Scout24 hast Du Zugang zu teils sensiblen, internen Daten. Gehe damit vertraulich um! Wenn Du Dir nicht sicher bist, ob eine Information dieses Kriterium erfüllt, frage nach. Bevor Du etwas veröffentlichst, kontrolliere nochmals, ob Du alles, was dort steht, mit Deinem Namen unterschreiben kannst und ob es mit unserer Social Web Guideline übereinstimmt. Solltest Du auch nur geringe Zweifel haben, nehme Dir einen Moment Zeit und finde heraus, was Dich stört. Im Zweifel besprche Dich mit Deinen Kollegen oder Deinem Vorgesetzten – eine zweite Meinung ist immer hilfreich und schafft Sicherheit für Dich.

Authentizität:
Im Social Web bist Du immer auch Persönlichkeit. Sei Du selbst und versuche nicht, Dich künstlich zu verstellen! Das fällt negativ auf Dich zurück.

Dialog:
Das Social Web ist keine Einbahnstraße. Es geht um Dialoge. Engagiere Dich in Online-Gesprächen zu Themen, die Dir und uns wichtig sind. Bemühe Dich immer, in Konversationen einen Mehrwert zu bieten. Besonders wichtig ist allerdings, dass Du zuhören kannst! Nehme die Anliegen anderer Nutzer ernst und gehe auf sie ein.

Beziehung:
Egal ob Kunde, Kollege oder Nachbar: Bemühe Dich stets, gute und fruchtbare Beziehungen aufzubauen. Schreibe über interessante Dinge und respektiere die Leserschaft. Persönliche Eindrücke können Beziehungen festigen.

Sun

Nach der Übernahme von Sun durch Oracle von eher historischem Wert, aber dennoch interessant, da sich die Entstehung auf das Jahr 2004 zurückdatieren lässt, sind die Richtlinien des Computerherstellers Sun Microsystems.

Sun News – Sun Blogs

(http://www.sun.com/aboutsun/media/blogs/policy.html)

Many of us at Sun are doing work that could change the world. We need to do a better job of telling the world. As of now, you are encouraged to tell the world about your work, without asking permission first (but please do read and follow the advice in this note). Blogging is a good way to do this.

Advice By speaking directly to the world, without benefit of management approval, we are accepting higher risks in the interest of higher rewards. We don't want to micro-manage, but here is some advice.

It's a Two-Way Street The real goal isn't to get everyone at Sun blogging, it's to become part of the industry conversation. So, whether or not you're going to write, and especially if you are, look around and do some reading, so you learn where the conversation is and what people are saying.

If you start writing, remember the Web is all about links; when you see something interesting and relevant, link to it; you'll be doing your readers a service, and you'll also generate links back to you; a win-win.

Don't Tell Secrets Common sense at work here; it's perfectly OK to talk about your work and have a dialog with the community, but it's not OK to publish the recipe for one of our secret sauces. There's an official policy on protecting Sun's proprietary and confidential information, but there are still going to be judgment calls.

If the judgment call is tough-on secrets or one of the other issues discussed here-it's never a bad idea to get management sign-off before you publish.

Be Interesting Writing is hard work. There's no point doing it if people don't read it. Fortunately, if you're writing about a product that a lot of people are using, or are waiting for, and you know what you're talking about, you're probably going to be interesting. And because of the magic of hyperlinking and the Web, if you're interesting, you're going to be popular, at least among the people who understand your specialty.

Another way to be interesting is to expose your personality; almost all of the successful bloggers write about themselves, about families or movies or books or games; or they post pictures. People like to know what kind of a person is writing what they're reading. Once again, balance is called for; a blog is a public place and you should try to avoid embarrassing your readers or the company.

Write What You Know The best way to be interesting, stay out of trouble, and have fun is to write about what you know. If you have a deep understanding of some chunk of Solaris or a hot JSR, it's hard to get into too much trouble, or be boring, talking about the issues and challenges around that.

On the other hand, a Solaris architect who publishes rants on marketing strategy, or whether Java should be open-sourced, has a good chance of being embarrassed by a real expert, or of being boring.

Financial Rules There are all sorts of laws about what we can and can't say, business-wise. Talking about revenue, future product ship dates, roadmaps, or our share price is apt to get you, or the company, or both, into legal trouble.

Quality Matters Use a spell-checker. If you're not design-oriented, ask someone who is whether your blog looks decent, and take their advice on how to improve it.

You don't have to be a great or even a good writer to succeed at this, but you do have to make an effort to be clear, complete, and concise. Of course, "complete" and "concise" are to some degree in conflict; that's just the way life is. There are very few first drafts that can't be shortened, and usually improved in the process.

Think About Consequences The worst thing that can happen is that a Sun sales pro is in a meeting with a hot prospect, and someone on the customer's side pulls out a print-out of your blog and says "This person at Sun says that product sucks."

In general, "XXX sucks" is not only risky but unsubtle. Saying "Netbeans needs to have an easier learning curve for the first-time user" is fine; saying "Visual Development Environments for Java sucks" is just amateurish.

Once again, it's all about judgment: using your weblog to trash or embarrass the company, our customers, or your co-workers, is not only dangerous but stupid.

Disclaimers Many bloggers put a disclaimer on their front page saying who they work for, but that they're not speaking officially. This is good practice, but don't count on it to avoid trouble; it may not have much legal effect.

Tools We're starting to develop tools to make it easy for anyone to start publishing, but if you feel the urge, don't wait for us; there are lots of decent blogging tools and hosts out there.

This site contains blogs written by Sun employees and is governed by company policies, including Sun's Blogging Guidelines *(siehe unten, Anmerkung des Autors)*. When employees leave Sun, blogs written during their employment normally remain in place here and are subject to the same policies. Sun Alumni are invited to continue blogging on the friends.sun.com/blogs site, where additional terms and conditions apply.

Die angesprochenen „Sun's Blogging Guidelines" finden sich hier:
http://www.sun.com/aboutsun/media/blogs/BloggingGuidelines.pdf:

> Speaking to the world in public has potential risks for you and for Sun and you need to understand them. Here are the big-picture risks.
> Posting the wrong thing on your blog could:
> – Lose Sun its right to export technology outside the U. S.
> – Get Sun and you in legal trouble with U. S. and other government agencies.
> – Lose Sun its trademark on key terms like Java and Solaris.
> – Cost us the ability to get patents.
> – Cost you your job at Sun.
>
> Most of these risks can be avoided by just being careful and responsible. Here is a summary of the important rules to follow to avoid getting in trouble. There is an applicable company policy for each of the items listed. Links to these policies are included in the internal version of this document located at https://akula.sfbay.sun.com:8443/blogs-admin/ Violation of any applicable company policy may result in disciplinary action up to and including termination of employment.
>
> Summary of the important rules:
>
> 1. Do not disclose or speculate on non-public financial or operational information. The legal consequences could be swift and severe for you and Sun.
>
> 2. Do not disclose non-public technical information (for example, code) without approval. Sun could instantly lose its right to export its products and technology to most of the world or to protect its intellectual property.
>
> 3. Do not disclose personal information about other individuals.
>
> 4. Do not disclose confidential information, Sun's or anyone else's.
>
> 5. Do not discuss work-related legal proceedings or controversies, including communications with Sun attorneys.
>
> 6. Always refer to Sun's trademarked names properly. For example, never use a trademark as a noun, since this could result in a loss of our trademark rights.
>
> 7. Do not post others' material, for example photographs, articles, or music, without ensuring they've granted appropriate permission to do this.
>
> 8. Follow Sun's Standards of Business Conduct and uphold Sun's reputation for integrity. In particular, ensure that your comments about companies and products are truthful, accurate, and fair and can be substantiated, and avoid disparaging comments about individuals.

Telstra

Als eines von bisher wenigen Telekommunikationsunternehmen hat Telstra seine Policies öffentlich gemacht: http://www.telstra.com.au/abouttelstra/download/document/social-media-company-policy-final-150409.pdf?red=/at/m/d/smcpf150409pdf.

Social Media – Telstra's 3 Rs of Social Media Engagement Company Policy

Relevant Business Principle: Communication of InformationPurpose
Social media offers the opportunity for people to gather in online communities of shared interest and create, share or consume content.

Globally the interest and participation in social media is growing at phenomenal rates. This interest also extends to corporations who are recognising that social media offers new opportunities to engage in conversations with customers and other communities with shared interests.

Telstra embraces social media as an important tool of corporate and business engagement. Telstra also encourages its employees to use social media in a personal capacity as a way to reach out and share information and views with friends and communities – both old and new.

With the rapid growth and application of social media, Telstra recognises the need to have a policy which ensures that employees who use social media either as part of their job, or in a personal capacity, have guidance as to the company's expectations where the social media engagement is about Telstra, its products and services, its people, its competitors and/or other business related individuals or organisations. Telstra's 3 Rs of Social Media Engagement are therefore 'guardrails' designed to protect the interests of employees and the company. In brief, the 3 Rs ask that when engaging in social media you be clear about who you are representing, you take responsibility for ensuring that any references to Telstra are factually correct and accurate and do not breach confidentiality requirements, and that you show respect for the individuals and communities with which you interact.

It is important to note that this policy does not apply to employees' personal use of social media platforms where the employee makes no reference to Telstra related issues.

Given the rapid development and uptake of social media and its growing relevance to corporate activity, this policy will be reviewed regularly to ensure it remains relevant and applicable.

Application
Telstra's 3 Rs of Social Media Engagement is a Company Policy of Telstra Corporation Limited and it applies to all Telstra employees and contractors and to any other person who is notified that this Company Policy applies to them. Subject to Telstra Business Principles and Company Policies, it applies to each of Telstra's 100 % owned Australian subsidiaries and their employees and contractors.

If you require clarification about aspects of this policy and how it applies to your own circumstances, please contact Mike Hickinbotham, Social Media Senior Advisor, Public Policy & Communications in the first instance.

Policy

Telstra appreciates the value in using social media to build more meaningful relationships with customers, communities and other relevant stakeholders. If you are officially accredited to represent Telstra in social media, or if you are discussing Telstra or Telstra business related issues in your personal use of social media platforms, you are required to follow this Policy. Social media tools include: social networking sites eg Facebook, MySpace, Bebo, Friendster video and photo sharing websites eg Flickr, YouTube micro-blogging sites eg Twitter weblogs, including corporate blogs, personal blogs or blogs hosted by traditional media publications forums and discussion boards such as Whirlpool, Yahoo! Groups or Google Groups online encyclopaedias such as Wikipedia any other web sites that allow individual users or companies to use simple publishing tools.

Telstra's 3 Rs of Social Media Engagement

Telstra's 3 Rs of Social Media Engagement are Representation, Responsibility and Respect. Telstra's 3 Rs apply when: you are authorised and accredited to represent Telstra on social media platforms and are using a social media platform for business purposes. Further information is outlined in section below.
you choose to make references to Telstra, its people, products or services, and/or other business related individuals or organisations when you are using a social media platform in a personal capacity. Further information is outlined in section 5 below.
Telstra's Social Media Engagement Policy does not apply to personal use of social media platforms where you make no reference to Telstra related issues.

Social Media Engagement for Business Purposes
Before you can become an authorised Telstra representative on a social media platform, you must have approval from your one-up manager and be accredited by Public Policy & Communications. This section outlines how Telstra's 3 Rs of Social Media Engagement apply if you are accredited to represent Telstra as part of your job responsibilities.

Representation
You are required to:
– disclose that you are a Telstra employee and be clear about which business unit you are representing and what your role and accountabilities are;
– disclose only publicly available information. You must not comment on or disclose confidential Telstra information (such as financial information, future business performance, business plans, imminent departure of key executives). If you require clarification about what Telstra information is in the public domain, you should refer to material such as telstra.com, nowwearetalking.com.au and Telstra's annual report. You could also consult with the Media Relations and Public Affairs teams in the Public Policy & Communications business unit and/or the Investor Relations Unit in the Finance & Administration business unit.

Responsibility

You are required to:

- complete the Telstra social media accreditation process before you can represent Telstra in social media;
- complete additional training to update your knowledge on emerging social trends and evolving best practice in social media, when requested to do so;
- ensure that any content you publish is factually accurate and complies with relevant company policies, particularly those relating to confidentiality and disclosure (see References section below);
- ensure you are not the first to make a Telstra announcement unless you have received the appropriate internal clearances and approvals in accordance with Telstra's policy for releasing information in the public domain (Policy 61);
- only offer advice, support or comment on topics that fall within your area of responsibility at Telstra. For other matters, alert the relevant topic expert who is accredited for social media engagement and, if the situation requires a real time response, let the other party know that the request has reached Telstra for response;
- ensure you do not post material that is obscene, defamatory, threatening, harassing, discriminatory or hateful to another person or entity, including Telstra, its employees, its contractors, its partners, its competitors and/or other business related individuals or organisations;
- ensure you do not disclose other people's personal information in social media venues, and comply with the Privacy Policy and the Marketing Privacy Policy.

Respect

You are required to:

- be respectful of all individuals and communities with which you interact online;
- be polite and respectful of others' opinions, even in times of heated discussion and debate;
- adhere to the Terms Of Use, and seek to conform to the cultural and behavioural norms, of the social media platform being used;
- respect copyright, privacy, financial disclosure and other applicable laws when publishing on social media platforms. Check with your BU General Counsel if you are not certain about what you can reproduce or disclose on social media platforms.

Other Uses of Social Media Platforms

This section outlines how Telstra's 3 Rs of Social Media Engagement are applied if you choose to make references to Telstra, its people, products or services, its competitors, and/ or other business related individuals or organisations when you are using a social media platform in a personal capacity. It is important in these circumstances that readers of your posts do not misconstrue your personal comments as representing an official Telstra position.

Representation

You are required to:

- identify yourself as a Telstra employee if you refer to Telstra, its people, products and services, its competitors and/or other business related individuals or organisations;
- ensure you do not imply in any way that you are authorised to speak on Telstra's behalf;
- ensure you do not knowingly use the identity of another Telstra employee or an employee of a Telstra business partner or competitor (including name or variation of a name);
- be mindful during your social media engagements of the importance of not damaging the corporation's reputation, commercial interests and/or bringing Telstra into disrepute;
- disclose only publicly available information. You must not comment on or disclose confidential Telstra information (such as financial information, future business performance, business plans, imminent departure of key executives). If you require clarification about what Telstra information is in the public domain, you should refer to material such as telstra. com, nowwearetalking.com.au and Telstra's annual report. You could also consult with the Media Relations and Public Affairs teams in the Public Policy & Communications business unit and/or the Investor Relations Unit in the Finance & Administration business unit;
- not include Telstra's logos or trademarks in your postings.

Responsibility

You are personally responsible for the content of your posts online. In this context, you have a responsibility to ensure that: any information about Telstra products and services that you provide is informed and factually accurate. If you wish to express your opinions please state they are your personal opinions.

if you are offering your personal perspective on a matter related to Telstra, be mindful that your commentary and opinion does not cause damage to Telstra or its commercial interests.

You are required to:

use a disclaimer to ensure that your stated views and opinions are understood to be your own and not those of Telstra. A disclaimer is required when you:

- refer to the work done by Telstra;
- comment on any Telstra-related or telecommunications issue; or
- provide a link to a Telstra website.

use a permanent disclaimer if you are referring regularly to Telstra or Telstra related issues. For irregular Telstra references, a disclaimer need only be used on a case by case basis. An example of a disclaimer is: "the views expressed in this post are mine only and do not necessarily reflect the views of Telstra."

adhere to Telstra's Policy on Acceptable Use of Telstra Provided Services and Information Systems if you are using Telstra provided services made available to you as an employee or contractor. In particular, limited personal use of Telstra provided services (such as email, internet access and instant messaging) is allowed, however it must be within reasonable limits and not interfere with your work;

reference only publicly available information such as that on telstra.com and nowwearetalk-ing.com.au, or in Telstra's annual report;

ensure you are not the first to make a Telstra announcement;

ensure you do not post material that is obscene, defamatory, threatening, harassing, discriminatory or hateful to another person or entity, including about Telstra, its employees, its contractors, its partners, its competitors and/or other business related individuals or organisations.

Respect
– You are required to:
– be respectful of all individuals and communities with which you interact online;
– be polite and respectful of other opinions, even in times of heated discussion and debate;
– adhere to the Terms Of Use, and seek to conform to the cultural and behavioural norms, of the social media platform being used;
– respect copyright, privacy, financial disclosure and other applicable laws when publishing on social media platforms. Check with your BU General Counsel if you are not certain about what you can reproduce or disclose on social media platforms.

Breach of Policy
As is the case with all of Telstra's company policies, if you do not comply with this Policy you may face disciplinary action under Telstra's Performance Improvement and Conduct Management (PICM) process. This disciplinary action may involve a verbal or written warning or, in serious cases, termination of your employment or engagement with Telstra.
Telstra may recover from you any costs incurred as a result of a breach of this Company Policy. If you break the law you may also be personally liable.

References
1. Telstra Business Principles and Company Policies
2. Policy 61 – Release of Information to the Public Domain
3. Acceptable Use of Telstra Provided Services and Information Systems Company Policy
4. Workplace Surveillance Company Policy
5. Privacy Company Policy
6. Marketing Privacy Company Policy

Definitions

Contractor
Any person, company or other contracting party engaged to provide services to or on behalf of Telstra under a contract of services, either directly or indirectly (for example, through a third party). This includes agency workers, consultants, agents and suppliers.

GMD
All personnel included in Band A of the Telstra Executive Team and includes the CEO of Sensis Pty Ltd and the Group General Counsel.

Confidential Information Includes:
– information derived from the performance of your work at Telstra
– opinions, knowledge and facts about Telstra, its employees, its business and its customers that have not been disclosed to the public.

Telstra verfügt auch über eine eingängige „Comic-Version" der Guidelines – als Online-Training mit Musik unterlegt und mit animierten Videos illustriert. Sehenswert unter: http://exchange.telstra.com.au/training/flip.html

Telstra Social Media Guidelines

Zudem existieren weitere Dokumente, die etwa Regelungen für die Telstra-Community „Telstra Exchange" enthalten (http://exchange.telstra.com.au/about/community-guidelines/):

The Telstra Exchange (exchange.telstra.com.au) website is designed to spark an exchange of views about Telstra, Australian telecommunications and broader technology issues.

All comments submitted via the Telstra Exchange website are reviewed by a moderator prior to publication.

By submitting a comment to the Telstra Exchange website, you consent to Telstra reproducing and publishing that content (either in whole or an edited version of the posting) to Telstra Exchange, and in other Telstra websites or Telstra publications.

All Telstra employees participating in Telstra Exchange should be aware of Telstra's Social Media Policy – Telstra's 3 Rs of Social Media Engagement (PDF – 61KB). This policy sets out three basic principles for social media engagement, Representation, Responsibility and Respect (the 3 Rs).

Moderation aims
Our community guidelines aim to ensure the Telstra Exchange blogs are inclusive and inviting.

Toward that end, moderators will ensure that user comments are relevant and appropriate, and may take any steps they deem appropriate to ensure content meets the site's Comment moderation policy, described below.

Standard operating hours for comment moderation
– The Telstra Exchange blogs will be monitored and actively moderated during standard operating hours only: Monday to Friday 9am–5.30pm AEST.
– During our standard operating hours we'll aim to review all comments within 2 hours.
– Comments submitted outside of standard operating hours, or over the weekend, will be reviewed on the next working day.

Comment moderation policy
Postings may be edited for reasons of space, clarity, to remove offensive, threatening or unlawful content, or to avoid repetition.

You will not be directly contacted if your post has been rejected.
– Please ensure you address the conversation (blog) topic
– Please respect the views of others
– You must supply a valid email address to post a comment. Your email address will not be published

Contributors may not submit content that: is threatening, abusive, defamatory, indecent, menacing, harassing, offensive, infringes any person's intellectual property rights, including copyright, impersonates anyone, misrepresents a relationship with any person or organisation, encourages others to commit unlawful acts, harasses anyone or is unlawful in any way.

It is in your interests, as well as ours, to ensure that all content is lawful.
You may face personal liability if content you submit is published and is unlawful.
For example, if you submit material which is defamatory and cannot be defended, then you could be sued by the person defamed. In addition, the following types of postings are not permitted:

– repetitive messages, including cross-posting, flooding, and spamming
– messages of excessive length (more than 1000 words or 2500 characters)
– viruses, files, or potentially harmful code
– advertising, promotions, or similar material

We reserve the right to reject posts that direct readers to third-party websites.

Community standards
To ensure the dialogue on Telstra Exchange remains relevant and engaging for all users, you're also expected to observe 10 simple principles. Our moderators apply these principles when reviewing your comments.

1. We welcome debate and dissent, but personal attacks (on blog authors, moderators, other users or any individual), persistent trolling and mindless abuse will not be tolerated. The key to maintaining Telstra Exchange as an engaging and inclusive space is to focus on intelligent discussion of relevant subjects.

2. We acknowledge criticism of Telstra's products, services, policies and performance, but will not publish persistent misrepresentation of the Telstra Corporation, our Board, our share-holders or our staff. For the sake of robust debate, we will distinguish between constructive, focused argument and propaganda or smear tactics.

3. We understand that people often feel strongly about the issues discussed on Telstra Exchange, but we may reject or remove any content that others might find offensive or threatening. Please be pleasant and respectful of the opinions and beliefs of others. Not everyone has a thick skin, so please consider the impact your comments may have on others.

4. We reserve the right to redirect or curtail conversations that descend into repetitive flame-wars based on ingrained personal opinion or generalisations. We don't want to stop you discussing issues you are passionate about, but we do ask users to find ways of sharing their views that do not feel alienating, threatening or toxic to others.

5. We will reject or remove any content that may put us (or you) in legal jeopardy, for example, this includes potentially defamatory comments, or material posted in potential breach of copyright.

6. Keep it relevant. We know that conversations can be wide-ranging, but if you submit commentary wholly unrelated to the original blog topic ("off-topic") then it may be rejected or removed, in order to keep the discussion on track.

7. Queries or comments about moderation will not be published. The moderator's decision is final and no correspondence will be entered into. Abusive posts will be deleted, as will posts asking 'why was my post deleted?'

8. Telstra Exchange does not supplant existing Telstra customer service or complaints resolution forums, but it is an arena for discussion and for two-way feedback. Please direct any individual customer service issues or complaints to the channels listed on our contact us page. Any individual service issue reported via Telstra Exchange may be forwarded to an appropriate Telstra representative who will attempt to contact you via email, or via the Telstra Exchange blogs, to resolve the matter.

9. Maintain a measured tone and don't shout. Any comments submitted in ALL-CAPS, or similar, may be rejected. Also be aware that you may be misunderstood, so try to be clear. Expect that people may understand your post differently than you intended. Tone of voice (sarcasm, humour and so on) doesn't always translate well online, so err on the side of caution.

10. The platform is ours, but the conversation belongs to everybody. We want this to be a welcoming space for intelligent discussion, and we expect participants to help us achieve this by notifying us of potential problems and helping each other to keep conversations inviting and appropriate. If you spot something problematic on our blogs, please report it.

Your use of the Telstra Exchange website is governed by the Terms of Use and Copyright & Trade Mark Matters of Telstra.com.

Sharing information is the essence of social media. However, many elements of the site such as text, pictures and logos are subject to copyright. To avoid infringing copyright, we ask that you link to material on the site rather than reproducing it. Quoting from a post in the context of a discussion is generally acceptable, but please do not copy and paste large sections of text on to third party websites.

If you wish to reproduce an entire post, a picture or a logo, or if you are unsure about whether your proposed use is acceptable, please email the Telstra Exchange team.

The Gazette
Einen Gegenentwurf zu den ausufernden Social Media Guidelines liefert die US-Zeitung „The Gazette" (zitiert nach: http://socialmediatoday.com/index.php?q=SMC/93569) Folgendes:

- If you're using an account for work purposes, identify yourself as an employee of The Gazette.
- If posting something would embarass you or the company, or call your professional reputation into question, DON'T POST IT.

Das ist zunächst alles. Es gibt jedoch noch einige Fallbeispiele als Ergänzung, die die beiden Punkte der Policy illustrieren sollen.

University of Salford (Manchester)

Wie oben bereits beim Beispiel Harvard Law School beschrieben, benötigen Hochschulen zunehmend Guidelines. Die hier als Beispiel genannte UK-Universität hat ihre Guidelines veröffentlicht unter http://www.slideshare.net/salfordwebmaster/university-of-salford-staff-guidelines-social-media.

Social media guidelines

Social media such as blogs, Twitter, and Flickr are a great asset to the University's activities with researchers, tutors and departments able to highlight their activities.
Marketing & Communications has compiled these guidelines based on those used by organisations such as the BBC and Opera, to give staff members confidence when using these applications.

If you have any questions, please get in touch with Jamie Brown, Press and PR Officer on 55361 or email j.brown@salford.ac.uk

And remember – social media is a great tool, so don't be afraid to use it.

Why bother?
– Get your course, research or department higher up on search engine rankings
– Establish yourself as an expert. Whatever your subject, people can follow your blog or come to you with questions – raising our reputation

Basics
– If you're talking about the University online whether in forums, your blog or anywhere else, declare that you work here to avoid conflict of interest or accusations of deception.
– Declare also that your views are not necessarily those of the University – in your biography for example.
– Don't reveal confidences of the University or its partners. This can involve work which hasn't been officially announced or completed, or conversations you've had. If in doubt – check with your line manager.
– Don't break the law! Don't libel people, swear, or post anything indecent or offensive.

Things you should be doing
– If you're using a University logo, make sure it's the correct one. The one to use is the one without the pips in the roundel. Contact Marketing for the current range.
– Have a conversation – reply to comments, tweets and so on. The more the University talks to people the better we'll be able to get our views across and establish partnerships.
– Express yourself! Blogs, Twitter and other social media can really enhance what the University offers to students, the media and other staff. They're a great way for us to reach out and let other people know what we're doing.
– Social media isn't an arcane or 'techie' preserve – it's another way of communicating with

people and the same principles apply. Remember your audience and use language they understand.

If you're concerned that anything you are doing gives rise to a conflict of interest then speak to your line manager.

Social media the University is already using
- Twitter – we have a profile available to view at www.twitter.com/salforduni and several other individuals and departments also run their own
- Flickr – both the Press Team and Student Life Directorate upload their pictures. The Press Team photo stream is here: http://www.flickr.com/photos/32104790@N02/
- Blogs. A number of staff and departments have their own blogs including:

http://www.careers.salford.ac.uk/blog
http://frederickroad.blogspot.com/
http://www.edu.salford.ac.uk/blogs/

Voestalpine

Voestalpine mit Hauptsitz in Linz (Österreich) ist nach Unternehmsangaben mit rund 360 Produktions- und Vertriebsgesellschaften in über 60 Ländern vertreten. Die Unternehmensgruppe besteht aus insgesamt fünf Divisionen. Der Umsatz betrug im Geschäftsjahr 2009/10 rund 8,6 Milliarden Euro, und die voestalpine beschäftigt weltweit fast 40.000 Mitarbeiter.
Voestalpine ist einer der führenden europäischen Partner der Automobil-, Hausgeräte- und Energieindustrie. Sie ist zudem Weltmarktführer in der Weichentechnologie, bei Werkzeugstahl und Spezialprofilen sowie Europas Nummer 1 bei der Herstellung von Schienen. Stahl der voestalpine findet sich in zahlreichen Produkten wie der neuesten Airbus-Generation, aber auch in Bauwerken wie etwa dem Brüssel Atomium, dem Londoner Wembley-Stadion oder dem Burj Dubai, dem höchsten Gebäude der Welt. Die voestalpine AG notiert seit 1995 an der Wiener Börse und ist eines der bestperformenden ATX-Unternehmen.
Bei Voestalpine ist Social Media Chefsache. Die Aktivitäten unterstehen direkt dem Leiter Konzernkommunikation und sind von Umfang, Verständlichkeit und Aufmachung vorbildlich – nicht nur für den B-to-B-Bereich. Alle Aspekte werden auf sieben leicht zu merkende Grundsätze heruntergebrochen:

„Das Social Media Manual gibt Infos zum Thema Social Media und Social Networks, stellt den Social-Media-Auftritt der voestalpine vor und gibt 40.000 Mitarbeiterinnen und Mitarbeitern weltweit eine Handlungsempfehlung mit sieben einfachen Grundsätzen für den Umgang mit Social-Media-Plattformen." So lautet die Eigendarstellung des Unternehmens zu dem aufwendig produzierten Manual.

Das Dokument beschreibt zunächst, was Social Media ist, erläutert dann die wesentlichen Aktivitäten (Blog auf der Corporate-Website, Twitter, Facebook, YouTube, Xing, Flickr und Slideshare) und definiert als Kern der Policy:

„7 Grundsätze für den Umgang mit Social Media"

Bevor Sie auf Social-Media-Plattformen aktiv werden, sollten Sie sich folgende Dinge überlegen:
- Wofür möchte ich Social Media nutzen (beruflich und/oder privat)?
- Welche Anwendungen oder Plattformen möchte ich für welchen Zweck einsetzen?
- Mit welchen Personen möchte ich in Kontakt treten?
- Welche Themen interessieren mich?
- Welche Informationen stelle ich online?
- Wie kommuniziere ich im Social Web?

Die folgenden 7 Grundsätze sollen Ihnen eine praktische Hilfestellung geben, um Ihr „Social Media Life" verantwortungsvoll zu gestalten.

(1) Sprechen Sie nur für sich
Bitte beachten Sie, dass Sie jegliche Web-Aktivitäten als Person und nicht als offizielle Instanz der voestalpine durchführen und dies auch deklarieren.
Wenn Sie z.B. einen Blog oder eine eigene Website haben, sollten Sie einen „Disclaimer" auf Ihrer Seite ergänzen.

Hier ein Beispiel dafür:
„Dies ist der persönliche Blog von [Name] und enthält nur persönliche Ansichten, Gedanken und Meinungen."

(2) Seien Sie authentisch
Kommunizieren Sie stets offen und ehrlich. Stellen Sie Ihre Meinung transparent dar und kommunizieren Sie immer aus Ihrer persönlichen Sicht. Gehen Sie mit Ihren Aussagen verantwortungsvoll um und behandeln Sie andere User respektvoll und aufrichtig.
Um authentisch zu sein, kommentieren Sie Artikel nicht anonym, sondern mit Ihrem eigenen Namen.
Stellen Sie sicher, dass Ihre Kommunikation für andere nachvollziehbar ist und dass Sie ein unverfälschtes Bild von Ihrer Person zeigen.
Gerade in Zeiten von Spam und gefälschten Accounts ist es wichtig, bei allen Social-Media-Aktivitäten authentisch zu sein und Vertrauen zu vermitteln.

(3) Bedenken Sie: Das Web hat ein Gedächtnis
Für all Ihre Aktivitäten im Social Web sind Sie selbst verantwortlich.
Die von Ihnen erstellten Inhalte (Kommentare, Links, Texte, Bilder, Videos etc.) sind über lange Zeit im Internet sichtbar und über Suchmaschinen auffindbar.

Auch von anderen Personen werden Inhalte erstellt, welche unter Umständen mit Ihnen in Verbindung gebracht werden.

Sie sollten keine Informationen veröffentlichen, die in Zukunft evtl. negative Auswirkungen haben könnten.

Durch das „Gedächtnis" des Internets und die zunehmende Vernetzung von Social Media ist es sehr schwierig, Daten zu löschen.

(4) Schützen Sie Ihre Privatsphäre

Alle Inhalte, die Sie erstellen, kommentieren oder weiterleiten, sind grundsätzlich für andere Benutzer sichtbar und auch für Suchmaschinen auffindbar. Überlegen Sie daher genau, was Sie publizieren und welche Informationen Sie zu Ihrer Person preisgeben.

Informieren Sie sich auch über die Einstellungen zur Privatsphäre von einzelnen Social-Media-Plattformen (Privacy-Einstellungen). Sie sollten regelmäßig prüfen, ob sich an diesen Bedingungen etwas geändert hat. Mitunter kann es vorkommen, dass Betreiber von Plattformen die Bestimmungen ändern, ohne eine direkte Zustimmung der Benutzer einzuholen.

(5) Beachten Sie Copyright

Geben Sie auf Social-Media-Webseiten nur jene Informationen preis, welche in Ihrer Expertise liegen und zu deren Publikation Sie autorisiert sind.

Verwenden oder verbreiten Sie keinerlei Informationen (insbesondere Bilder und andere schützenswerte Inhalte), über deren Copyright Sie nicht verfügen.

Verbreiten Sie keinerlei Informationen, die vertraulich sind.

Beachten Sie bitte – sofern für Sie gültig – auch die weiteren Konzernrichtlinien in geltender Fassung (im Intranet abrufbar unter http://voestalpine.net/konzernrichtlinien.aspx).

(6) Respektieren Sie die Marke „voestalpine"

Die Nutzung der Marke „voestalpine" im Zusammenhang mit Online- oder Social-Media-Aktivitäten obliegt der Abteilung Corporate Communications der voestalpine AG.

Sämtliche Informationen, die über diese Kanäle verbreitet werden, gelten als Kommunikationsbotschaften des Konzerns.

Die Publikation von Unternehmensinformationen ist in der konzernalen Kommunikationsrichtlinie (siehe http://voestalpine.net/konzernrichtlinien.aspx) festgelegt.

Im Zweifelsfall und wenn es um Inhalte betreffend rechtlicher, wirtschaftlicher oder medienrelevanter Themen geht, sollten Sie Ihren Vorgesetzten oder die Abteilung Corporate Communications kontaktieren.

Wenn Sie für Ihr Unternehmen Social-Media-Kommunikation oder Marketing betreiben oder betreiben wollen, gelten gesonderte Bedingungen. In diesem Fall bitte um direkte Kontaktaufnahme mit der Abteilung Corporate Communications.

(7) Kommunizieren Sie verantwortungsvoll

Bevor Sie aktiv in eine Diskussion im Social Web einsteigen, sollten Sie überlegen, was Ihre Botschaft bewirken könnte.

Insbesondere wenn es um Informationen zum voestalpine Konzern, einem voestalpine Standort oder um Ihre Position als voestalpine-MitarbeiterIn geht, sollten Sie verantwortungsvoll handeln.

Auch in Bezug auf Kunden, Lieferanten oder Wettbewerber sollten Sie sehr vorsichtig sein und abwägen, ob und wie Sie darüber Ihre Meinung zum Ausdruck bringen. Handeln Sie im Zweifelsfall stets im Sinne des Unternehmens oder klären Sie die Situation mit Ihrem Vorgesetzten, um ggf. die Diskussion im eigenen Unternehmen zu suchen und nicht über Social-Media-Kanäle auszutragen.

Beachten Sie auch sogenannte Netiquette-Regelungen oder Hinweise zur Nutzung von Kommentarfunktionen einzelner Social-Media-Plattformen – siehe Hinweise zu Kommentaren auf der voestalpine Innovation Microsite: http://www.voestalpine.com/innovation/inhalt/hinweise-zu-kommentaren.

So weit der Auszug aus dem Dokument.

Das Voestalpine Social Media Manual ist vollständig auf Slideshare ansehbar unter http://www.slideshare.net/voestalpine/voestalpine-social-media-m.

Washington Post

Vom Spannungsfeld zwischen klassischen Medien und Social Media war bereits oben die Rede. Auch die Guidelines der Washington Post zeigen dies auf (http://www.slideshare.net/femiadi/20336238-the-washington-post-social-networks-guidelines):

The following are effective immediately:

Newsroom Guidelines for Use of Facebook, Twitter and Other Online Social Networks

Social networks are communications media, and a part of our everyday lives. They can be valuable tools in gathering and disseminating news and information. They also create some potential hazards we need to recognize. When using social networking tools for reporting or for our personal lives, we must remember that Washington Post journalists are always Washington Post journalists. The following guidelines apply to all Post journalists, without limitation to the subject matter of their assignments.

Using Social Networking Tools for Reporting
When using social networks such as Facebook, LinkedIn, My Space or Twitter for reporting, we must protect our professional integrity. Washington Post journalists should identify themselves as such. We must be accurate in our reporting and transparent about our intentions when participating. We must be concise yet clear when describing who we are and what information we seek.

When using these networks, nothing we do must call into question the impartiality of our news judgment. We never abandon the guidelines that govern the separation of news from opinion, the importance of fact and objectivity, the appropriate use of language and tone, and other hallmarks of our brand of journalism.

Our online data trails reflect on our professional reputations and those of The Washington Post.
Be sure that your pattern of use does not suggest, for example, that you are interested only in people with one particular view of a topic or issue.

Using Social Networking Tools for Personal Reasons
All Washington Post journalists relinquish some of the personal privileges of private citizens. Post journalists must recognize that any content associated with them in an online social network is, for practical purposes, the equivalent of what appears beneath their bylines in the newspaper or on our website.

What you do on social networks should be presumed to be publicly available to anyone, even if you have created a private account. It is possible to use privacy controls online to limit access to sensitive information. But such controls are only a deterrent, not an absolute insulator. Reality is simple: If you don't want something to be found online, don't put it there.

Post journalists must refrain from writing, tweeting or posting anything – including photographs or video – that could be perceived as reflecting political, racial, sexist, religious or other bias or favoritism that could be used to tarnish our journalistic credibility. This same caution should be used when joining, following or friending any person or organization online. Post journalists should not be involved in any social networks related to advocacy or a special interest regarding topics they cover, unless specifically permitted by a supervising editor for reporting and so long as other standards of transparency are maintained while doing any such reporting.

Post journalists should not accept or place tokens, badges or virtual gifts from political or partisan causes on pages or sites, and should monitor information posted on your own personal profile sites by those with whom you are associated online for appropriateness.

Personal pages online are no place for the discussion of internal newsroom issues such as sourcing, reporting of stories, decisions to publish or not to publish, personnel matters and untoward personal or professional matters involving our colleagues. The same is true for opinions or information regarding any business activities of The Washington Post Company. Such pages and sites also should not be used to criticize competitors or those who take issue with our journalism or our journalists.

If you have questions about any of these matters, please check with your supervisor or a senior editor.

NOTE: These guidelines apply to individual accounts on online social networks, when used for reporting and for personal use. Separate guidelines will follow regarding other aspects of Post journalism online.

Wal-Mart

Der US-Einzelhändler – hierzulande vor einigen Jahren eher erfolglos am Markt – ist in seinem Heimatmarkt Marktführer, steht aber vielfach wegen Löhnen und Arbeitsbedingungen unter Kritik.

Wal-Mart regelt explizit den Umgang mit Twitter in den „Walmart's Twitter External Discussion Guidelines" (http://walmartstores.com/9179.aspx)

> Twitter asks a very basic question of its users: "What are you doing?" And we know the answer to that question – we're working every day to help people save money and live better.

> On Twitter we encourage dialogue with customers about the products, brands and initiatives discussed by the writers. We welcome your thoughts and @replies on any and all of those topics. While we'll do our best to reply to your comments, generally, we won't be able to reply to store or service issues through Twitter. If you'd like to comment about customer service or any other issue please visit: Walmart Stores Feedback or call 1-800-Walmart.

> A few notes:
> – While many of our 2.2 million associates around the world are using Twitter and other social networks, all official Walmart Twitter users will be identified on this landing page and will have a link back to this page from their Twitter profile.
> – Unless otherwise noted, U. S.-based Walmart approved Twitter users will follow the following naming conventions of "business unit + name/category." For example, "walmartmeeting," "samsclubrobert," and "walmartgames."
> – We won't reply to off topic @replies. Personal attacks and foul language = FAIL. Adding to the discussion = WIN.
> – @replies should contribute to the dialogue. Please support any claims with links to sources whenever possible. We love opinions. We love it even more when you back them up.

> The posting and presence of content on Twitter and on this site does not necessarily mean that Walmart agrees with the content, ensures its accuracy or otherwise approves of it. Nothing in any Twitter page constitutes a binding representation, agreement or an endorsement on the part of Walmart. Please review the site terms of use carefully.

Wilde Beuger Solmecke Rechtsanwälte

RA Christian Solmecke von WBS-Law.de bietet im Rahmen seiner Website ein kommentiertes Muster für eine Social Media Guideline an, die als Muster für eigene Anpassungen dienen soll (http://www.wbs-law.de/internetrecht/muster-fuer-social-media-guidelines-5718/) und ausdrücklich – mit Quellenangabe – weitergegeben werden kann:

Muster für Social Media Guidelines

Verfasser: RA Christian Solmecke

Social Media Guidelines
Die folgenden Richtlinien sollen als Anleitung für die Mitarbeiter des Unternehmens zur privaten wie beruflichen Nutzung von Social-Media-Kanälen wie Facebook, Twitter, Blogs, Foren, YouTube, Flickr etc. dienen. Ziel ist insbesondere, sowohl das Unternehmen als auch Sie als Mitarbeiter vor den Folgen unbedachter und möglicherweise geschäftsschädigender Aktivitäten zu schützen.

Einleitend sollte kurz definiert werden, welche Ziele mit den folgenden Richtlinien verfolgt werden sollen. Abhängig davon, ob und in welchem Umfang das Unternehmen selbst im Social-Media-Bereich aktiv ist, kann eine solche Einleitung durchaus auch ausführlicher gestaltet werden. Insbesondere können an dieser Stelle auch die positiven Erwartungen im Hinblick auf die Darstellung des Unternehmens im Web 2.0 formuliert werden.

Nutzungsumfang von Social Media
Aktive Teilnahme an Social Computing in all seinen Facetten kann sehr zeitaufwendig sein. Achten Sie daher darauf, dass Ihre eigentlichen Aufgaben innerhalb des Unternehmens nicht unter Ihren Social-Media-Aktivitäten leiden.

Der Abschnitt zum Umfang der Social-Media-Nutzung ist an dieser Stelle bewusst kurz gehalten, da die diesbezügliche Gestaltung ganz besonders von den Vorgaben des jeweiligen Unternehmens abhängt. Außerdem bestehen oftmals bereits Vereinbarungen über die private Internetnutzung der Mitarbeiter, sodass eine entsprechende Regelung in den Social Media Guidelines entbehrlich ist. Wichtig ist, dass der obige Passus keinesfalls verwendet wird, wenn die private Internetnutzung z. B. in einer Betriebsvereinbarung oder im Arbeitsvertrag gänzlich ausgeschlossen worden ist.

Eigenverantwortlichkeit
Grundsätzlich sind Sie für jegliche Äußerungen privater oder beruflicher Natur selbst verantwortlich. Einmal eingestellte Inhalte sind gerade im Internet oftmals sehr lange verfügbar. Wägen Sie daher vor der Veröffentlichung von Beiträgen sorgfältig deren Inhalt ab.

Die Eigenverantwortlichkeit hinsichtlich der Online-Aktivitäten ist eigentlich ebenso selbstverständlich wie die Achtung von gesetzlichen Vorschriften und allgemeinen Verhaltensregeln. Dennoch sollte auf die entsprechenden Hinweise keinesfalls verzichtet werden, da sie in der scheinbaren Anonymität des Netzes oftmals verdrängt werden. Hieran knüpft dann auch der nächste Punkt an.

Gesetzliche Vorgaben

Beachten Sie auch bei der Nutzung von Social Media geltende gesetzliche Vorgaben wie beispielsweise des Datenschutz-, Urheber- und Markenrechts.

Netikette

Auch im Internet sind die allgemeinen Regeln des Anstands zu beachten. Verhalten Sie sich also respektvoll etwa gegenüber anderen Diskussionsteilnehmern oder Wettbewerbern. Informieren Sie sich darüber hinaus über die jeweiligen Verhaltenskodizes der von Ihnen genutzten Plattformen.

Transparenz

Transparenz und Offenheit sind sowohl im privaten als auch im geschäftlichen Bereich unerlässlich für den Aufbau vertrauensvoller Beziehungen. Verstecken Sie sich daher nicht hinter einem Pseudonym oder gar vollkommener Anonymität. Transparentes Auftreten umfasst neben der Nennung des richtigen Namens sowie der Unternehmenszugehörigkeit auch einen entsprechenden Umgang mit Fehlern. Gestehen Sie diese offen ein, indem Sie beispielsweise bereits veröffentlichte Beiträge offen korrigieren und nicht einfach kommentarlos löschen.

Ein transparentes Auftreten ist eng mit den inhaltlichen Richtlinien verknüpft, da es mehr Bewusstsein für das eigene Handeln schafft. Darüber hinaus wird das Unternehmen so in die Lage versetzt, Vorfälle im Zusammenhang mit Internetveröffentlichungen besser aufklären zu können.

Kenntlichmachung privater Meinungen

Wenn Sie öffentlich einen Kommentar im Zusammenhang mit unserem Unternehmen abgeben, tun Sie dies in der ersten Person Singular („ich", nicht „wir"). Kennzeichnen Sie darüber hinaus, dass es sich um die Äußerung einer privaten Meinung handelt, indem Sie an geeigneter Stelle einen entsprechenden Hinweis hinterlegen. Dies gilt ebenfalls für die Abgrenzung von Meinungsäußerungen gegenüber geäußerten Tatsachen.

An dieser Stelle können auch Vorschläge bzw. Vorgaben dahingehend gemacht werden, wie der entsprechende Hinweis zu gestalten bzw. zu platzieren ist, etwa im Impressum eines privaten Blogs.

Unternehmensschädigende Äußerungen

Denken Sie auch bei Ihren Social-Media-Aktivitäten an Ihre Verbundenheit gegenüber dem Unternehmen. Kritische und ggf. geschäftsschädigende Äußerungen sind insbesondere im beruflichen Bereich zu unterlassen. Aber auch privat geäußerte Kritik kann negative Folgen für den geschäftlichen Erfolg des Unternehmens und damit auch für seine Mitarbeiter haben. Gleiches gilt für Aussagen über Partner oder Kunden. *Soweit es sich um bewusste Geschäfts- oder Rufschädigungen, Drohungen und Beleidigungen, falsche Tatsachenbehauptungen oder den Betriebsfrieden ernstlich gefährdende Äußerungen handelt, sind diese auch durch den Arbeitgeber sanktionierbar. Durch das Aufzeigen entsprechender Konsequenzen (Abmahnung, Kündigung) kann diesem Abschnitt daher noch mehr Nachdruck verliehen werden. Der Hinweis, dass auch eine in aller Regel zulässige, da von der Meinungsfreiheit gedeckte kritische Auseinandersetzung im privaten Bereich negative Folgen für Unternehmen und Mitarbeiter haben kann, schärft insoweit das Bewusstsein der Belegschaft.*

Verschwiegenheitspflicht
Vertrauliche Informationen des Unternehmens sowie von Kunden sind ebenso zu behandeln. Achten Sie daher auch und insbesondere bei der Nutzung von Social Media auf die Wahrung von Betriebs- und Geschäftsgeheimnissen.

Auch bzgl. der Verschwiegenheitspflicht kann sich ein Aufzeigen der ggf. gravierenden Folgen einer Zuwiderhandlung anbieten. So berechtigt das Verraten von Betriebs- oder Geschäftsgeheimnissen den Arbeitgeber im Einzelfall zur fristlosen Kündigung. Die Verschwiegenheitspflicht ergibt sich aus dem Arbeitsvertrag und ist immer dann anzunehmen, wenn ein berechtigtes betriebliches Interesse des Arbeitgebers an der Geheimhaltung vorliegt. Insofern kann es aber im Einzelfall sinnvoll sein, den Umfang der Verschwiegenheitsverpflichtung näher zu konkretisieren.

Ansprechpartner
Sollten Sie im Rahmen des Web 2.0 auf positive oder negative Beiträge oder Reaktionen, die das Unternehmen und/oder seine Produkte betreffen, stoßen, teilen Sie dies bitte [Kontaktdaten des Ansprechpartners] mit. An die gleiche Stelle können Sie sich auch wenden, wenn Unsicherheiten oder Fragen bzgl. der Umsetzung dieser Richtlinien bestehen.

Stand: Februar 2011

Yahoo

Online-Anbieter Yahoo hat naheliegenderweise ebenfalls seit Jahren Guidelines, die ursprünglich allein auf Blogs fokussiert waren. Verwunderlich bei einer Online-Company ist die starke Fokussierung auf juristische Aspekte und Verantwortlichkeiten.

Yahoo! Personal Blog Guidelines: 1.0 (http://jeremy.zawodny.com/yahoo/yahoo-blog-guidelines.pdf)

Yahoo! believes in fostering a thriving online community and supports blogging as a valuable component of shared media. The Yahoo! Personal Blog Guidelines have been developed for Yahoos who maintain personal blogs that contain postings about Yahoo!'s business, products, or fellow Yahoos and the work they do. They are also applicable to Yahoos who post about the company on the blogs of others. The guidelines outline the legal implications of blogging about the company and also include recommended best practices to consider when posting about Yahoo!.

LEGAL PARAMETERS: The following two bullets cover your legal responsibilities and non-disclosure obligations. Failure to abide by these two guidelines can result in serious ramifications for individual bloggers and/or individuals who post on the blogs of others.

Legal Liability

When you choose to go public with your opinions via a blog, you are legally responsible for your commentary. Individual bloggers can be held personally liable for any commentary deemed to be defamatory, obscene (not swear words, but rather the legal definition of "obscene"), proprietary, or libelous (whether pertaining to Yahoo, individuals, or any other company for that matter). For these reasons, bloggers should exercise caution with regards to exaggeration, colorful language, guesswork, obscenity, copyrighted materials, legal conclusions, and derogatory remarks or characterizations. In essence, you blog (or post on the blogs of others) at your own risk. Outside parties actually can pursue legal action against you (not Yahoo!) for postings.

Company Privileged Information

Any confidential, proprietary, or trade secret information is obviously off-limits for your blog per the Proprietary Information Agreement you have signed with Yahoo!. To obtain a copy of your agreement, please contact your HR manager. The Yahoo! logo and trademarks are also off-limits per our brand guidelines. Anything related to Yahoo! policy, inventions, strategy, financials, products, etc. that has not been made public cannot appear in your blog under any circumstances. see Yahoo! Guides 2. Disclosing confidential or proprietary information can negatively impact our business and may result in regulatory violations for the company.

Press Inquiries

Blog postings may generate media coverage. If a member of the media contacts you about a Yahoo!-related blog posting or requests Yahoo! information of any kind, contact PR (pr-corp@yahoo-inc.com or 415-318-4120) You should also reach out for PR for clarification on whether specific information has been publicly disclosed before you blog about it.

BEST PRACTICE GUIDELINES: These four recommendations provide a roadmap for constructive, respectful, and productive dialogue between bloggers and their fellow Yahoos. These are not "rules" and thus they can't be broken. There is no hidden meaning or agenda. We consider these to be "best practices guidelines" that are in the spirit of our culture and the best interest of all Yahoos, whether they blog or not. We encourage Yahoos to follow these guidelines, but it is not mandatory to do so. It's your choice. We really mean that.

Be Respectful of Your Colleagues

Be thoughtful and accurate in your posts, and be respectful of how other Yahoos may be affected. All Yahoo! employees can be viewed (correctly or incorrectly)as representative of the company, which can add significance to your public reflections on the organization (whether you intend to or not). Yahoos who identify themselves as Yahoo! employees in their blogs and comment on the company at any time, should notify their manager of the existence of their blog just to avoid any surprises. To be clear, you are not being asked to alert your manager of your posts, just to consider letting them know you have a blog where you may write about Yahoo!. Whether your manager chooses to occasionally read your blog or not, the courtesy head's up is always appreciated.

Get Your Facts Straight

As a Yahoo! employee with intranet access, you have the opportunity to contact the Yahoos who are responsible for the products, services, or other initiatives that you may want to write about. To ensure you are not misrepresenting your fellow Yahoos or their work, consider reaching out to a member of the relevant team before posting. This courtesy will help you provide your readers with accurate insights, especially when you are blogging outside your area of expertise. If there is someone at Yahoo! who knows more about the topic than you, check with them to make sure you have your facts straight.

Provide Context to Your Argument

Please be sure to provide enough support in your posting to help Yahoos understand your reasoning, be it positive or negative. We appreciate the value of multiple perspectives, so help us to understand yours by providing context to your opinion. Whether you are posting in praise or criticism of Yahoo!, you are encouraged to develop a thoughtful argument that extends well beyond "(insert) is cool" or "(insert) sucks".

Engage in Private Feedback:

Not everyone who is reading your blog will feel comfortable approaching you if they are concerned their feedback will become public. In order to maintain an open dialogue that everyone can comfortably engage in, Yahoo! bloggers are asked to welcome "off-blog" feedback from their colleagues who would like to privately respond, make suggestions, or report errors without having their comments appear your blog. Bloggers want to know what you think. If you have an opinion, correction or criticism regarding a posting, reach out for the blogger directly. Whether privately or on their blog, let the blogger know your thoughts.

ZF Friedrichshafen

Die ZF Friedrichshafen AG entwickelt, produziert und prüft weltweit Technologien für Antriebs- und Fahrwerktechnik. Auf der Weltrangliste der Automobilzulieferer gehört ZF zu den führenden Unternehmen – Umsatz 2010: 12,9 Milliarden Euro (Eigendarstellung).

Die ZF Social Media Guidelines sind unter http://www.zf.com/corporate/de/meta/social_media_guidelines.html öffentlich zugänglich.

Die Besonderheit hier: Diese gelten ausschließlich für die Freizeit. Gleichzeitig wird an das Verbot der privaten Internetnutzung erinnert. Aktiv nutzt ZF das Thema Social Media vor allem in der Personalarbeit/-ausbildung; hier der Orginaltext:

Warum Social Media Guidelines?

Das Internet hat sich gewandelt. Vom Nachschlage-Medium ist es in den vergangenen Jahren immer stärker zum Mitmach-Medium geworden. Anfangs waren es Online-Kunden, die ihre gekauften Waren beurteilt haben. Oder Computer-Nutzer, die über Foren Hinweise ausgetauscht haben. Aus diesen Foren und Gästebüchern ist inzwischen eine eigene Medienwelt entstanden: die Social Media. Sie leben sehr stark von den Inhalten und vom Engagement der Nutzer. Ganz gleich, ob es um Filme auf YouTube, um Bilder bei flickr, um persönliche Profile bei Facebook und MySpace, Kurznachrichten bei Twitter oder um Business-Netzwerke wie Xing oder LinkedIn geht: Immer sind es die Nutzer, die die entsprechenden Anwendungen interessant machen. Sie geben dabei auch viel von sich selbst und aus ihrem jeweiligen sozialen Umfeld preis.

Zum sozialen Umfeld gehören natürlich auch der Beruf und der Arbeitgeber. Immerhin können Sie aus der Innensicht das Unternehmen ZF besser darstellen als Außenstehende: Mit Ihrem Expertenwissen bereichern Sie Diskussionen im Internet und im Austausch mit Mitarbeitern anderer Firmen finden Sie vielleicht Anregung, die Sie für die eigene Arbeit nutzen können.

Es ist daher im Interesse der ZF Friedrichshafen AG, wenn Sie sich bei Social Media engagieren. Da es im Umgang mit diesen Kommunikationsformen noch viele Unsicherheiten gibt, möchten wir Sie über die Möglichkeiten und Risiken der Nutzung informieren – insbesondere für den Fall, dass Sie sich zu ZF äußern. Wir haben die folgenden Hinweise als kleine Hilfestellung zusammengestellt. Soweit es dabei nicht um gesetzlich oder arbeitsrechtlich vorgeschriebene Dinge geht, handelt es sich ausdrücklich nicht um Gebote, sondern um Empfehlungen, die Ihnen beim Umgang mit Social Media helfen sollen.

Diese Hinweise gelten für Ihre Aktivitäten in der Freizeit. Privates Surfen im Internet ist bei ZF während der Arbeitszeit grundsätzlich nicht erlaubt.

Für die deutschen Standorte ist die Nutzung von Internet und E-Mail außerdem in den Konzernbetriebsvereinbarungen 01/2007 und 01/2008 geregelt.

8 Tipps für den Umgang mit Social Media

1. Das Internet vergisst nichts (so schnell)
Wenn Sie Inhalte in Social-Media-Anwendungen einstellen, haben Sie anschließend nur noch bedingt Kontrolle darüber. Bedenken Sie das ganz generell, vor allem bei Inhalten, die

mit Ihrem Namen verknüpft sind. Es empfiehlt sich auch, die Bestimmungen des jeweiligen Anbieters gründlich zu lesen – häufig können Sie über einige Grundeinstellungen (etwa bei Xing oder bei Facebook) selbst festlegen, ob Ihre Inhalte von Nicht-Mitgliedern gelesen oder von Suchmaschinen verschlagwortet werden können.

2. In Ihrem Alltag halten Sie sich bereits an die Konzernrichtlinien – das gilt auch für Ihre Aktivitäten im Social Web. Geheime ZF-Informationen würden Sie niemals am Stammtisch ausplaudern? Dann tun Sie es bitte auch nicht im Internet. Es mag verführerisch sein, in Diskussionsforen, bei Xing oder auf dem eigenen Blog mit Insider-Informationen wie einem neuen Kundenprojekt oder einem Firmenkauf zu „glänzen". Aber es gilt: Geheim ist geheim und soll es auch bleiben.

Für den Fall, dass Journalisten oder Blogger über Social Media mit Ihnen in Kontakt treten, um Informationen über ZF zu bekommen (oder zu überprüfen), verweisen Sie an die offizielle Pressestelle in der ZF-Konzernkommunikation:
Martin Demel, Leiter Unternehmens- und Wirtschaftskommunikation
Tel. +49 7541 77-2528, martin.demel@zf.com

3. Beachten Sie geltendes Recht
Veröffentlichen Sie keine verleumderischen, beleidigenden oder sonstwie rechtswidrigen Inhalte. Stellen Sie keine fremden Inhalte ohne entsprechende Urheberverweise ins Netz und beachten Sie Copyrights.
Respektieren Sie das Recht von Dritten am eigenen Bild. Zeigen Sie Respekt vor Kollegen, Kunden und Wettbewerbern.

4. Seien Sie authentisch!
Das beginnt bei der Erkennbarkeit mit Namen und Firmenzugehörigkeit und setzt sich bei Stil und Ton fort: Bleiben Sie auch im Social Web erkennbar Sie selbst. Haben Sie keine Angst, eine eigene Meinung zu vertreten – machen Sie aber klar, dass Sie für sich selbst und nicht für ZF sprechen. Vermeiden Sie Äußerungen, die den Betriebsfrieden gefährden und die weitere Zusammenarbeit mit Arbeitgeber und Kollegen unzumutbar machen.

5. Seien Sie auch als Privatperson professionell und höflich
Wer etwas im Netz veröffentlicht, übernimmt für diese Inhalte die Verantwortung. Das bedeutet auch, dass Sie sich als Autor schon mal der Kritik anderer User aussetzen – die Sie dann als ungerecht empfinden könnten. Bleiben Sie in diesem Fall aber auf dem Boden und gehen Sie mit Kritik sachlich und grundsätzlich höflich um. Lassen Sie sich nicht provozieren. Wenn Sie den Eindruck haben, eine Diskussion entgleitet in Beschimpfungen, brechen Sie sie lieber ab, als sich daran weiter zu beteiligen.

6. Korrigieren Sie sich, wenn nötig
Das Social Web lebt von Diskussionen – und zu deren Ergebnissen gehört auch, dass man sich und eventuelle Fehler korrigiert. Scheuen Sie davor nicht zurück, es wird Sie in den Augen viele User sogar sympathischer machen.

7. Seien Sie ehrlich

Manipulationen, Weglassungen oder Lügen haben im Internet oft keine Chance, weil es immer User gibt, die einen Sachverhalt überprüfen können – und ihn dann auch richtigstellen. Seien Sie also ehrlich, wenn Sie sich an Diskussionen beteiligen – auch wenn es um ZF geht (Ausnahme: Interna, siehe Punkt 2).

8. Achten Sie auf Qualität

Banale Äußerungen gibt es im Internet und vor allem in den Social Media schon genug. Achten Sie auf Qualität Ihrer Beiträge, tragen Sie zu intensiver und wertvoller Konversation durch hochwertigen Inhalt bei.

Für weitere Fragen zum Thema Social Media Guidelines stehen wir Ihnen zur Verfügung: ZF Friedrichshafen AG, Martin Demel, Leiter Unternehmens- und Wirtschaftskommunikation, Tel. +49 7541/77-2543, martin.demel@zf.com

Der Social Media Workshop

Die Versuchung ist groß, sich anhand der obigen Empfehlung und der anschließenden Auflistung von Social-Media-Richtlinien einfach an eine branchenähnliche Policy anzulehnen beziehungsweise diese schlicht zu übernehmen.

Zu beobachten ist, dass etwa die Policy von IBM vielfach als Vorlage dient und in der Pharmabranche die von Roche als Messlatte verwendet wird, während in puncto B-to-B-Aufmachung und -Inhalt voestalpine häufig als Vorbild genannt wird.

Aufgrund der Vielfalt der gelisteten Beispiele ist es natürlich denkbar, für die meisten individuellen Gegebenheiten in Ihrem Unternehmen mit hoher Wahrscheinlichkeit auch möglich, eine entsprechende Policy zum „Anlehnen" zu finden. Dennoch wäre der empfehlenswerte Weg – ausgehend von der hier gewonnenen Übersicht –, eigene Kriterien zu definieren und daraus eine Policy abzuleiten. Je nach Organisation kann dies unter Umständen gemeinschaftlich online in einem Wiki (siehe oben das Beispiel Rotes Kreuz Austria) erfolgen oder in einem Workshop, bei dem Unternehmensvertreter aus Öffentlichkeitsarbeit, Marketing, Personalwesen und anderen in Ihrer Organisation von Social Media tangierten Bereichen gemeinsam – gegebenenfalls unter externer Anleitung – im Rahmen eines ein- bis zweitägigen Workshops zusammen eine Policy entwickeln. Sollten im Unternehmensumfeld private Social-Media-Initiativen festgestellt worden sein, empfiehlt es sich, auch deren Protagonisten mit einzubeziehen.

Dass die Social-Media-Richtlinien vor Inkrafttreten – wegen möglicher juristischer Komplikationen – mit der eigenen Rechtsabteilung oder einem Vertragsanwalt abzustimmen sind, versteht sich dabei von selbst.

Vorbereitende Arbeiten für den Workshop (Ergebnisse sollten zu Workshop-Beginn vorliegen):

Sammlung und Sichtung aller existierenden Social-Media-Aktivitäten im Unternehmen sowohl offizieller als auch inoffizeller Natur.
Zu den offiziellen Arbeiten zählen alle Aktivitäten, die vom Unternehmen selbst ausgehen, zum Beispiel der Unternehmens-Blog der Kommunikationsabteilung. Entsprechend bedeutet inoffiziell eine auf Initiative eines Mitarbeiters oder einer Gruppe von Mitarbeitern in Eigenregie gestartete Online-Aktivität mit Bezug zum Unternehmen, also etwa eine selbst erstellte Facebook-Fanpage oder ein privat betriebener Twitter-Account, der Unternehmens- oder Markenbezug aufweist.
Zudem sollte überprüft werden, ob und inwieweit Kunden, Fans oder gegebenenfalls Konkurrenten in Sozialen Medien mit Relevanz für das eigene Unternehmen oder eigene Produkte bereits weitergehende Äußerungen getätigt oder bereits Websites, Twitter-Accounts etc. eingerichtet haben.

Folgende Fragestellungen sollten in einem Social Media Policy Workshop adressiert werden (Reihenfolge und genauer Ablauf dienen lediglich als Empfehlung, von der im Einzelfall abgewichen kann):

Welche Ziele verfolgt das eigene Unternehmen mit Social Media?
Für die erfolgreiche Bewältigung des Workshops ist es sinnvoll, zunächst anhand dieser Frage ein gemeinsames Verständnis von den Social-Media-Zielen des Unternehmens herzustellen.

Auf welche Medien bezieht sich die Social Media Policy?
Welche Medien sind relevant?
Social Media ist vielfältig. Die großen Plattformen wie Facebook und Co. nehmen zwar in der öffentlichen Diskussion bei Weitem die dominierende Rolle ein. Dennoch spielen sich die für das Unternehmen relevanten Diskussionen unter Umständen in kleinen Fachforen ab. Diese zu identifizieren und in die Policy zu integrieren ist Aufgabe dieser Teilfrage.
Auch die Frage, ob einzelne Dienste Gegenstand separater Policies sein sollten (siehe oben), ist hier zu diskutieren.

Welche Zielgruppe(n) sollen adressiert werden?
Nicht immer ist die Zielgruppe so klar auszumachen, wie es auf den ersten Blick scheint. Nehmen wir einen Autozulieferer, der besondere Hi-Fi-Lautsprechersysteme an die Autoindustrie liefert, die der Endkunde beim Fahrzeugkauf beim Händler aus der Aufpreisliste mitbestellt – oder eben nicht (Nachrüstung nicht möglich). Für die Social-Media-Aktivitäten des Anbieters kann der Endkunde eine wesentliche Zielgruppe sein. Im Idealfall geht dieser nämlich beim Neuwagenkauf mit dem festen Vorsatz „Ich brauche dieses Hi-Fi-System" zum Händler („Demand-Pull"). Die Zielgruppe kann aber auch der Autoverkäufer sein („Push").
Wie an diesem Beispiel zu erkennen ist, können es durchaus unterschiedliche Zielgruppen sein, die die Social-Media-Aktivitäten eines Unternehmens tangieren. Die Diskussion dieser Frage im Workshop soll helfen, hier Klarheit zu schaffen.

Wie wird die Zielgruppe angesprochen? Tonalität/Netiquette
Kernfrage hierbei ist hierbei die Frage nach dem „Du". Im Internet und insbesondere auf Social-Media-Plattformen ist ein vertraulicher Umgang, der sich im „Du" ausdrückt, vielfach an der Tagesordnung.
Ein vorschnelles Du kann aber vom Nutzer auch als plumpe Aufdringlichkeit ausgelegt werden, und selbst wenn es die „richtige" Ansprache für die Kernzielgruppe ist, was ist mit den „Streuverlusten"? Wie also agieren?

Wer ist Absender der Nachricht?
Hier ist sie wieder, die oben bereits aufgeworfene Frage Personalisierung versus Institutionalisierung der offiziell genutzten Accounts: Arbeitet man bewusst mit dem Zusatz „Organisation/Einheit" und liefert damit einen unpersönlichen Touch, oder baut man eine Person (oder mehrere) zum Sprecher auf und riskiert damit, dass diese unter Umständen das Unternehmen verlässt? Und wem gehört dann der Account?

Wie geht man mit externen Inhalten um?
Gerade in Social Media muss man davon ausgehen, dass man die Meinungshoheit nicht besitzt. Im Workshop sollte daher auch adressiert werden, wie mit abweichenden oder falschen Inhalten von Dritten umgegangen wird. Ebenfalls zu planen wäre, inwieweit Mitarbeiter angehalten werden sollen, „Scouting" nach derartigen Inhalten zu betreiben und diese zu melden.

Welche Materialien dürfen verwendet werden?
Ein Toolkit der Materialien (Grafiken, Logos etc.), die verwendet werden dürfen, sollte den Mitarbeitern bereitgestellt werden. Dies dient nicht nur einer einheitlichen Symbolsprache, sondern hilft, Urheberrechtsverletzungen und andere Rechtsprobleme zu vermeiden.

Wie differenziert man persönliche und professionelle Nutzung?
Je nach Ausgangslage wäre hier zu diskutieren:
– der Bezug zu einer existierenden Internet Policy (wenn etwa die private Internetnutzung im Unternehmen generell ausgeschlossen ist, hat dies erhebliche Konsequenzen für die Möglichkeiten der Ausgestaltung einer Social Media Policy);
– Stellung und besondere Regelungen für Mitarbeiter als „Markenbotschafter";
– [...]

Welchen Begrenzungen unterliegen die Kommunikationsinhalte?
Denkbare Ansätze sind:
– Negativliste: Worüber darf nicht gesprochen werden?
– Positivliste: Worüber darf gesprochen werden?
Beide Ansätze haben Vor- und Nachteile.

Welche Folgen hat eine Verletzung der Social Media Policy?
Von Arbeitsrechtlern wird immer wieder darauf hingewiesen, dass es gesonderter Rege-

lungen nicht bedarf, da bei der Verletzung einer Policy zumeist auch arbeitsvertragliche Pflichten verletzt werden. Dennoch kann es zur Präzisierung sinnvoll sein, Sanktionen auch in den Policies zu verankern.

Wer ist verantwortlich für Social Media?
Auch grundlegend dezentrale Aktivitäten von Mitarbeitern, die unter Umständen im Rahmen der Policy weitgehend autonom agieren, brauchen eine Führung oder zumindest eine letztinstanzliche Clearing-Stelle für Zweifelsfälle.

Wie lange ist die Social Media Policy gültig?
Trotz der Kurzlebigkeit einzelner Plattformen haben Social-Media-Richtlinien unter Umständen eine lange Lebensdauer (Beispiel sind die in diesem Buch beschriebenen Blogging Policies, die teilweise aus 2004 und 2005 stammen). Ob und inwieweit man Review-Zyklen einbaut, sollte hier diskutiert werden.

Soll die Social Media Policy veröffentlicht werden?
Die Schlussfrage der Workshop-Themen zum Thema Social Media lautet: Soll man die eigene Policy veröffentlichen? Diese ist durchaus legitim. Denn unter Umständen gelingt es, mit einer gut gemachten Policy einen gewissen Marketingeffekt zu erreichen. Wenn man die durch Social Media geforderte Offenheit konsequent lebt, kommt man eigentlich auch nicht daran vorbei.

Die Zukunft von Social Media im Unternehmen

Die explosionsartige Verbreitung von Social Media ändert die Erwartung von Endanwendern über die Kommunikation mit Unternehmen. Kunden erwarten und fordern zunehmend einen echten Dialog – in Echtzeit.

Da wird es Zeit für Unternehmen, die Gestalt der Kundenbeziehungen neu zu durchdenken.

Auch wenn Facebooks Vizepräsidentin für Europa, Mittlerer Osten und Afrika Joanna Shields laut Wallstreet Journal vom 04.05.2011 schon mal vom „engagiertesten Publikum, das es jemals gab" spricht und damit Social Media und wohl vor allem die Facebook-Nutzer meint, bleiben Fragen offen.

Etwa Fragen nach der „Conversion Rate". Wie viele Twitter-Followers oder wie viele Facebook-Fans sind oder werden Kunde? Denken Sie etwa an Porsche – mit über einer Million Fans bei Facebook und gut 100.000 Fahrzeugen Jahresproduktion.

Das ZDF berichtete unlängst in einer Serie zum Thema Social Media von einer Berliner Band mit immerhin rund 20.000 Fan,s die zu einem Gratiskonzert geladen hatte. Es kamen 2 (in Worten: zwei) Fans.

In Summe lässt sich die Entwicklung jedoch nicht mehr umkehren. Was ein Unternehmen ausmacht, wird zunehmend von „der Community" mitdefiniert.

Organisationen tun daher gut daran, sich nicht nur aufs Zuhören zu beschränken.

In einer universell vernetzten Welt ist jeder Mitarbeiter in gewisser Weise Repräsentant seines Unternehmens. Das ist jeder Mitarbeiter mit Kundenkontakt sonst natürlich auch – wie etwa der unfreundliche „Schalterbeamte" als Repräsentant der Post wahrgenommen wird. Der Unterschied ist dabei lediglich die – potenziell – unbegrenzte Außenwirkung von Social Media. Die obigen Beispiele haben dies gezeigt.

Letztendlich sollen und können die in diesem Buch diskutierten Social-Media-Richtlinien nicht mehr und nicht weniger sein als eine Basis für eine Social-Media-Kultur im Unternehmen bei dem jedem Mitarbeiter klar ist, was richtig und was falsch ist.

Glossar

App

Eigentlich Kurzform von „Applikation". Gemeint sind aber Anwendungsprogramme, die auf einem Smartphone laufen und zumeist über einen in das Betriebssystem integrierten Online-Shop („App Store") bezogen werden können. Apps gibt es auch für den Zugriff auf Social Networks wie Xing oder Facebook.

Blog

Weblogs oder einfach Blogs sind elektronische Tagebücher im Internet. Mit regelmäßig neuen Einträgen liefert der Betreiber des Weblogs – der Blogger – Informationen aus seinem Leben und/oder Inhalte zu einem ganz bestimmten Themengebiet aus dem privaten oder geschäftlichen Umfeld. Im Unterschied zu einfachen persönlichen Websites erlauben Blogs Diskussionen und vertieften Gedankenaustausch durch die Kommentarfunktion und die Verknüpfung mit anderen Webseiten und Weblogs (über Hyperlinks und sogenannte Trackbacks).

Online-Foren, die eine themenbezogene Diskussion erlauben, sind altbekannte Verwandte der Weblogs. Im Unterschied zu Letzteren fehlt den Foren aber die zentrale Rolle (beim Blog ist das der Blogger) und damit derjenige, der die Themenausrichtung allein bestimmt. Weblogs haben innerhalb weniger Jahre eine enorme Popularität erlangt. Mitentscheidend für die hohe Akzeptanz ist sicherlich die einfache Bedienbarkeit (eine Weblog-Software wie etwa „Wordpress" ist im Prinzip nichts anderes als ein browserbasiertes, funktionsreduziertes und auf einfache Benutzbarkeit hin optimiertes Web-Content-Management, das zudem meist fertig installiert im Rahmen eines Blog-Accounts oder eines Webhosting-Dienstangebotes kostenlos oder kostengünstig genutzt werden kann). Während Weblogs zunächst im privaten Bereich ihren Siegeszug antraten, werden neuere Aktivitäten in diesem Umfeld primär von Unternehmen betrieben. Zahlreiche Unternehmen nutzen Blogs, um die mehr oder weniger persönlichen Ansichten von Führungskräften oder Schlüsselmitarbeitern aus dem Technikumfeld ihren Kunden bekannt zu machen. Auch intern – im Intranet eines Unternehmens – können Weblogs als gesteuerte Diskussionsplattform eingesetzt werden.

Cloud

Bezeichnung für Rechnerkapazitäten, Dienste und Speicherplatz, die netzbasiert, das heißt im Internet, als Dienstleistung angeboten werden.

Co-Creation
Von Co-Creation spricht man, wenn ein Kunde an der Entstehung eines Produktes mitwirkt. Diese Mitwirkung beschränkt sich zumeist auf gestalterische Aspekte, etwa in der Designentwicklung, kann aber auch darüber hinausgehen und in Einzelfällen auch der Auslöser für Neuentwicklungen im Unternehmen oder gar des Ankaufs der Kundenideen durch das Unternehmen sein.

Cyberwar
Wortschöpfung aus den Begriffen Cyberspace und War. Bezeichnet eine Auseinandersetzung im Internet und in anderen Netzen. Das denkbar einfachste Ziel in einem solchen, auch als Information Warfare bezeichneten Konflikt ist die Störung von Verbindungen und das Lahmlegen von Rechnersystemen. Fortgeschrittenere Ziele können das Manipulieren von Systemen beinhalten.

Digitale Reputation
Glaubwürdigkeit einer Person oder auch eines Unternehmens innerhalb einer Online-Community. Diese wird durch entsprechende Äußerungen und Beiträge in Foren und Weblogs begründet. Nur selten wird berücksichtigt, dass diese Äußerungen auch nach Jahren noch auffindbar sind – etwa für Kunden, Interessenten, Geschäftspartner, Personalchefs oder Journalisten. Was die persönliche Reputation angeht: Innerhalb von Communities besteht eine zunehmende Tendenz, den Wert der Beiträge einer Person zu ranken und so ein mechanistisches Hilfsmittel – quasi als Messverfahren für Reputation – zu implementieren. Unbedachte Äußerungen von Mitarbeitern können – auch wenn sie in einem privaten Kontext geschehen – auf die Reputation des Unternehmens zurückstrahlen.

Digital Natives – Digital Immigrants
Digital Natives oder „Eingeborene des Internets" ist eine gängige Bezeichnung für die Altersklasse, die mit Internet (und Mobiltelefon) aufgewachsen ist. Im Allgemeinen werden darunter die ab 1980 Geborenen gefasst. Ihnen wird – nicht immer zu Recht – ein fortgeschrittener Umgang mit dem Internet zugeschrieben als den „digitalen Immigranten", den Älteren, die erst später im Studium oder Berufsleben mit den neuen Medien konfrontiert wurden.

Echtzeitsuche
Oberbegriff für verschiedene neuartige Suchtechnologien, die anders als die klassische Websuche zeitnah (beinahe in Echtzeit) Nachrichten und Meldungen aus Social Networks durchsuch- und auswertbar machen.

Identitätsdiebstahl
Missbräuchliche Nutzung personbezogener Daten durch einen Dritten. Im Regelfall erfolgt die Aneignung der Identität einer anderen Person mit dem Ziel, einen eigenen Vorteil zu erlangen (etwa durch betrügerische Bestellung von Waren und Dienstleistung) oder die Person gezielt zu schädigen (etwa durch Verbreitung von Unwahrheiten).

Location Based Services
Zumeist im Kontext mit Mobilfunknetzen erbrachte Dienstleistungen mit Orts- beziehungsweise Ortungsbezug, wie etwa Navigation.

Long-Tail-Effekt
Auf der Heavy-Tail-Verteilung basierende Theorie über die Netzökonomie. Die Grundidee ist sehr einfach. Demnach kann man im E-Commerce auch mit Artikeln Geld verdienen, die im stationären Umfeld als Ladenhüter keine Beachtung finden und im Kampf um den dort begrenzten Regalplatz nicht gelistet und daher nicht verkauft werden. Online ist jedoch Regalplatz im Prinzip unendlich vorhanden, das heißt, auch Produkte mit einer geringen Umschlagshäufigkeit können Erfolg bringen – die Masse macht's. Dies gilt ganz besonders auch für digitale Güter. Digitale Güter sind Produkte oder Dienstleistungen, die sich mithilfe von Informationssystemen entwickeln, vertreiben oder anwenden lassen.

M2M–Machine2Machine
Bezeichnung für automatisierte Transaktionen, die ohne menschliches Zutun direkt von einem Rechnersystem an ein anderes weitergegeben werden, etwa die automatische Nachbestellung von Teilen beim Unterschreiten einer bestimmten Vorratsmenge.

Mashup
Bezeichnung für das Zusammenmischen und Verknüpfen von Informationen aus verschiedenen Webanwendungen. Im Web-2.0-Umfeld gängige Vorgehensweise, die von Webseiten-Betreibern durch das Zurverfügungstellen von Programmierschnittstellen teilweise aktiv gefördert wird. Populärste Basis für Mashup sind die von Google bereitgestellten Geografieinformationen (Google Maps/Google Earth), die etwa von Hotspot-Anbietern genutzt werden, um eine Karte mit allen von diesem Dienst offerierten WLAN-Hotspots im Web darzustellen.

Mass Customization
Herstellung eines nach Kundenwunsch individualisierten Produkts mit den Methoden der Massenfertigung. Dieser Ansatz versucht, die Vorteile der Massenfertigung mit hohem Individualisierungsgrad zu verbinden. Häufig soll durch eine Art Baukastenfertigung

(Modularisierung) oder durch Anpassung von Designs oder Passformen eine derartige Individualisierung erreicht werden. Insbesondere bei Softwareprodukten wird eine Individualisierung (etwa der Benutzeroberfläche eines Webportals) oft außerhalb der eigentlichen Herstellung durch den Endanwender vorgenommen. Ein weiterer Schritt für die künftige Weiterentwicklung des Mass-Customization-Konzeptes wäre die Integration von Innovationen der Kundenseite in die Produktentstehung (siehe auch Co-Creation).

Mechanical Turk
Bezeichnung für einen vermeintlichen Schachautomaten aus dem 18. Jahrhundert. Dieser Begriff wird vom Internetanbieter Amazon für ein innovatives Webprojekt verwendet, bei dem menschliche Arbeit über das Internet koordiniert wird.

Netiquette
Kunstwort aus Network und Etiquette. Bezeichnet informelle Verhaltensregeln im Internet, kein festes Regelwerk. Dennoch gibt es Versuche einzelner Online-Gemeinschaften, selbst Verhaltensregeln zu definieren und diese auch schriftlich niederzulegen. Verstöße werden entsprechend von Moderatoren einer Community verfolgt und mit Löschung der Beiträge oder – in extremeren Fällen – Ausschluss aus einer Community „geahndet".

Netzwerkeffekt
Beschreibung für die Beobachtung, dass der Nutzen eines Standards oder Netzwerks mit der Zahl der Nutzer wächst. Durch steigende Nutzerzahlen erhöht sich die Attraktivität für weitere Nutzer. Dies wird auch als positive Rückkopplung bezeichnet. Mit Erreichen einer kritischen Masse kann die Nutzerzahl exponentiell anwachsen.

Ökonomie der Aufmerksamkeit
Eine von Georg Franck entwickelte wissenschaftliche Theorie, nach der Aufmerksamkeit (etwa in den Massenmedien) ein knappes Gut ist, das eine ähnliche Funktion erfüllen kann wie eine Bezahlung. Bei Social-Media-Initiativen geht es häufig um die Nutzung von viralen Effekten (siehe: Virale Effekte) zur Generierung von Aufmerksamkeit.

Open Innovation
Öffnung des Innovationsprozesses in einem Unternehmen für Einflüsse von außerhalb zu dem Zweck, das eigene Innovationspotential zu vergrößern und „Betriebsblindheit" zu vermeiden.

Smartphone
Mobiltelefon mit hoher Prozessorleistung, das PC-ähnliche Zusatzfunktionen und die Installation von Applikationen (siehe: Apps) erlaubt sowie einen Internetzugang bereitstellt. Gängige Betriebssysteme für Smartphones sind Symbian, Android, iPhone OS und Windows Mobile. Viele Smartphones setzen auf Touchscreen-Bedienung.

Social Media/Social Web/Social Software
Oberbegriff für alle Programme und Systeme, die menschliche Kommunikation und soziale Interaktion über das Internet unterstützen und fördern. Wird teilweise als Synonym für „Web 2.0" gebraucht.

Social Commerce
Begriff für die Beteiligung der Nutzer an E-Commerce-Aktivitäten, zum Beispiel durch Ranking, Empfehlungen und Mitgestaltung von Produkten.

Social Networks
Online-Communities, die als Basis für die Pflege bestehender sozialer Kontakte und das Eingehen neuer Beziehungen im Internet dienen – zumeist auf einzelne Gruppen und deren Bedürfnisse zugeschnitten, etwa für Studenten, Berufstätige, Mütter/Väter oder Singles.

Statusmeldung
Hier: kurze Textnachricht, mit der sich Nutzer eines Social Networks mitteilen.

Viraler Effekt
Hier: Eine Information, ein Link, eine Nachricht, ein Sonderangebot etc., wird innerhalb kürzester Zeit von Mensch zu Mensch weitergetragen. Die Ausbreitung verläuft dabei ähnlich wie bei einem biologischen Virus. Man unterscheidet dabei zwischen erwünschten (etwa im Social-Media-Marketing) und unerwünschten viralen Effekten.

Virus
Ein Virus (auch: Computervirus) ist ein sich selbst verbreitendes Computerprogramm, das andere Dateien befällt und sich mit deren Benutzung weiterverbreitet.

Web 2.0
Vom Verleger Tim O'Reilly geprägter Oberbegriff für neuere, interaktive, nutzerzentrierte Techniken und Dienstangebote im Internet. Auch als „Social Software" bezeichnet (siehe: Social Software).

Web-Bug
Möglichkeit zur statistischen Erfassung und Nachverfolgung der Nutzerbewegung auf Internetseiten durch Einbau eines einzelnen Seitenelements. Ist ein solches Element in hinreichend viele Websites integriert, so kann die Bewegung eines Nutzers im Internet über verschiedene Seiten hinweg weitgehend nachvollzogen werden.

Wiki
Ein Wiki, auch WikiWiki oder WikiWeb genannt, ist eine Sammlung von Webseiten, bei denen jeder Nutzer nicht nur lesenden, sondern auch schreibenden Zugriff hat. Mit einer in die Wiki-Software integrierten Bearbeitungsfunktion kann der Anwender – ähnlich wie in einem Web-Content-Management-System – Inhalte bearbeiten und etwa einzelne Beziehungen durch Querverweise (Hyperlinks) kenntlich machen. Der Name stammt von wikiwiki, dem hawaiischen Wort für „schnell". In Entstehung wie Bedeutung kann man Wikis den Wissensmanagementwerkzeugen zuordnen. Wikis können im Internet oder Intranet eingesetzt werden, um das Wissen zu einzelnen Themengebieten – etwa einem Entwicklungsprojekt – auf einfache Weise zu sammeln. Aufgrund der einfachen – browserorientierten – Bedienbarkeit ist die Einstiegsschwelle für eigene Beiträge gering. Viele Unternehmens-Wikis haben daher eine weit höhere Akzeptanz als herkömmliche Intranetanwendungen für Wissensmanagement. Ähnlich wie bei Weblogs spielt auch bei Wikis der persönliche Faktor, d.h. die Möglichkeit, sich bei einer aktiven Beteiligung Respekt innerhalb der Gemeinschaft oder Gruppe zu erarbeiten, eine treibende Rolle.

Wikipedia
Auf Basis des Wiki-Prinzips (siehe: Wiki) konzipiertes Online-Lexikon, bei dem jeder Besucher auch eigene Beiträge erstellen kann (http://www.wikipedia.org).

Weitere aktuelle Begriffe aus Internet, Informationsverarbeitung und Telekommunikation finden Sie in Thomas R. Köhler „IT von A bis Z" (Frankfurter Allgemeine Buch 2008).

Schlagwortverzeichnis

Über den Autor

Thomas R. Köhler, Jahrgang 1968, gilt als einer der führenden Online-Experten. Seit 1994 ist er nicht nur »Serial Entrepreneur«, sondern auch gefragter Vortragsredner bei Fach- und Firmenveranstaltungen. Wenn es um die Chancen und Risiken von Internet und Social Media geht, weiß er aus erster Hand zu berichten.

Köhler ist Autor zahlreicher Standardwerke zu Technologiethemen. In seinem jüngsten Buch »Die Internetfalle« (Frankfurter Allgemeine Buch 2010) beschäftigt er sich mit den Risiken und Nebenwirkungen von Social Media für den Einzelnen wie für Unternehmen (Blog zum Buch: internetfalle.net).

Als Geschäftsführer der CE21 – Ges. für Kommunikationsberatung mbH in München berät Köhler mit seinem Team Unternehmen bei der Auswahl und dem Einsatz neuer Technologien (www.ce21.de).

Thomas R. Köhler
Social-Media-Management

FSC
www.fsc.org
MIX
Papier | Fördert
gute Waldnutzung
FSC® C083411

Zeitfracht Medien GmbH
Ferdinand-Jühlke-Straße 7
99095 Erfurt, Deutschland
produktsicherheit@kolibri360.de